A *Short Course in Windows NT 4 for Beginners*

Stewart Venit

California State University
Los Angeles

Scott/Jones, Inc., Publishers

P. O. Box 696, El Granada, CA 94018
scotjones2@aol.com
(650) 726-2436 *or* Fax: (650) 726-4693
http://www.scottjonespub.com

A Short Course in Windows NT 4 for Beginners
Stewart Venit

ISBN 1-57676-013-8

Book Production: The Canfield Bookworks
Text Design: V & J Enterprises
Composition: Stewart Venit
Book Manufacturing: Malloy Lithographing, Inc.

0 9 8   X Y Z

ADDITIONAL TITLES OF INTEREST FROM SCOTT/JONES

A Short Course in Windows 95
The Windows 95 Textbook: Standard Edition
The Windows 95 Textbook: Extended Edition
The Windows 98 Textbook (forthcoming)
> by Stewart Venit

Access 97 Guidebook
> by Maggie Trigg and Phyllis Dobson

Building Applications with Microsoft Office and Visual Basic
> by Ron Gilster and Karen Braunstein-Post

Microsoft Word for Office 97: Economy Pack
> by Paula Ladd and Ralph Ruby

QuickStart to the Internet, HTML, and VB Script
> by Forest Lin

QuickStart to Internet Explorer 4
> by Debby Tice and Leslie Hardin

Contents

Contents

Preface

A Short Course in Windows NT 4 for Beginners provides an introductory look at the interface and capabilities of this operating system. The text supplies detailed information about basic concepts (such as using menus, dialog boxes, and the help system), working with applications and documents, and managing files and folders. It also discusses some ways to customize the Windows environment, briefly describes a few of the built-in "accessories", and presents a few other special topics.

A Short Course in Windows NT 4 for Beginners is intended for those who have little or no experience with computers; or those who are familiar with DOS, Windows 3.1, or Windows NT 3.51, but not with Windows 95 or NT 4. This text can be used in a short course on Windows NT or to complement another text in a computer literacy, applications, or operating system course that uses NT 4.

Students who master the content of *A Short Course in Windows NT 4 for Beginners* will acquire a solid foundation in its use and should be well-prepared to learn other aspects of Windows on their own.

Organization of the Text

We have organized this text to provide as much flexibility as possible in choosing topics and the order in which they are presented. A pictorial representation of the text's organization is shown in the Chapter Dependency Flowchart on the next page. Here is a more detailed description:

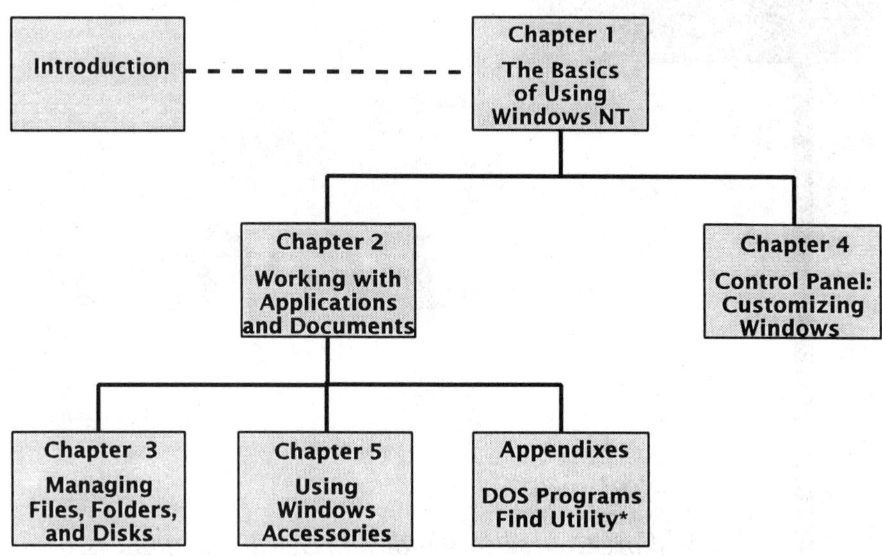

Chapter Dependency Chart

- An Introduction provides general information about computer hardware and software. It is intended primarily for those students who have little or no experience with computers, but may also be useful reading for others.

- Chapter 1, covering the basics of using Windows NT, is the normal jumping-off point for students who have some familiarity with computers, but none with NT version 4. Most of the concepts that are discussed here should be familiar to those who have used Windows 3.1 or NT 3.51; for these students, this chapter can be covered quickly. Be aware, however, that the terminology and techniques discussed in Chapter 1 are used throughout the text.

- Chapter 2 covers some fundamental material on working with applications and documents, and typically would be the next material covered. However, those instructors who want to follow a more gentle path can instead jump to Chapter 4, which deals with some of the ways to customize Windows.

- After completing Chapter 2, Chapter 3, 4, or 5 can be covered next. Chapter 3 is the most difficult of these, but also contains the most important material.

Features of the Text

End-of-section tutorials

1. Certainly, the best way to learn Windows NT is to use Windows NT. With this in mind, we have written the text in a way that encourages students to follow along at the computer. Moreover, most sections end with a brief Tutorial that reviews the material by leading the student through hands-on exercises.

No delay in starting up

2. The text introduces Windows' terminology and techniques immediately; we start up Windows on the first page of the first chapter. On the other hand, for those courses that require it, the Introduction provides general information on using personal computers.

Objectives

3. Each chapter (and the Introduction, as well) begins with a brief overview and list of objectives.

Chapter exercises

4. The text contains three types of exercises at the end of every chapter:

   - True/false, multiple choice, and completion Review Exercises test the students' knowledge of facts presented in the chapter. Answers to the odd-numbered exercises are provided in Appendix C.

   - The last Review Exercise in each chapter asks the student to "Build Your Own Glossary" — to provide definitions for a given list of important terms introduced in that chapter. (To facilitate this task, the listed terms are boldfaced when they first appear.)

   - Lab Exercises require the students to perform the kinds of tasks they will encounter in using Windows on an everyday basis.

TIPs

5. TIPs appear periodically throughout the text. These short notes provide insight into, or specialized knowledge about, the topic at hand. A fact or technique may be called a TIP because it is especially important or because it is interesting or unusual.

WARNINGs

6. Other specialized notes are designated as WARNINGs. They caution the reader against taking certain actions, which in some circumstances could lead to extreme regret.

Margin notes

7. Occasional brief phrases in the left margin of the text make it easy for the reader to locate subtopics and important procedures.

Supplements

8. The following ancillary material is available for this textbook:

   - A *Student Disk* that contains the files referenced in the

Tutorials and Lab Exercises accompanies the text.

- The answers to the even-numbered Review Exercises are available to instructors directly from the publisher[*].

A Few Words about Homework

This text, through its end-of-chapter exercises, provides an ample supply of homework problems. The Review Exercises can usually be answered with a single word (or letter, in the case of the multiple choice problems), and the Lab Exercises contain frequent questions that require a brief answer or explanation. (The Lab Exercises also occasionally call for an optional screen capture.)

In a computer course, it is desirable to provide students, as quickly as possible, with the ability to use the computer for printing solutions to their homework problems. With this in mind, we introduce, relatively early in the text, the basics of WordPad (Section 2.2) and the techniques for capturing windows and screens (Section 2.3). Once this material has been completed, students will be able to hand in computer-printed homework.

Acknowledgments

I would like to thank the many people who helped bring this project to fruition. Special thanks goes to the instructors who provided insight and feedback about their Windows NT courses:

Wade Graves
Grayson County Community College

Dennis Hansen
Southeastern Community College

Peter Maggiacomo
Sinclair Community College

Bruce Martin
Oakland Community College

Matt McCaskill
Brevard Community College

Pat Rodihan
Union City College

Phillip Smith
Marshall University

Richard White
Miami-Dade Community College

Floyd Winters
Manatee Community College

---

[*]The address and telephone numbers of the publisher appear on the back cover.

My publisher, Richard Jones, gave enthusiastic and unwavering support for this text, and managed, as usual, to make criticism sound like praise. I would like to thank my wife, Corinne, and my daughter, Tamara, for understanding that a project of this sort requires the author to spend countless hours glued to the computer. Finally, special mention should be made of my dogs, Maggie and Abby, who usually kept me company, sleeping peacefully next to the humming computer.

Introduction

We are living in a world that is becoming increasingly dependent on the electronic computer. Computers help run our businesses and institutions, design and build manufactured products, provide instantaneous worldwide communication, publish our newspapers, magazines, and books, and supply all sorts of educational and recreational activities. Many forms of employment now require some kind of **computer literacy** — an understanding of how to use a computer effectively.

In this introduction, we will describe, in general terms, the computer's *hardware* and *software* — the components and programs that make it work. Although this material is not essential for an understanding of Windows NT, it may help with certain topics and will probably increase your computer literacy. More specifically, you will learn about:

1. Computers in general and personal computers in particular.

2. The components of a computer: its central processing unit, internal memory, mass storage, and input and output devices.

3. Types of computer applications.

4. The function of an operating system.

5. The various versions of Microsoft Windows.

Personal Computers

Everyone who uses a computer on a daily basis becomes accustomed to dealing with special computer-related terminology. Yet, to a beginner, many of these terms can be confusing and even intimidating. There are floppy disks and hard disks, kilobytes and megabytes, mice and monitors, and much, much more. In this section, we will try to take some of the mystery out of computer terminology.

What is a Computer?

As with any evolving technology, precisely defining the term *computer* is not easy. Computers can take many different forms and their capabilities are constantly expanding. Yet, all computers perform the same basic operations. Every **computer** can input, store, manipulate, and output vast quantities of data at very high speed. Moreover, all computers are *programmable* — they can follow a list of instructions (a **program**) and act upon intermediate results without human intervention.

A **personal computer** (or **PC**) is a relatively small type of computer, intended for use by one person at a time. (Larger machines — known as *minicomputers*, *mainframes*, and *supercomputers*, in order of increasing size and power — can be simultaneously shared by many users, connected to the computer by cables or telephone lines.) All personal computers are small enough to fit on a desktop; portable PCs are even smaller — usually no larger than a looseleaf binder. A drawing of a typical PC is shown in Figure 1.

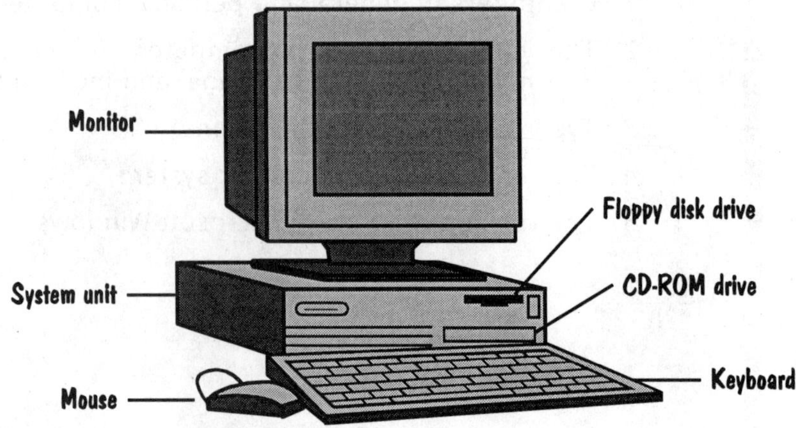

Figure 1   A Typical Personal Computer

Components of a computer

As the definition implies, a computer must have the ability to input, store, manipulate, and output data. These functions are carried out by the five main components of a computer system:

1. The central processing unit (CPU)

2. Internal memory (RAM and ROM)

3. Mass storage devices (such as disk, CD-ROM, and tape drives)

4. Input devices (such as keyboard and mouse)

5. Output devices (such as monitors and printers)

In a personal computer, the first two types of components (and usually the third as well) are located in the **system unit** (see Figure 1). The input and output devices are housed in their own enclosures and are connected to the system unit by cables. Components like these, that are used by a computer but located outside the system unit, are sometimes called **peripherals**. All the physical equipment that makes up the computer system is known as **hardware**.

The Central Processing Unit

The **central processing unit** (also called the **processor** or **CPU**) is the brain of the computer. It receives all program instructions, performs the arithmetic and logical operations necessary to execute them, and controls all the other computer components. In a personal computer, the processor consists of millions of transistors residing on a single *chip* about the size of a postage stamp, and plugged into the computer's main circuit board, the *motherboard*.

More than any other component, the CPU distinguishes one computer from another. If the kind of computer you are using is *IBM-compatible*, then the processor is probably made by Intel Corporation and referred to as either a 486 (pronounced "four-86") or *Pentium*. If you are using a computer that is not IBM-compatible, then it probably contains an Alpha, Power PC, or MIPS processor.

The power of a processor is determined largely by two factors: its speed, measured in *megahertz* (MHz), and the amount, or number of *bits*, of data it can process at a time. (A **bit** is the smallest piece of information a computer can manipulate; its value is represented by either a 0 or 1.) For example, Pentiums are 64-bit chips that vary in speed from 60 MHz to (as of this writing) 333 MHz. To use Windows NT, you need a computer with at least a 32-bit chip, and the more speed the better.

Internal Memory

A computer uses its **internal memory** to store the instructions and data to be processed by the CPU. In a personal computer, memory resides on a series of chips either plugged directly into the motherboard or into one or more smaller circuit boards connected to the motherboard.

ROM and RAM

Internal memory is divided into two types: ROM and RAM. **ROM** stands for *Read-Only Memory*. It contains an unalterable set of instructions that the computer consults during its start-up process and during certain other basic operations. **RAM** (*Random Access Memory*), on the other hand, can be both read from and written to. (Think of ROM as a reference sheet, while RAM is a scratchpad — a very large scratchpad.) RAM is used by the computer to hold program instructions and data. Whereas ROM is a permanent form of memory storage, all the information stored in RAM is lost when the computer is turned off.

Memory is usually measured in *kilobytes* and *megabytes*; one **byte** consists of eight bits and is the amount of memory used to store one character of information. (Loosely speaking, a *character* is any symbol you can type, such as a letter, a digit, or a punctuation mark.) One **kilobyte**, abbreviated KB, is 1,024 (= 2^{10}) bytes and one **megabyte** (MB) is 1,024 kilobytes. For example, a computer with sixteen megabytes of RAM, a typical amount nowadays, can store 16,777,216 (= $16 \times 1,024 \times 1,024$) characters of information.

Mass Storage Devices

In addition to ROM and RAM, a computer needs **mass storage**, another form of memory, which stores programs and data semi-permanently. Data remain in mass storage until you decide to erase them. However, to make use of any information stored on a mass storage device, the computer must first *load* (copy) that information into RAM.

Hard and floppy disk drives

On personal computers, the primary type of mass storage device is the **disk drive**. Most PCs contain a *hard disk drive* and a *floppy disk drive* housed within the system unit. The latter drive is accessible from the outside (see Figure 1) so that disks can be inserted and removed from it. To store information, the hard disk drive makes use of a constantly spinning magnetic platter — the **hard disk** — which is sealed within the drive. **Floppy disks** (or **diskettes**), on the other hand, are stored away from the computer and, when needed, are inserted into the diskette drive.

Modern personal computers use floppy disks that are 3½ inches in diameter (see Figure 2) and store 1.44 megabytes of data. (You may encounter diskettes of other sizes and/or capacities on older, less powerful PCs.) Hard drives hold much more data than floppies. Modern personal computers come equipped with hard drives that exceed 1,024 megabytes — one **gigabyte** (GB) — of storage capacity.

Write-protecting a diskette

If you want to prevent the accidental erasure of data on a floppy disk, you can *write-protect* it. A write protected diskette can be read from, but not written to or erased. To write-protect a 3½-inch diskette, throw its write-protect switch so that the hole under it is exposed (see Figure 2).

Write-protect switch

Figure 2 Floppy Disk

You may be wondering why computers contain both hard and floppy drives. Typically, the hard drive is used to store most of the programs and data to be used by a PC. Floppy drives, which are much slower in operation, are typically used in the following ways:

- To transfer newly purchased programs from the distribution disks to the computer's hard disk.

- For *backup* purposes — to make copies of valuable hard disk data in the event that the hard disk becomes damaged.

- To help transfer information from one computer to another.

- For *archival* purposes — to move information from the hard disk to floppies when it is unlikely to be needed in the foreseeable future.

CD-ROM drives

Virtually all PCs sold today are equipped with another type of mass storage device, the **CD-ROM drive**. These drives use disks that are similar to audio compact discs (hence the "CD" in the name). Like floppies, CD-ROMs are removable and portable, but, unlike floppies, they hold large amounts of information — about 600 MB each. Because CD-ROM drives are read-only devices (hence the "ROM" in the name), they are used primarily:

- To distribute large applications to the computer user (instead of using dozens of floppies).

- To run applications that require an unusually large amount of storage space, such as encyclopedias and graphics-intensive games.

However, even CD-ROMs do not have the capacity needed to run certain modern computer applications, such as those that use large amounts of video and sound. For this reason, the *digital versatile disk*, or DVD, was developed. A DVD has more than seven times the storage capacity of a CD-ROM. DVD drives, which can also read CD-ROMs, are slowly replacing the latter in computer systems.

Other mass storage devices

Floppy disk drives and CD-ROM drives are referred to generically as *removable media* devices since, unlike hard drives, their disks are inserted into the drive before use and removed from it afterwards. Other types of removable media drives have recently become popular; they have large storage capacities, yet preserve the floppy's ability to *write* data to the disk. The most common of these is the *Zip* drive made by Iomega Corporation, which holds 100 megabytes of information. Other drives of this type can store as much as two *gigabytes* of data.

Another fairly common mass storage devices is the **tape drive**, which uses media that resemble audio cassettes. It can be used to copy (back up) the entire contents of a hard disk onto a magnetic tape. Should the information on the hard disk become inaccessible for any reason, the data could then be retrieved from the backup tape. A tape drive works slowly, but this isn't too important considering its intended role.

Input Devices

The computer uses its **input devices** to receive data from the outside world. For this purpose, every computer includes a typewriter-like **keyboard** (see Figure 3). To enter information into the computer, you simply type it at the keyboard in the same way you would using an ordinary typewriter. The characters you type will simultaneously appear on the computer's display screen.

Special keys

Computer keyboards contain quite a few keys not found on a typewriter. (Figure 3 shows a common keyboard layout for IBM-compatible machines.) These "extra" keys include:

- Twelve *function keys* labeled F1 through F12 are arrayed across the top of the keyboard. They perform special tasks that vary from program to program.

- Just to the right of the large block of typewriter-like keys are ten *cursor control keys*: the four *Arrow keys* (↑, ↓, ←, and →) plus Insert, Home, etc. These keys allow you to move the *cursor*, which indicates the current typing position, around the screen.

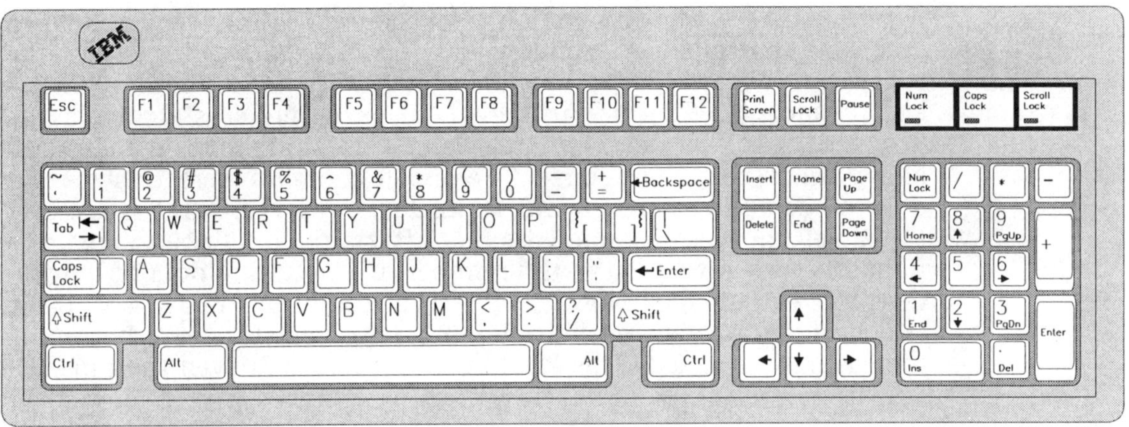

Figure 3   A Typical Keyboard Layout

- A *numeric keypad*, at the far right of the keyboard, allows you to enter numbers quickly. If the *Num Lock* light (above the keypad) is off, pressing one of these keys does not input a number — it performs the secondary function indicated on the key (for example, Home or ↑). To turn the Num Lock light on or off, press the Num Lock key.

You may notice a few other special keys (such as Esc and Print Screen) here and there on the keyboard. We will explain their functions at the appropriate time later in the text.

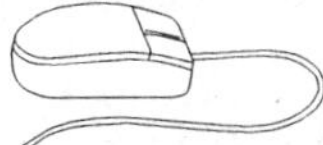

Another standard input device is the **mouse**, a hand-held object containing two or three buttons, which (together with the cable that connects it to the computer) vaguely resembles a long-tailed rodent. When you roll the mouse around on the desk top, a pointer moves correspondingly on the screen. For example, if you roll the mouse to the left, the pointer moves left. Once the pointer is positioned appropriately on the screen, pressing a mouse button (*clicking the mouse*) performs a program function. The mouse can speed up many Windows operations, but it lacks the versatility of the keyboard.

Output Devices

Whereas input devices allow us to communicate with the computer, **output devices** make it possible for the computer to "talk" to us. The most common output devices are *monitors* and *printers*.

A **monitor** is a high resolution television-like screen enclosed in a case and controlled by circuitry — the *video adapter* — within the computer. (The screens on portable computers use an entirely different technology; they are usually *LCD* — liquid crystal display — *panels.*) As is the case with televisions, monitor size is measured along the screen's diagonal. The most common screen sizes for desktop computers are 14 and 15 inches, but larger screens are also available. Another characteristic that affects the quality and cost of a monitor is its *resolution* — the number of *pixels* (tiny dots of light) it uses to create images. Nowadays, screen resolutions of 1024 × 768 — 768 horizontal rows, each containing 1,024 pixels — are becoming increasingly common. This kind of resolution puts even the finest of televisions to shame.

Unfortunately, output to the screen is both impermanent (it disappears when the power is turned off) and not terribly portable (you'd need a pretty long extension cord to take your screen output home from school). If you want to make a permanent copy of a program's output on paper, you need to use a **printer**.

The text and pictures produced by virtually all printers are composed of tiny dots of ink or an ink-like substance. The size of these dots and how closely they are packed together determines the quality of the output. Currently, two types of printers dominate the market:

- *Laser printers* have become the standard for business use. They produce excellent-looking black-and-white text and graphics at a high rate of speed, and are remarkably reliable. Laser prices start at about $400, but they cost relatively little to run and maintain. *Color* laser printers are not as common as their monochrome brethren, mainly because of their considerable cost.

- *Ink jet printers* spray incredibly tiny drops of ink on the paper creating surprisingly clear images. Moreover, most ink jets produce pretty good color output as well. Although, generally speaking, ink jet printers cost less to buy than lasers, they are slower and have a higher cost of operation. For these reasons, ink jets are more common in the home than in the office.

Software, Operating Systems, and Windows

The most powerful hardware cannot accomplish anything by itself. It needs **software** — computer programs — to bring it to life. Software provides instructions for the central processing unit and, in so doing, allows the computer user to write letters, calculate loan balances, draw pictures, play games, and perform countless other tasks.

Applications Software

Software can be divided into two general categories: applications software and system software. **Applications** are programs you use to enhance your productivity, solve problems, supply information, or provide recreation. To be able to run programs like these is the reason one learns to use a computer.

Here are some of the most commonly used applications:

Some types of applications

- *Word processors* help you create, edit, and print documents such as letters, reports, memos, and so on.

- *Database managers* allow you to enter, access, and modify large quantities of data. You might use a database program to create a personal phone directory. A business can use this kind of application to maintain customer lists and employee records.

- *Spreadsheet programs* simplify the manipulation and calculation of large amounts of tabular data (spreadsheets). These programs are often used by businesses to try to foresee the effect of different strategies on their bottom line.

- *Drawing and painting programs* allow one to use the computer to (as you may have guessed) draw or paint pictures — *graphics* — on the screen and print them on paper.

- *Multimedia applications* make extensive use of graphics, sound, and sometimes video images to provide information or entertainment.

Applications are developed and published by many different companies and are sold by retail stores and mail order firms. Each software package consists of a *user's guide* together with one or more diskettes or CDs that contain the application *files* — the programs, data, and documents needed by the application. Before you can use a software package, it must be *installed* — the computer must copy files from the floppies or CDs to the hard disk and supply certain information about the application to the operating system.

The Operating System

The second general software type is **system software**, the programs used by the computer to control and maintain its hardware and to communicate with the user. The most important piece of system software is the **operating system** — the computer's master control program. An operating system has two general functions:

1. It helps the application you are using to communicate with the computer hardware. Applications are written to run under a specific operating system, which supplies easy ways for the programmers to access the computer's disk drives, memory, and so on.

2. It provides an *interface* — a link — between you and the computer that allows you to install and start up applications, manipulate disk files, and perform other very basic tasks.

DOS   The central processing unit may be the brain of the computer, but the operating system gives the machine its personality. For years, the most common operating system for IBM-compatible computers was **DOS** (for *disk operating system*), which was developed by Microsoft Corporation for the original IBM Personal Computer introduced in 1981. Despite major changes made to it over the intervening years, DOS retains much of the awkwardness of its distant past, and as a result, its popularity has waned considerably in the 1990s.

An immediate clue to an operating system's personality is its *start-up screen*, the one you see after you turn on the computer and it has gone through its preliminary functions. With pure, unadorned DOS, you are presented with a few lines of mysterious-looking text ending with the **DOS prompt** (most likely, C:\>) followed by a blinking underline (the *cursor*). This is DOS' way of asking you to enter a command. For example, if you want to start up your word processor, you might type the following two lines (pressing the Enter key at the end of each):

```
CD \WP51\DATA
\WP51\WP
```

This kind of **command line interface** is classic DOS. In order to direct DOS to perform a function, the computer user must memorize (or have a handy list of) a large number of arcane commands. This is certainly not a *user-friendly* system.

GUIs   A vast improvement in user-friendliness is the **graphical user interface** (GUI, pronounced "gooey") popularized by the Apple Macintosh line of computers. In a GUI, the start-up screen contains a collection of small stylized pictures called **icons** (see Figure 4) together with a set of **menus** that supplies available options. (The menus in Figure 4 are entitled *File, Options, Window,* and *Help.*) With a graphical user interface, you can start up applications and perform other operating system functions as easily as moving the mouse pointer to the corresponding icon or menu item and pressing a mouse button. The keyboard can also be employed to carry out functions, but using a GUI is much easier with a mouse.

Microsoft Windows

Windows is a very sophisticated piece of software, originally developed in 1985 by Microsoft Corporation, that employs a graphical user interface to help make IBM-compatible computers easier to use. Although Windows sold slowly at first, version 3.0 (introduced in 1990) and especially version 3.1 (1992) were wildly popular. The latter version established Windows as the standard operating environment for IBM-compatible computers.

Advantages of Windows

Using Windows provides many advantages over plain old DOS:

- Its graphical user interface is much easier to use than DOS' command line interface. (Figure 4 shows the Windows 3.1 start-up screen.)

- Windows has *multitasking* capabilities — you can run more than

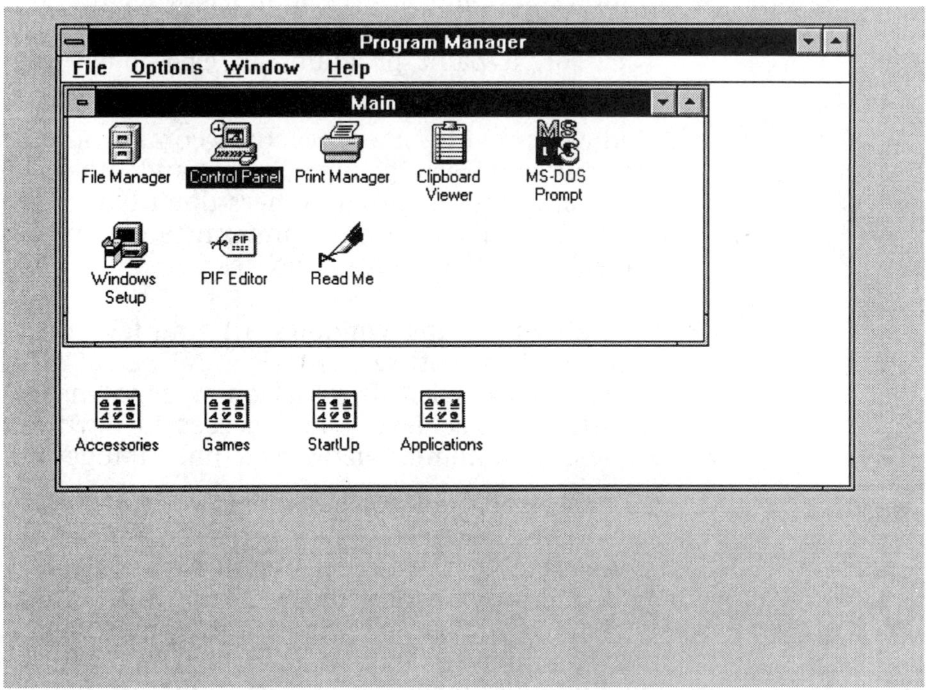

Figure 4   A Typical Windows 3.1 Start-up Screen

one application at a time, each occupying its own area on the screen. For example, you can start up a paint program to draw a picture without closing down the word processor that is already running.

■ You can easily transfer data from one application to another. For example, the picture you've just completed in the paint program can be inserted by Windows into your word processing document.

■ Windows provides uniform standards for the look and feel of applications developed to run under it. (Such programs are called *Windows applications*; those not designed specifically for Windows are called *DOS applications*.) This is of great benefit to the computer user, making it easier to learn and use new applications.

■ The Windows user interface is highly customizable; you are given a great amount of control over the way that it looks and acts. For example, you can design your own start-up screen, choose your own screen colors, position and size the areas on the screen in which your applications are running, and much, much more.

■ Windows supplies a large number of useful small and medium-sized applications. These include an on-screen calculator, a word processor, a paint program, an easy-to-use file manager, and even a few games.

■ Windows provides modules that control a wide assortment of different monitors, printers, mice, and other peripherals. As a result, applications programmers don't have to worry about writing their own software to communicate with the huge variety of available input and output devices.

Microsoft also used the Windows 3.1 interface on a more sophisticated variant of the software, *Windows NT* 3.51. ("NT" stands for New Technology.) Although this variation was not nearly as popular as version 3.1, it did achieve some success in environments that consisted of many computers *networked* (linked) together.

Windows NT 4 In 1995, Microsoft brought out a new version of Windows, *Windows 95*, which had a completely new interface and many other improvements. About a year later, Microsoft also updated Windows NT to version 4, and provided it with the Windows 95 interface. (Its start-up screen is shown in Figure 5.) As with the previous versions of NT, the new one was intended to be used primarily by businesses and other organizations that made use of large computer networks.

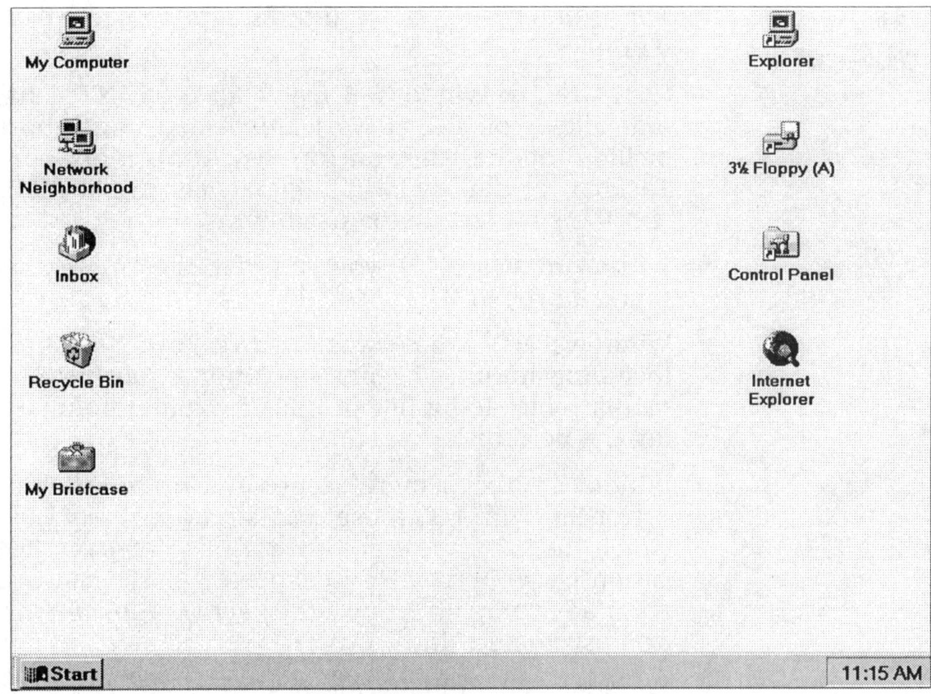

Figure 5   A Typical Windows NT 4 Start-up Screen

Windows NT 4 comes in two versions: *Workstation* and *Server*. Although they have the same user interface and most of the core features are the same, there are significant differences between the two:

- **Windows NT Workstation** is intended for use on a computer that serves the needs of an individual user. Although a computer running NT Workstation may be connected to a network, it can also function as a *standalone* machine — one that need not make use of network resources.

- **Windows NT Server** is intended for use on a network *server* — a computer that controls the operation of the network. NT Server is a more complicated operating system than NT Workstation. In addition to performing all the functions of the latter, Server supplies tools that allow the network administrator to manage the network itself.

Windows NT 4 has the following advantages over previous versions of Windows:

Advantages of Windows NT 4

- The Windows 95/NT 4 interface is easier to use than that of Windows 3.1/NT 3.51.

- Compared to Windows 3.1 and NT 3.51, NT 4 has new features that allow you to get work done faster and more easily. These include the Start button for easy startup of your programs, the Taskbar for quickly switching between applications, and Desktop shortcuts for frequently used items.

- With Windows NT 4, you can give files more reasonable names than allowed in Windows 3.1.

- Windows NT 4 has most of Windows 95's built-in programs, including improved communications, more sophisticated multi-media tools, and a few utilities for maintaining and better utilizing the hard disk.

- Windows NT 4 is more secure and more reliable than Windows 3.1 or 95. With NT, a user can set up a secret password, without which the system cannot be started. Moreover, should one application *crash* (terminate unexpectedly), NT can usually prevent it from adversely affecting other active applications and the operating system itself.

- Windows NT, unlike Windows 3.1 or 95, can be used with many computer systems that are not IBM-compatible.

To be sure, Windows NT 4 is not for everyone. In particular, Windows 95 may be a better choice for some computer users because it has the following features that NT lacks:

Disadvantages of Windows NT

- Windows NT requires a faster processor, more disk space, and more RAM than Windows 95.

- Windows NT does not successfully run as many Windows 3.1 or DOS applications as Windows 95.

- It is usually easier to add new hardware, such as a modem or printer, to a system that is running Windows 95.

- Windows 95 has better support for portable computers.

CHAPTER 1

The Basics of Using Windows NT

In the introduction to this text, we discussed the *what* and *why* of Windows NT. Recall that one of the goals of this powerful operating system is to make the computer easier to use. In this chapter, you will begin to see some of the things that Windows can do and how easily they are done. More specifically, you will learn to:

1. Recognize the elements of the Windows NT Desktop.

2. Use the mouse to perform basic Windows operations.

3. Choose items from menus.

4. Move, resize, minimize, maximize, and close windows.

5. Scroll through the contents of a window.

6. Use dialog boxes to indicate preferences.

7. Shut down Windows NT.

If you have worked with Windows 3.1 or NT 3.51, you should be familiar with most of the material presented in this chapter. Nevertheless, it's probably still a good idea to read through it; the review might be beneficial and there are a few new concepts in Sections 1.1 and 1.5.

1.1   *The Windows NT Desktop*

**Starting
Windows NT**

If Windows NT is installed on your computer, when you turn on the machine, you will see some messages flash across the screen. Then:

1. If the message "Please select the operating system to start" appears, use the Up Arrow or Down Arrow key to highlight the Windows NT Workstation entry (if it isn't already highlighted) and press the Enter key.

2. After a short while, you will see the Windows NT logo and then the message "Press Ctrl+Alt+Delete to log on". To proceed, hold down the Ctrl and Alt keys, tap the Delete key, and then release Ctrl and Alt. A small window, called the Logon Information dialog box, will be displayed on the screen.

3. In the Logon Information dialog box, type your user name and password (which were set up by your system administrator or when you installed Windows NT) in the appropriate boxes[*] and press the Enter key.

The startup process will continue and a window with the message "Welcome to Windows NT" may appear. If it does, press the Enter key to remove it from the screen. Finally, the Windows NT opening screen, like the one shown in Figure 1, will be displayed. (Depending on how your computer has been set up, its opening screen might look quite different from the one pictured here.)

The entire screen area is referred to as the Windows **Desktop**. Just like a regular desk top, it's the place on which you will do your work. Currently (in Figure 1), there are only a few objects on the Desktop. After we begin working with a program or two, however, most of the Desktop will be covered by *windows* of various sorts, and the objects you see here (except the Taskbar) will usually become obscured.

**Items on
the Desktop**

The **Start button**, located in the lower left corner of the screen in Figure 1, is the jumping off point for a typical Windows session. It provides access to all the applications (programs) installed on your computer. We will discuss the use of the Start button at the beginning of Chapter 2.

The labeled pictures displayed on the screen are called **icons**. These icons (and others like them throughout the Windows environment) provide easy access to various aspects of Windows NT. For example, as

---

[*]If you are not sure how to do this, consult Sections 1.2 and 1.4, which discuss using the mouse and dialog boxes.

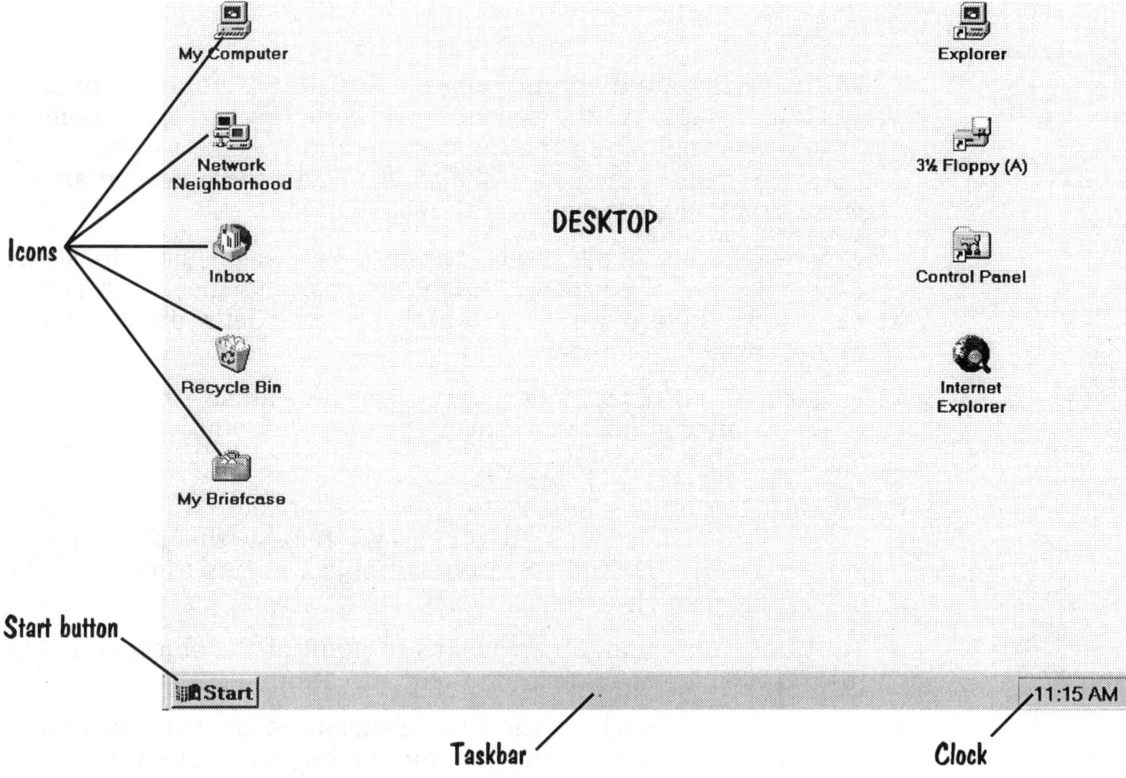

Figure 1   The Windows NT Desktop

you will see in Chapter 3, the icon labeled "My Computer" allows you to work with virtually every piece of hardware and software that is part of your computer system.

The **Taskbar** displays the applications and documents that you are currently using. Because there are no applications currently running, the only item on the Taskbar in Figure 1 (other than the Start button) is the Clock utility, which displays the time of day.

1.2   Of Mice and Menus

As you know, one of the primary advantages of working with Windows is that it is easy to use. This is due, in part, to its extensive use of the mouse and menus.

Using the Mouse

When a mouse is moved around on a flat surface, its pointer moves in a corresponding way on the screen. The shape of the mouse pointer depends on the application that is running and the use to which it is being put. The pointer may look like an arrow, a double-headed arrow, an I-beam, or a hand, among other things.

In Windows and its applications, the mouse can be used to select items displayed on the screen, initiate actions, and move and resize certain objects. Before we illustrate these uses, let's discuss some important mouse terminology.

Mouse terminology

- To *point at* an object means to move the mouse so that its on-screen pointer is positioned over the specified object and held in place for a few moments.

- To *click* the mouse means to press and release the left mouse button. To *right-click* is to press and release the right mouse button. To click (or right-click) *on* an object means to point at the object and then click (or right-click)*.

- To *double-click* on an object means to point at the object and click the left mouse button twice in rapid succession.

- To *drag* an object with the mouse means to point at the object, press (but not release) the left mouse button, move the mouse pointer to a new location, and then release the button. To *right-drag* an object is to perform the same actions using the right mouse button instead of the left.

To illustrate these operations, let's return to the computer screen shown in Figure 1. If we double-click on the My Computer icon, the **window** — boxed-in area on the screen — shown in Figure 2 appears. (Your My Computer window may look quite different from the one pictured here. Don't worry; for the purposes of the current discussion, it does not matter.)

If you double-click on an object and it doesn't initiate an action, you may have moved the mouse slightly between clicks or perhaps you didn't follow the first click by the second quickly enough. Try double-clicking again.

---

*If the functions of your left and right mouse buttons seem to be reversed, they can easily be restored to their "normal" settings. Either ask your lab coordinator to do this for you or see Section 4.4. (If you want to try it yourself, first finish reading Chapter 1.)

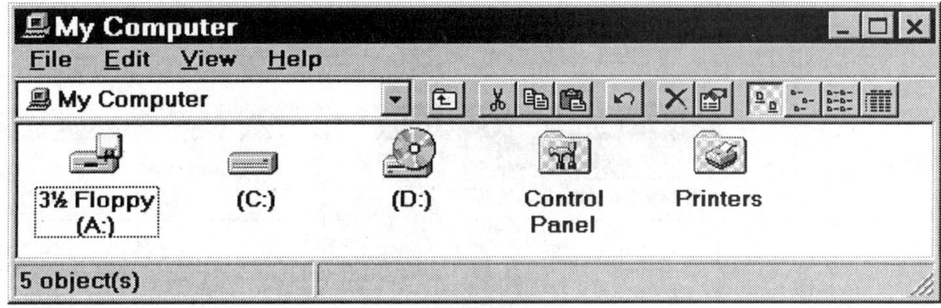

Figure 2   The My Computer Window

Using Menus

The first line of the My Computer window (Figure 2) is called its **title bar**; it contains the name of the window together with some symbols that we'll discuss in Section 1.3. Below the title bar is the My Computer **menu bar**:

Opening a menu

The words that appear on the menu bar are the names of **menus** — lists of commands — that can be used to manipulate the contents of the My Computer window. To *open* (display) a menu, simply click on its name. For example, if you click on the word *View*, the menu pictured in Figure 3 (on the next page) appears. Because this kind of menu looks as if it were pulled down, like a window shade unrolling from the word View, it is called a **pull-down menu**.

Selecting a menu option

Once a menu has been opened, you can choose one of the options listed by clicking on that item. (Doing so will also close the menu.) For example, to choose the "Line up Icons" option from the View menu in Figure 3, move the mouse pointer straight down until it is positioned over this item (it will become highlighted) and click the left button.

NOTE

If you prefer, the options listed on a pull-down menu can be accessed using the keyboard. Notice that each name on the menu bar has one letter underlined; for example, the *V* in View. To display a pull-down menu, hold down either Alt key, press the key corresponding to the underlined letter, and then release the Alt key. (We will write this sequence of actions as — if the underlined letter is V — "press Alt+V".) Then, to select an option on that menu, either:

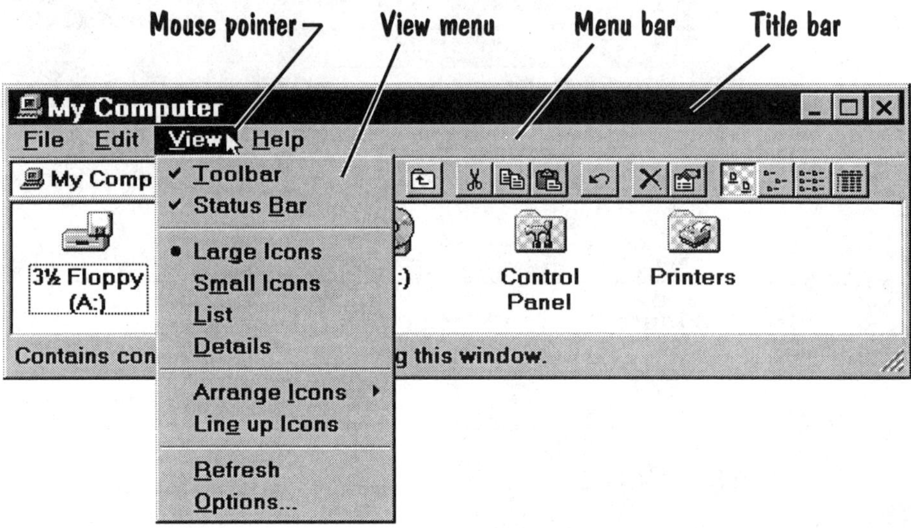

Figure 3   A Typical Pull-down Menu

- Press the key corresponding to the underlined letter in the desired option.

or

- Press the Down Arrow key (↓) until the desired option is highlighted and then press the Enter key.

For example, to display the View menu shown in Figure 3, hold down the Alt key, press the key labeled V, and release Alt. Then, to select the Line up Icons option, *either* press the E key *or* press the Down Arrow key several times until the option is highlighted and then press the Enter key.

Closing a menu   If you want to close a menu without selecting any of the options, just click on any other part of the screen. As an alternative, press the Escape key.

Types of Menu Items

Let's take a closer look at the View menu that is displayed in Figure 3. Notice that some options on this menu are preceded or followed by a special symbol, such as a check mark or bullet (see Figure 4).

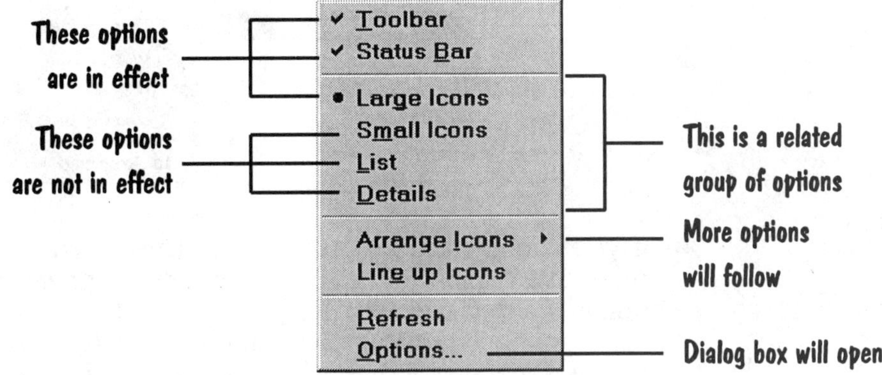

Figure 4   Special Symbols for Menu Options

These symbols have a consistent meaning throughout Windows and its applications:

Menu symbols

- If a *check mark* (✔) appears next to a menu option, it indicates that this item or characteristic is currently in effect. For example, in Figure 4, the check marks next to Toolbar and Status Bar indicate that both these objects are displayed in the My Computer window. If you click on Toolbar, the menu will close and the Toolbar will disappear from the window. (Try it!) Then, the next time you pull down the My Computer View menu, you'll notice that the check mark next to Toolbar has disappeared as well — this option is no longer in effect. To get it back, choose Toolbar again. We call this kind of option a *toggle*: if the Toolbar *is* currently displayed, choosing the menu option turns it off; if it is *not* displayed, choosing the option turns it on.

- A *bullet* (•) next to a menu option not only means that this option is in effect, but also indicates that the rest of a group of related items are *not* in effect. (The horizontal lines within a menu — see Figure 4 — divide it into these groups.) For example, the bullet on the Large Icons option in Figure 4 describes the contents of the My Computer window (see Figure 3). This window does *not* contain Small Icons, a List, or Details. Only one bulleted item within its group can be in effect at any given time.

- A *triangle symbol* (▸) next to a menu item indicates that a *submenu* of additional options will appear if you "point at" this item. For example, if you move the mouse pointer over the Arrange Icons option in Figure 4 and hold it steady for a few moments, the following submenu is displayed at its right:

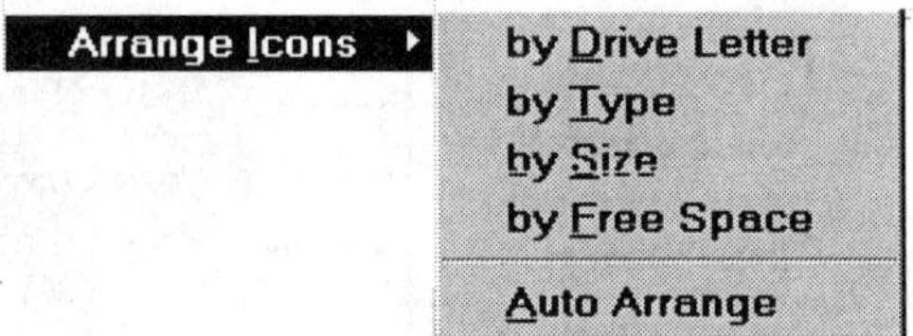

- If you choose a menu name that is followed by an *ellipsis* (three consecutive periods), a *dialog box* will appear requesting additional information. (Dialog boxes are discussed in Section 1.4.) For example, choosing the Options item from the View menu of Figure 4 displays a dialog box presenting the available options. (If you open this dialog box, you can close it, removing it from the screen, by clicking on the button labeled Cancel.)

Before we close this section, let's pull down My Computer's Edit menu (by clicking on the word Edit on the menu bar) to illustrate a couple of additional points. This menu is shown in Figure 5.

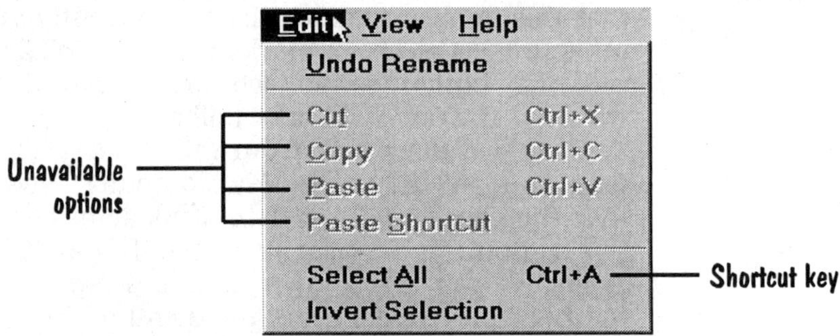

Figure 5   The My Computer Edit Menu

In Figure 5, notice that:

- The second group of options is *dimmed* — it appears to be "faded out". This indicates that these options are temporarily not available. If you click on one of these items, nothing will happen!

- Keystrokes (such as Ctrl+A) appear next to several menu items. These keystrokes are called **shortcut keys**. They provide a quick way of choosing the corresponding menu option *without displaying the menu itself.* For example, to select all the objects in the My Computer window without displaying the Edit menu, just press Ctrl+A; that is, hold down the Ctrl (Control) key, type A, and then release Ctrl.

NOTE

If you have been following along at the computer and you now want to close the My Computer window, click on the little box marked with an **X** in the upper-right corner of this window. To shut down Windows NT, which is wise to do before turning off your computer, follow the instructions in Section 1.5.

TUTORIAL

Try the following exercise on your own.

1. Turn on your computer (if it's not already on) to start Windows NT. If the My Computer window is open, close it by clicking (tapping the left mouse button) on the little box marked with an **X** in the upper-right corner of this window.

2. *Click* on the My Computer icon (by moving the mouse pointer — an arrow shape — over this icon, then tapping the left mouse button). The words *My Computer* should now be highlighted.

3. *Drag* the My Computer icon to another location on the Desktop. (Position the mouse pointer over the icon; press, but do not release, the left mouse button; move the pointer to a new location on the screen, and release the mouse button.)

4. Drag the My Computer icon back to its original location.

5. *Double-click* on the My Computer icon (by clicking twice in rapid succession on this icon). The My Computer window should open. If not, try double-clicking again, being sure not to move the mouse as you do so.

6. Click on the word *View* on the menu bar. The View menu should open.

7. On the View menu, there will be a *bullet* next to one of the options in the second group (beginning with "Large Icons"). Click on one of the other three items in this group. The View menu should close. Notice the change in the My Computer window.

8. Open the View menu and *point at* Arrange Icons by moving the mouse pointer over these words and holding it still for a few moments. A submenu should appear. Note whether or not the option Auto Arrange is checked on this submenu.

9. Now click on the Auto Arrange option. The two menus will close. Reopen the View menu and the Arrange Icons submenu. If Auto Arrange was originally "checked", it should now be "unchecked", and vice-versa.

10. Reopen the View menu and click on the "Options..." item. A new window — a dialog box — will open. Close it by pressing the Escape key or by clicking on the box marked with an **X** in the upper-right corner of this window.

11. If you want to quit, to shut down Windows NT see the NOTE that precedes this tutorial.

1.3   Windows within Windows

While working at your desk (say, doing homework), you might have several documents open at once — perhaps a textbook, a reference book, and your notebook. This is often the case on the Windows Desktop as well. Here, the documents and other related objects are contained in *windows*. Depending on what you're doing at the moment, you might want to move some of these windows around, make one of them bigger, or perhaps take some of them off the Desktop. In this section, we will describe how to perform these actions — how to move, resize, and close windows.

Operations on Windows

Before we explain *how* to move or resize a window, let's look at a few reasons *why* you might want to perform these operations. For one thing, it's usually much easier to use the contents of a window when it occupies the entire screen; you can view more information and, in some cases, see more detail as well. Often, however, when a window opens, it just occupies part of the Desktop. (This was the case with our My Computer window in Section 1.2.) In such a case, you might want to increase the size of the window, perhaps **maximizing** it so that it uses as much screen real estate as possible.

The disadvantage of maximizing a window is that it then might obscure everything else on the Desktop. Even when not maximized, it might cover vital information in another window or on the Desktop itself. Thus, at times you will want to reduce the size of a window or even **close** it, which takes it off the Desktop. Instead of closing a window, it is sometimes possible to **minimize** it, which also removes it from the screen. The difference between closing and minimizing a window is a subtle one:

- *Closing a window* removes its contents from the computer's internal memory, RAM (see the Introduction).

- *Minimizing a window* keeps its contents in RAM and reduces the window to a button on the Taskbar, allowing us to restore the window quickly and easily.

Manipulating Windows

To illustrate the different ways in which we can manipulate a typical window, let's open the My Computer window by double-clicking on the My Computer icon, as we did in Section 1.2. Figure 6 shows the parts of the title bar that are involved in moving, minimizing, maximizing, and closing a window.

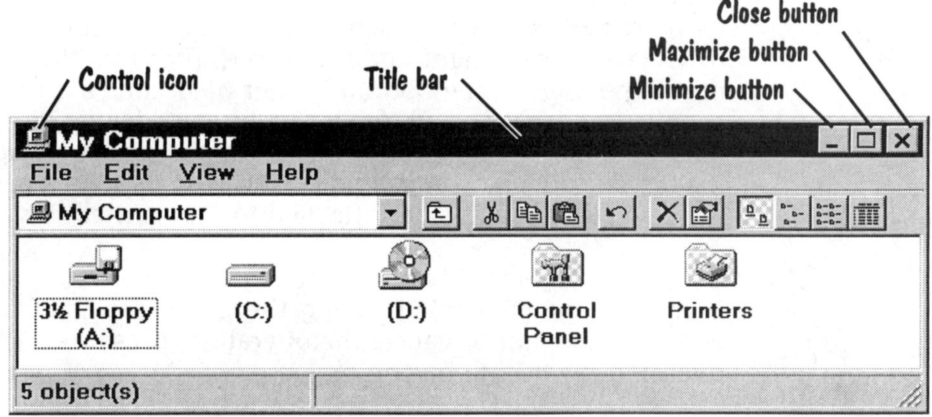

Figure 6   Parts of the Title Bar

Moving a Window   To *move* a window, drag its title bar to the new location. More specifically, position the mouse pointer over the title bar, press (but don't release) the left mouse button, and move the mouse in the direction you want the window to move.

As you do so, an outline of the moving window may appear on the screen. When this outline, or the window itself, is positioned to your liking, release the mouse button.

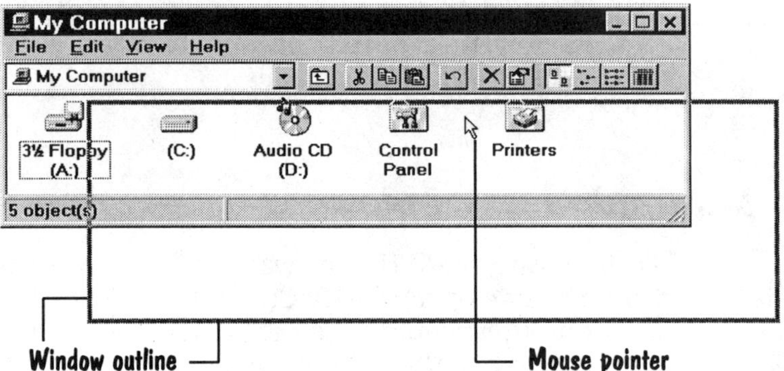

Resizing a Window   To *resize* a window, drag its border or corner to a new position. For example, to increase the height of a window, position the mouse pointer on the bottom border (it becomes a two-headed arrow, as pictured above) and drag the border down. When the window outline* indicates that you've achieved the desired height, release the mouse button; the window will redraw to its new size. (If you drag a window *corner*, both sides attached to that corner move at once.)

If you change your mind during the process of moving or resizing a window and want to cancel the operation, press the Escape key before releasing the mouse button.

Minimizing, Maximizing, or Closing a Window   To *minimize*, *maximize*, or *close* a window, click on the **minimize button**, **maximize button**, or **close button**, respectively (on the right end of the title bar).

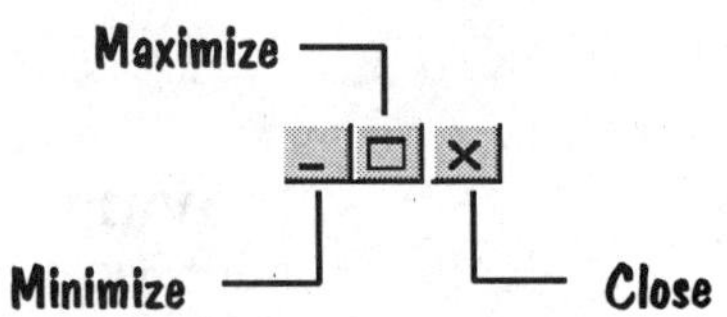

Note that:

- When a window is minimized, it is removed from the screen but its name and icon continue to appear on a button on the Taskbar. To reopen a minimized window, click on its Taskbar button.

---

*Instead of an outline, you may see the actual window, together with its contents, move as you drag the mouse pointer. (A setting in Control Panel's "Display" utility determines which of these occurs.)

- When a window is maximized, it expands to its largest possible size and the maximize button is replaced by a **restore button.** Clicking on the latter, **restores** the window, returning it to its former position and size. 

- When a window is closed, it disappears from the screen.

You can also *maximize* a window by double-clicking on its title bar. Once a window is maximized, the same operation —double-clicking on the title bar — restores it. A window can also be *closed* by double-clicking on its Control icon (see Figure 6), but since every Windows NT window has a close button, this fact is useful for little more than impressing your friends, and it's not likely to do even that.

Although using the mouse is easier, Windows NT does allow you to use the keyboard to perform the move, resize, maximize, minimize, and close operations on a window. These operations (when available) are listed on the window's **Control menu**. To open the Control menu using the keyboard, press Alt+Spacebar or Alt+Hyphen, whichever works. (Remember: The notation "Alt+*keystroke*" means "hold down the Alt key, type the keystroke, and then release the Alt key".) The Control menu will appear in the upper left corner of the window, as shown in the following figure:

(You can also open its Control menu by right-clicking on the window's title bar or by clicking on its Control icon — see Figure 6 — if the window has one.) Choosing the Minimize, Maximize, Close, or Restore option performs the indicated task. Choosing Move or Size requires some maneuvering with the Arrow keys to complete the task; for these two operations, it's *a lot* easier to use the mouse!

Scroll Bars

When a window is not large enough to view all its contents at once, one or two **scroll bars** will be displayed to allow you to move through the contents without increasing the size of the window. For example, if we decrease the size of the My Computer window shown in Figure 6 so that the icons are partially or completely covered, the resulting window will look similar to the one in Figure 7.

Figure 7   Scroll Bars Visible in a Window

Scrolling in a window
If the contents of a window — let's call it a *document*, even if it's just a collection of icons — is only partly visible, you have to **scroll** to see the rest of it. To understand how this works, imagine that the entire document is lying on the Desktop, but the window acts like a "cutout", allowing us to see only part of it. To see more (without increasing the window's size), we have to move the cutout around. For example, when you *scroll down*, imagine the cutout moving in a downward direction so that a lower part of the document comes into view. (In actuality, the window stays fixed on the screen and, figuratively speaking, the document itself moves around.)

You can use the mouse to scroll through the contents of a window by clicking on various parts of a scroll bar (see Figure 7): the *horizontal* scroll bar scrolls the window left or right; the *vertical* scroll bar scrolls it up or down. Let's take a closer look at a vertical scroll bar (shown at the right).

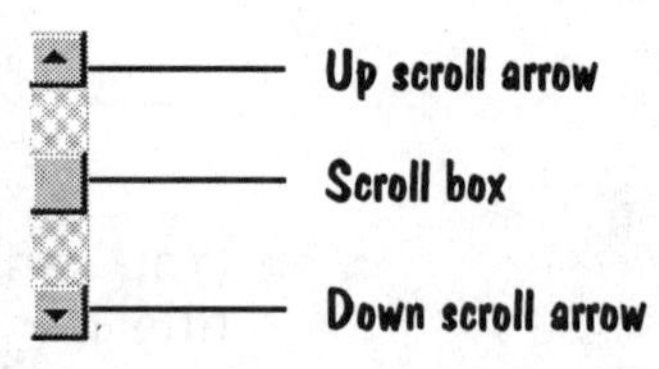

Here's how this scroll bar is used. (A horizontal scroll bar works in an analogous way.)

- Clicking on the up or down scroll arrow scrolls the window up or down one "step". Holding down the mouse button while pointing at the up or down scroll arrow scrolls the window continuously in that direction until you release the button.

- Clicking on the scroll bar above or below the scroll box scrolls up or down one window's worth of information.

- Dragging the scroll box up or down scrolls the window proportionally within the document. For example, if you drag the scroll box to the middle of the scroll bar, the window will scroll to a point about halfway through the document.

NOTE

The horizontal and vertical scroll bars also give visual clues to the size of the document in the window and your current location within it:

- The *length* of a scroll box is proportional to the amount of the document you are viewing. For example, the horizontal scroll box in Figure 7 is roughly 80% of the length of the corresponding scroll bar; we can deduce from this that we are seeing about 80% of the width of the underlying "document". The vertical scroll box in Figure 7 is about half the length of its scroll bar; we are viewing about half the height of the document.

- The *position* of a scroll box along its scroll bar gives your relative location in the document. For example, in Figure 7, the horizontal scroll box is positioned at the left of its bar and the vertical scroll box is positioned at the top of its bar; we conclude that we are viewing the upper-left part of the underlying "document".

TUTORIAL

Try the following exercise on your own.

1. Start up your computer (if necessary) and open the My Computer window by double-clicking on its icon.

2. If the My Computer window is maximized (occupies the entire screen above the Taskbar), restore it by double-clicking on the title bar.

3. Minimize this window by clicking on its minimize button, toward the right end of the title bar. The title *My Computer* and its icon continue to appear on a button on the Taskbar.

4. Reopen the My Computer window by clicking on its Taskbar button.

5. Move the My Computer window to the upper-left corner of the screen by positioning the mouse pointer on the title bar and dragging the window to the appropriate place.

6. Make the window as small as possible in the horizontal direction. To do so, position the mouse pointer over the right window border (the pointer is placed properly when it turns into a "double arrow") and drag the border to the left as far as it will go. The horizontal scroll bar (and possibly the vertical one, as well) should appear.

7. Scroll across the window by positioning the mouse pointer over the right scroll arrow and holding down the left mouse button until the scroll box reaches the right end of the scroll bar. Now scroll back the other way by dragging the scroll box to the left end of the scroll bar. Increase the window to its former size.

8. Maximize the My Computer window by clicking on the maximize button, toward the right end of the title bar. 

9. Pull down the Control menu by clicking on the Control icon (which looks like a computer) on the left end of the title bar (or by pressing Alt+Spacebar). Notice that the Maximize option is dimmed.

10. Restore the My Computer window by clicking on the Restore option on the Control menu.

11. Close the My Computer window by clicking on the close button on the right end of the title bar. (Should you now want to shut down your computer, see Section 1.5.) 

1.4   Conversing with Dialog Boxes

As you may recall, choosing a menu item followed by an ellipsis (...) displays a dialog box. A **dialog box** is a special type of window that presents groups of related options from which you can make selections. As you work with Windows NT and its applications, you will encounter a seemingly infinite variety of dialog boxes. Yet, all dialog boxes have certain things in common. In this section, we will discuss these common features.

A Typical Dialog Box

To illustrate the features of a dialog box, let's take a look at a very interesting one. (Although we will discuss the types of objects in this dialog box here, a description of its capabilities will come later, in Chapter 4.) If you right-click (click the right mouse button) on an empty area of the Desktop, the following menu appears:

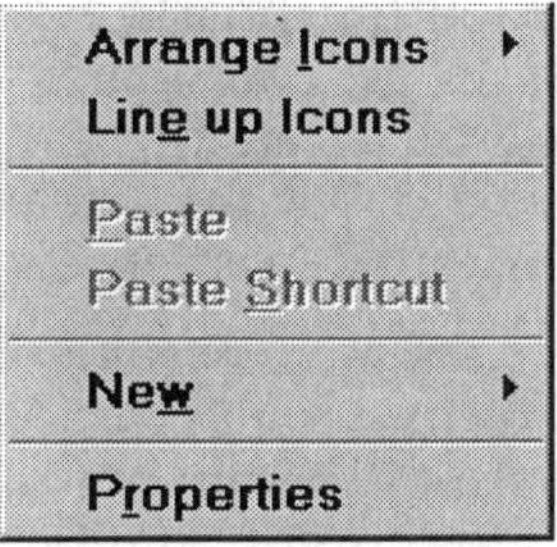

Choosing the Properties option from this menu opens the Display Properties dialog box shown in Figure 8. (Notice that there isn't any ellipsis next to the Properties option on the menu!)

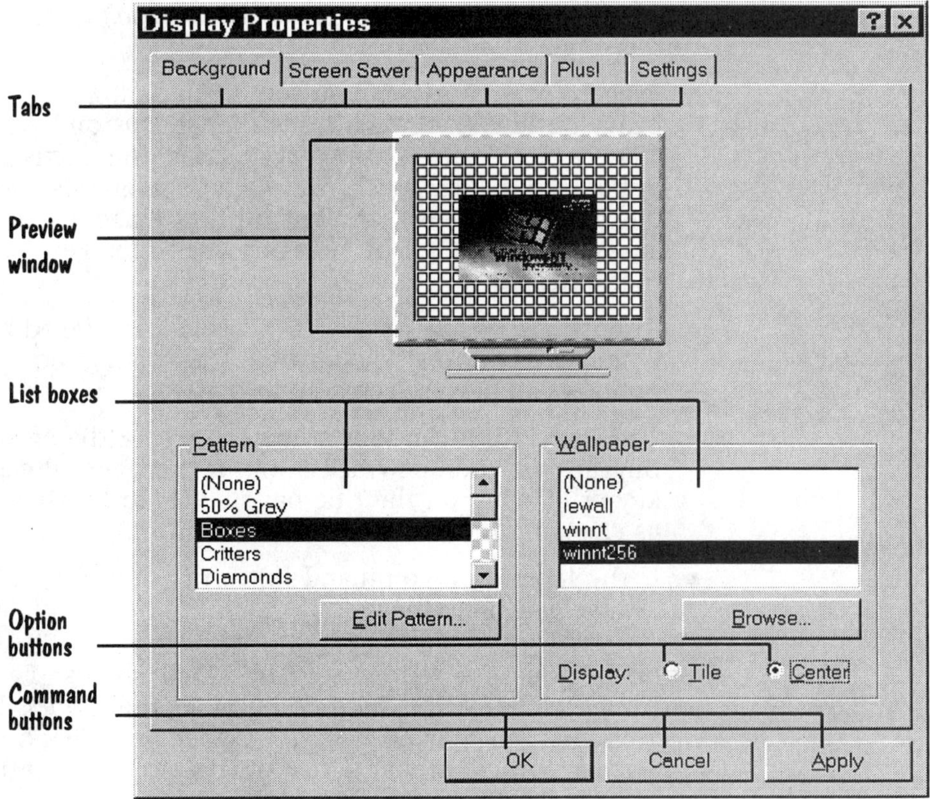

Figure 8   A Typical Dialog Box

At the top of this dialog box is the familiar title bar, which supplies the name of the window. It also contains a close button (marked with an X) and a help button (marked with a ?), but not a minimize or maximize button. In general, dialog boxes cannot be resized in any way; in particular, they cannot be minimized or maximized. Dialog boxes *can* be moved about the screen; as with any window, just drag its title bar to the desired location.

Most objects in a dialog box allow the user (that's you!) to specify preferences or execute commands. These objects (for example, the tabs, command buttons, option buttons, and list boxes of Figure 8) are arranged in related groups and associated with easily recognized symbols. Each symbol indicates a different function, as described below.

Command buttons are represented by large labeled rectangles. When you click on a command button, it initiates an action. For example, clicking on the Browse button in Figure 8 opens another dialog box. (Notice the ellipsis following the word *Browse.*) Here are a few special features of command buttons:

- Exactly one command button in a dialog box is enclosed in a heavy outline. (In Figure 8, it's the OK button.) We say that this is "the default button" or that it "has the focus". As you select options in a dialog box, the focus sometimes moves to another button. Nevertheless, the button that currently has the focus can always be activated by pressing the Enter key (or by clicking on that button).

- Almost all dialog boxes have a button labeled "OK" or "Close". When this button is activated, the dialog box closes and the options you have selected go into effect.

- The Cancel button allows you to close a dialog box without putting any of your new selections into effect. (Pressing the Escape key or clicking on the title bar's close button has the same effect as choosing the Cancel command button.)

- If the label on a command button is dimmed, this option is not available at this time.

Option buttons are represented by small circles. These buttons are sometimes called *radio buttons* because they work like the station selection push buttons on a radio — when you click on one of them, it is *selected* (turned on) and the others are automatically *deselected* (turned off). For this reason, in a group of these buttons, exactly one of the corresponding options is selected at any given time. The currently selected option button is indicated by a "bullet". For example, in Figure

8, the Center option is currently selected. If you click on the Tile button, it will acquire the bullet (indicating that this option has been selected), and the Center option will be deselected.

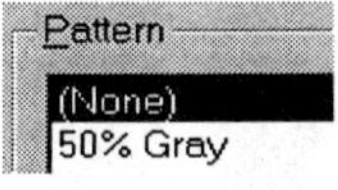

A **list box** is a rectangular box that contains a list of items from which you can choose. To select an item, click on its name. If the list is too long to fit in the box, a scroll bar will be displayed so that you can scroll through the entire list. The currently selected item in the list is highlighted. For example, in Figure 8, the selected item in the Pattern list box is "Boxes" and the selected Wallpaper is "winnt256".

Tabs, which resemble file folder tabs, always appear at the top of a dialog box (if they appear at all). The currently selected tab (which is "Background" in Figure 8) appears to be in front of the others. The name on the tab provides a short description of the group of options currently visible in the dialog box. To select another tab, click on it; a new "page" of options will become available. Figure 9 shows the result of clicking on the Screen Saver tab in the dialog box of Figure 8.

NOTE

Some dialog boxes also display written or pictorial information for the user. For example, the dialog box in Figure 8 contains a *preview window* that shows the effect your selections will have on the Windows Desktop should you choose the OK (or Apply) command button.

Additional Dialog Box Features

If you click on the Screen Saver tab in the Display Properties dialog box of Figure 8, most of the contents of this window change, providing a new set (*page*) of options from which to choose. The result is shown in Figure 9 (on the next page), which illustrates additional features of a dialog box.

A **check box** is represented by a small square, which may or may not contain a check mark. When the check box is selected, the check mark is present; when it is deselected, the check mark does not appear. For example, the deselected check box in Figure 9 indicates that this screen saver is not "password protected". A check box is a toggle:

- If you click on it when it's deselected, then it becomes selected (and a check mark appears).

- If you click on it when it's selected, then it becomes deselected (and the check mark disappears).

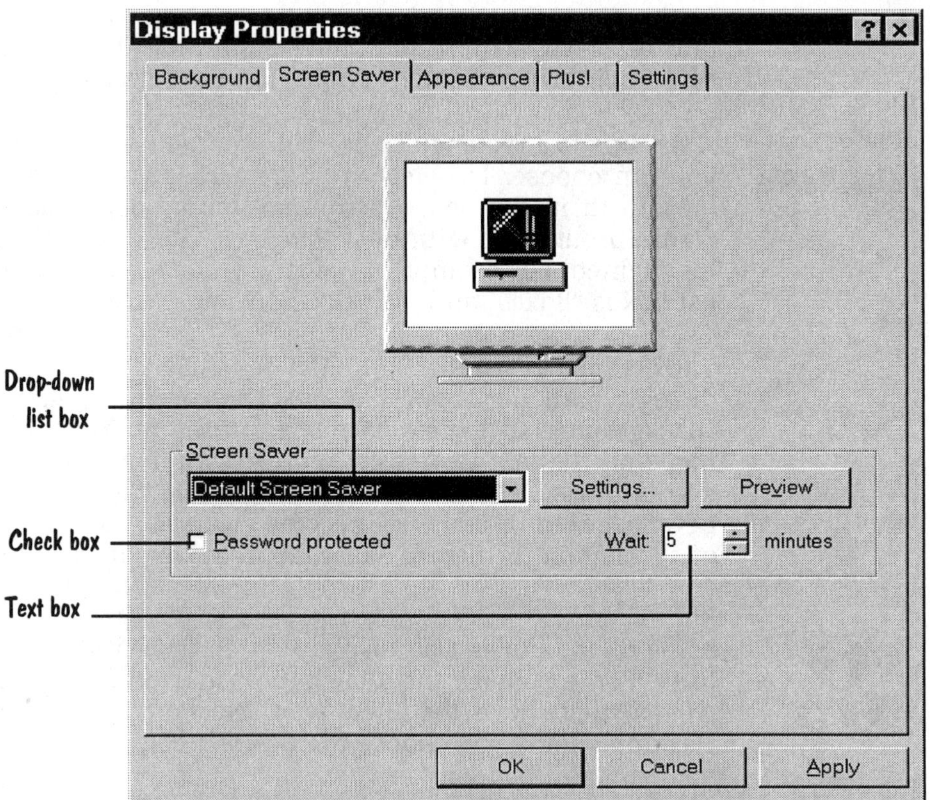

Figure 9   Additional Features of a Dialog Box

 A **text box** allows you to input a number or name into a dialog box. It is symbolized by a rectangle that contains the *current value* for that option — the number or name that is used if you don't change it. For example, in Figure 9, "5" is the current value for the Wait text box. To change it, click on the text box, press the Backspace key to erase the current value, and then type a new one. (Do not press the Enter key after typing unless you want to activate the command button that has the focus!) Some text boxes, like the one in Figure 9, contain up and down arrows which provide an alternate way to change the current value. Here, each click on the appropriate arrow moves the time up or down one minute.

A **drop-down list box** is a special type of list box. Here, only one of the listed items (the current value) is initially visible. To see the rest of the list, click on the downward-facing triangle at the right end of the box. Then, to select an item from the list, click on that item. The list will close and the new item will be the one displayed.

TUTORIAL

Try the following exercise on your own.

1. Start up your computer (if necessary) and/or close any open windows by clicking on their close buttons.

2. Open the Display Properties dialog box by right-clicking on (an empty area of) the Desktop and then selecting Properties from the resulting menu.

3. If the Center option button is not selected (if it doesn't have a darkened center), select it by clicking on it.

4. From the Wallpaper text box, select the *winnt256* wallpaper. To do so, scroll down the list until "winnt256" appears and then click on this item. The "screen" in the preview window should look like the one shown in Figure 8.

5. Select the Tile option button. You should see a difference in the appearance of the preview window.

6. Click on the Screen Saver tab to view a new page in the dialog box. It should look similar to the one in Figure 9.

7. Open the Screen Saver drop-down list by clicking on the down triangle in this box.

8. Select *3D Flying Objects* from this list (by clicking on it) and click on the Preview button to view the Flying Objects screen saver. To return to the Display Properties dialog box, click the mouse.

9. Change the time in the Wait text box to 3 minutes by clicking on this box and then on its up or down arrow until "3" appears in the text box.

10. Choose Cancel by clicking on the Cancel command button or by pressing the Escape key. If you now want to shut down your computer, follow the instructions in Section 1.5.

1.5   Shutting Down Windows NT

All good things (in fact, all things in general) must come to an end. At some point, you're going to want to quit working with Windows NT and turn off your computer.

WARNING

If you want to turn off your computer, you should first shut down Windows NT. Doing so ensures that all open files will be properly closed. As a result, you are much less likely to inadvertently lose data or your preferred Windows settings.

To shut down or restart Windows NT:

1. Close all applications that are currently running. If an application's window is open on the Desktop, click on its close button (see Section 1.3); if the application has been minimized, right-click on its Taskbar button and then choose Close from the resulting menu. If you have used an application to modify a document and have not saved these changes to disk, Windows will display a message warning you of this fact. (We will discuss saving documents in Section 2.2.)

2. Click on the Start button, at the left end of the Taskbar. This action opens the **Start menu** (shown below). If the Start button is not visible anywhere on the Desktop, you can open the Start menu by pressing Ctrl+Esc; that is, hold down the Ctrl key, press the Esc (Escape) key, and then release Ctrl.

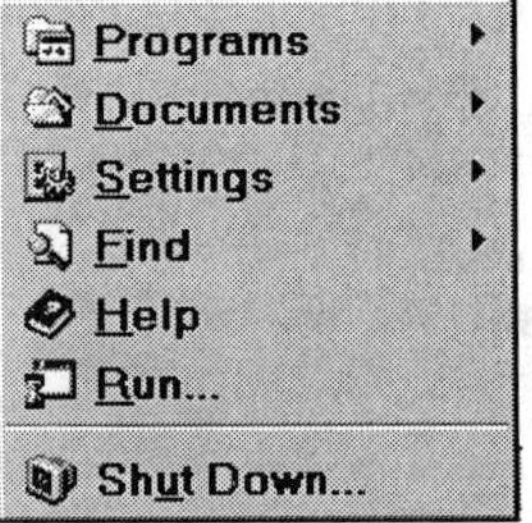

3. Click on the Shut Down option on the Start menu. The dialog box shown in Figure 10 will open.

4. Now select an option by clicking, if necessary, on the appropriate option button and choosing the Yes command button. Or, close this dialog box and return to Windows by choosing No (or by pressing the Escape key).

   - The first option, "Shut down the computer?", should be selected when you want to turn off your computer. Activating this option eventually displays the message: "It's now safe to turn off your computer." (You can restart Windows at this point by clicking on the Restart command button.)

   - Activating the second option, "Restart the computer?", restarts Windows, reinitializing all its settings. This option may

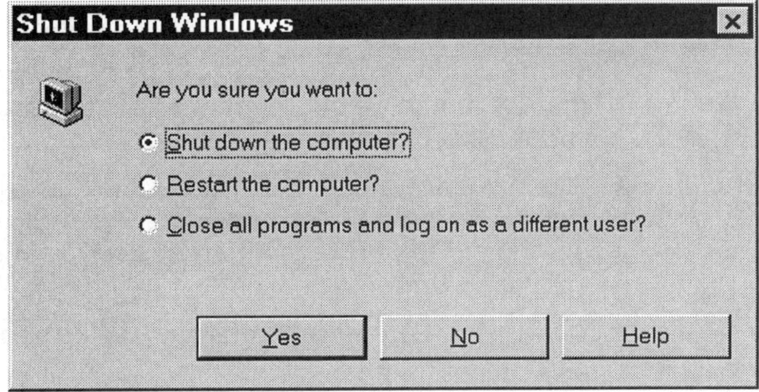

Figure 10   The Shut Down Windows Dialog Box

be useful after a program *crashes* (terminates abruptly) and/ or Windows itself does not seem to be responding properly to your commands.

- The third option, "Close all programs and log on as a different user?" closes all applications, disconnects your computer from the network (if any), and then displays the Logon Information dialog box so that you can log back onto Windows.

Here are a couple of shortcuts for shutting down Windows:

- You can display the Shut Down Windows dialog box after closing all applications by pressing the Alt+F4 keystroke combination.

- You can activate the "Shut down the computer?" option in the Shut Down Windows dialog box even if there are applications running. In this case, Windows will attempt to close these applications and, if successful, shut down your computer. (If you try this approach, you may see a message prompting you to save changes in a document or requesting that you close certain applications yourself.)

Try the following exercise on your own.

1. Turn on your computer, if necessary, to start Windows NT. If Windows is already running, close all windows by clicking on their close buttons.

2. Restart Windows NT: Open the Start menu by clicking on the Start button (if you can't find this button, press Ctrl+Esc to open the Start menu); choose Shut Down from the menu; select the "Restart the computer?" option button in the resulting dialog box; and choose the Yes command button.

3. When Windows NT starts again, press Alt+F4 to open the Shut Down Windows dialog box. This time, select the "Close all programs and log on as a different user?" option and choose the Yes command button.

4. When the Logon Information dialog box appears, enter your password to log back onto NT.

5. Now, open the Shut Down Windows dialog box, select the "Shut down the computer?" option button, and choose Yes. When the message "It's now safe to turn off your computer." appears, do just that.

Review Exercises

Section 1.1

1. A(n) ____________ is a small stylized picture used to represent a Windows NT object.

2. The ____________ button is positioned at the left end of the Taskbar.

3. True or false: You cannot start Windows NT unless you enter the proper password.

4. The Windows *Desktop* refers to:

    a. The area occupied by your computer, keyboard, and mouse.
    b. The windows that are currently open.
    c. The application that is currently running, including its menus, icons, and so on.
    d. None of the above is the Windows Desktop.

Section 1.2

5. To click on an object on the screen, move the mouse pointer over that object and press the ____________.

6. To open an application's View menu, you can click on the word ____________ on the menu bar.

7. If the name of a menu item is followed by an ellipsis (...), then choosing that menu item opens a(n) ____________.

8. True or false: When double-clicking the mouse, you should pause for a second or two between clicks.

9. True or false: To use a shortcut key to perform a task, open the menu that lists that task, and then press the shortcut key.

10. True or false: To right-drag an object, move the mouse pointer over it and click the right button.

11. When you position the mouse pointer over an object, hold down the left button, and move the pointer to a new location, it is called

    a. Clicking on the object.
    b. Double-clicking on the object.
    c. Dragging the object.
    d. Pointing at the object.

12. If an item on a menu is dimmed, clicking on that item

    a. Opens a dialog box.
    b. Opens a submenu.
    c. Closes the menu.
    d. Does nothing at all.

Section 1.3   13. To move a window, drag its ____________ to the desired location on the screen.

14. Clicking on a window's __________ increases the window's size as much as possible.

15. To increase the width of a window without increasing its height, drag its ____________ to the right or its ____________ to the left.

16. True or false: You can close a window by clicking on its menu bar.

17. True or false: When a window is minimized, the window disappears from the screen.

18. True or false: When a window opens, horizontal and vertical scroll bars are always displayed.

19. Which part of a window contains its maximize, minimize, and close buttons?

    a. Its title bar.
    b. Its menu bar.
    c. Its toolbar.
    d. Its status bar.

20. If an application is maximized, from its Control menu, you *cannot*

    a. Open the application's window.
    b. Close the application's window.
    c. Minimize the application's window.

    d. Restore the application's window.

In Exercises 21 and 22, identify the indicated parts of the window shown in Figure 11. Your answers should come from the following list:

Close button	Control icon
Horizontal scroll bar	Maximize button
Menu bar	Minimize button
Title bar	Vertical scroll bar

21. Identify the components of the window in Figure 11 that are marked A, B, C, and D.

22. Identify the components of the window in Figure 11 that are marked E, F, G, and H.

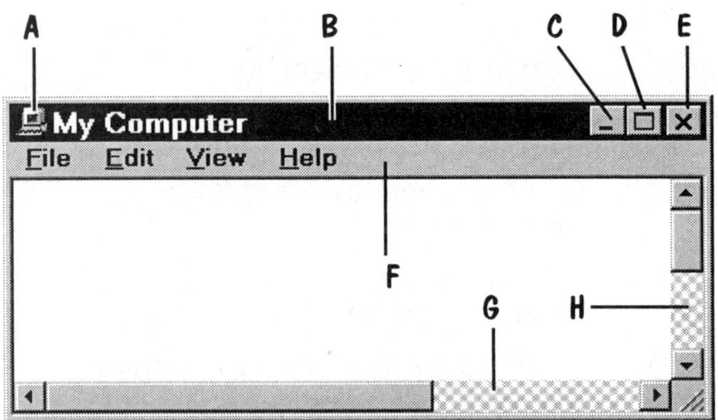

Figure 11   Window for Exercises 21 and 22

Section 1.4   23. When you click on the command button labeled ____________ in a dialog box, the box closes and the selected options go into effect.

24. In a dialog box, instead of clicking on the Cancel button, you can press the ___________ key.

25. In a dialog box, a ___________ allows the user to turn an option on or off without affecting other options.

26. True or false: Dialog boxes can be moved around the screen.

27. True or false: A drop-down list box only displays a single item until you click on the appropriate symbol to "open" it.

28. True or false: In a group of related option buttons, only one button can be selected at any given time.

29. Which of the following objects appears on the title bar of a dialog box?

    a. A minimize button.
    b. A maximize button.
    c. A close button.
    d. A Control icon.

30. Dialog boxes never contain:

    a. Command buttons.
    b. Restore buttons.
    c. Option buttons.
    d. Tabs.

Section 1.5   31. The Shut Down option, which allows us to shut down Windows NT, appears on the ____________ menu.

32. The Shut Down Windows dialog box gives us the option of shutting down or ____________ Windows NT.

33. True or false: It is a good idea to shut down Windows NT before turning off your computer.

34. True or false: To display the Start menu, even if the Start button is not visible on the screen, press Ctrl+Esc.

35. You can display the Shut Down Windows dialog box after closing all applications by pressing the keystroke combination:

    a. Alt+Spacebar
    b. Alt+Hyphen
    c. Alt+F4.
    d. None of these keystrokes works.

Build Your Own Glossary   36. The following words and phrases are important terms that were introduced in this chapter. (They appear within the text in bold-face type.) Write a definition for each term. After you learn to use WordPad (in Section 2.2), you should enter these definitions into the Glossary file on the Student Disk.

Check box	List box	Restore button
Close a window	Maximize a window	Scroll
Close button	Maximize button	Scroll bar
Command button	Menu	Shortcut key
Control icon	Menu bar	Start button
Control menu	Minimize a window	Start menu
Desktop	Minimize button	Tab (in a dialog box)
Dialog box	Option button	Taskbar
Drop-down list box	Pull-down menu	Title bar
Icon	Restore a window	Window

Lab Exercises

Work each of the following exercises at your computer. Begin by turning the machine on (if necessary) to start Windows NT. Then, close all open windows by clicking on the button labeled with an X on the title bar of each window. If you want to shut down the computer after completing an exercise, follow the instructions in Section 1.5.

**Lab Exercise 1
(Section 1.2)**

a.   *Right*-click (click with the right mouse button) on an empty part of the Desktop. On the resulting menu:

Which options (if any) are dimmed?
Which options (if any) will open a dialog box when selected?
Does a bullet appear next to any option?

b.   Point at the Arrange Icons option to open its submenu. Notice that there is an Auto Arrange item on the submenu. (Don't click on it!) The Auto Arrange item is a toggle. Is it selected? How do you know?

c.   Point at the New option on the original menu. In the submenu that appears, click on Folder. What is the name of the new icon that has appeared on the Desktop?

d.   Click on an empty part of the Desktop. Then, *right*-drag the new icon to another part of the Desktop. How many items are listed on the menu that appears when you release the mouse button?

e.   Select the Copy Here option. How many copies of the new icon now appear on the Desktop?

f.   Drag each copy of the new icon on top of the Recycle Bin icon. What happens each time?

**Lab Exercise 2
(Section 1.2)**

a.   Double-click on the Recycle Bin icon to open its window. List the names of the menus that appear on the menu bar.

b.   Open the Edit menu. What is the shortcut key for the Cut option? Is this option dimmed?

c.   Press Ctrl+A, the shortcut key for the Select All option. Why didn't anything happen?

d.   Cancel the Edit menu (close it without choosing any item). What mouse action or keystroke did you use?

e.   Open the View menu. How many items have bullets next to them? How many items have submenus?

f.   Choose the Toolbar menu item. The View menu will close. What else happened?

g.   Reopen the View menu. Is the Toolbar menu item "checked" now?

h.   *Right*-click (click with the right button) on the Status Bar item. What, if anything, happened?

i.   Click on the word *View* to close this menu. Then, click on the button labeled with an X in the upper-right corner of the Recycle Bin window to close it.

Lab Exercise 3
(Section 1.3)

a.   Click on an empty part of the Desktop, then press the F3 function key to open the Find window. Does this window have a Control icon on its title bar?

b.   If the Find window is maximized, restore it. Then, decrease its width as much as possible. Is the entire window title visible now? Did any scroll bars appear?

c.   Try to increase or decrease the height of this window. Was it possible to do either?

d.   Maximize the Find window. Does it occupy the entire screen?

e.   Right-click the title bar to display the Control menu. List the items that appear on this menu. Cancel the Control menu by clicking elsewhere in the window.

f.   Move the window in a *horizontal* direction. Was the restore button replaced by a maximize button? If not, click on the restore button.

g.   Minimize the window to a button on the Taskbar; then restore it to a window. Is it the same size as it was before being minimized?

h.   Resize the Find window to the approximate size it had when you began this exercise and close this window.

Lab Exercise 4
(Section 1.3)

a.   Right-click on an empty part of the Desktop; then select Properties from the resulting menu to open the Display Properties window.

b.   Notice that this window (a *dialog box*) does not contain a minimize or maximize, button or a Control icon. Try to maximize the window by double-clicking on its title bar. Did this work?

c.   Can this dialog box be: Moved? Resized? Minimized?

d.   Open the window's Control menu. What mouse action or keystroke combination did you use? What items are listed on the Control menu? Cancel this menu.

e.   In the small window entitled *Pattern*, use the vertical scroll bar to scroll to the bottom of the list. What name appears there? Why isn't a *horizontal* scroll bar displayed?

f.   Try closing the Display Properties window by pressing Alt+F4. Did it work? If not, close it by clicking on the close button.

Lab Exercise 5 (Section 1.4)

a.   Double-click on the Clock on the Taskbar to open the Date/Time Properties dialog box. (If you can't find the Taskbar, press Ctrl+Esc to display it.)

b.   Try to change the year displayed in the Date text box to 1800. Were you able to do this?

c.   Using the up and down arrows in the Date text box, determine the allowable range of years. What is it?

d.   Click on the Time Zone tab to change to this set of options.

e.   Open the drop-down list and scroll to the bottom. What place is given for the "GMT+12:00" entry? Close the drop-down list.

f.   Click on the ? button on the title bar; then click on the text to the right of the check box. What happened?

g.   Close this dialog box by clicking on the Cancel button or pressing the Escape key.

Lab Exercise 6 (Section 1.4)

a.   Click on an empty part of the Desktop; then press the F3 function key to open the Find window.

b.   Deselect the *Include subfolders* check box. Did the text in the *Look in* drop-down list box change?

c.   Click on the Date Modified tab. Notice that the *All files* option button is selected.

d.   Select the *between* option button. What happened to the *All files* button?

e.   Select one of the *previous* option buttons. Try to enter the number 0 in the corresponding text box. Could you do this?

f.   Click on the Advanced tab and open the drop-down list. Why is a vertical scroll bar necessary here? What name is at the bottom of the list?

g.   Close the Find window by clicking on its close button.

Lab Exercise 7
(Section 1.5)

a. Open the Shut Down Windows dialog box; then close it without shutting down or restarting the computer. How did you do this?

b. Reopen the Shut Down Windows dialog box and activate the "Restart the computer?" option. Was the Windows NT logo displayed before Windows restarted?

c. Open the Shut Down Windows dialog box and activate the "Close all programs and log on as a different user?" option. Do any messages appear on the screen before the Logon Information dialog box is displayed?

d. Log back on to Windows.

e. Open the Shut Down Windows dialog box and activate the "Shut down the computer?" option. What message is displayed prior to "It's now safe to turn off your computer"?

f. Turn off your computer.

Working with Applications and Documents

In Chapter 1 we discussed the structure and general use of some basic Windows NT objects — the Desktop, menus, windows, and dialog boxes. In this chapter, we will concentrate on how to use Windows NT to run your **applications** (programs) and manipulate your **documents** (the work created by an application). To be more specific, you will learn:

1. Various ways to start and close applications.

2. How to use the WordPad application to create simple word processing documents.

3. How to open, save, print, and close documents.

4. How to switch among the applications that are running.

5. How to transfer information from one document to another.

6. How to "capture" windows and screens.

7. How to install and uninstall applications.

8. How to add Windows components to your hard disk.

9. How to use the online Windows NT Help system to locate information about a desired topic.

10. How to obtain online context-sensitive help.

After completing this chapter, you will be able to use Windows NT to print a copy of your homework!

2.1   *Starting and Closing Applications*

Windows NT supplies a myriad of ways to start (or *open*) and exit (or *close*) applications. In this section we will describe most of these techniques.

Using the Start Menu

Recall that if you click on the Start button at the left of the Taskbar or press the Ctrl+Esc keystroke combination, the Windows NT Start menu opens (Figure 1). In Section 1.5, we discussed how to use the last item on this menu to shut down or restart Windows NT. Here, we will describe how to use the Start menu to open the applications available on your computer.

Figure 1
The Start Menu

The Programs option

Usually, the most straightforward way to open a program is to select the **Programs option** from the Start menu. When you point at this item (holding the arrow-shaped mouse pointer steady for a moment or two), a submenu listing specific applications and groups of applications will be displayed, as shown in Figure 2. (Your list of programs will undoubtedly be different from the one that appears here.)

On the submenu, the items followed by a right-facing triangle (such as Accessories, at the top in Figure 2) represent *groups* of applications; if you point at one of these items, another submenu will open, presenting further applications and possibly groups of applications. A submenu item that is not followed by a right triangle (such as Windows NT Explorer at the bottom of the list) represents a program. To start a program, just click on it! The Start menu will close and the program will begin running.

For example, suppose you want to open WordPad, a word processor that is included with the Windows NT software package. To do so, click on the Start button to open the Start menu (Figure 1) and point at the Programs option to open its submenu (Figure 2). Then, point at the Accessories option, which opens another submenu, and finally click on the WordPad item at the bottom of the latter. After a few moments, the WordPad opening screen will be displayed.

Figure 2
Pointing at the
Programs Option
on the Start Menu

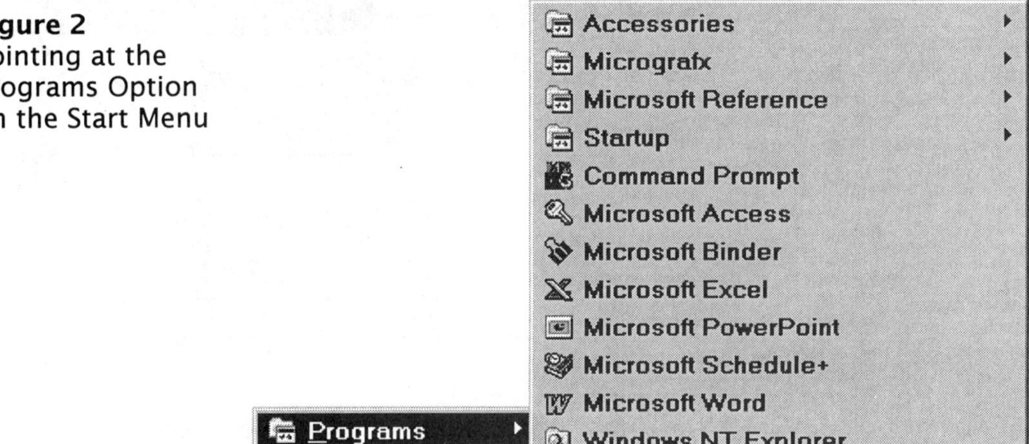

The Documents option

Using the **Documents option** on the Start menu can sometimes be a real time-saver. Pointing at this item (see Figure 3) displays a submenu containing a list of up to 15 documents that you recently saved to disk*. (We will discuss saving documents in Section 2.2.) Clicking on one of the listed documents starts the application that created it and also displays (*opens*) the designated document within it.

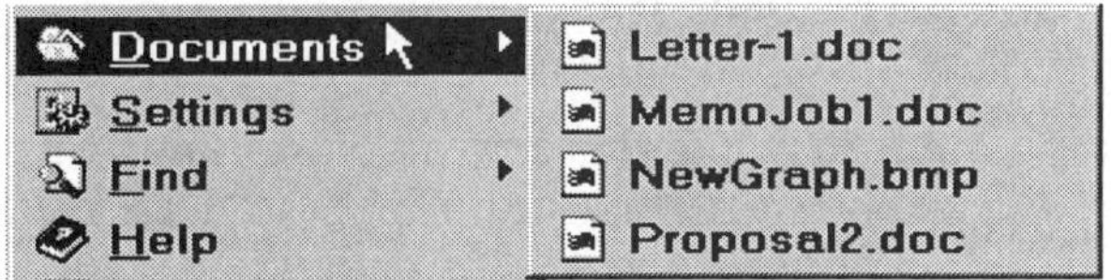

Figure 3   Pointing at the Documents Option

The Run option

The techniques we have just described for starting an application are quick and easy, but require that the program, or a document created by it, appear on one of the Start submenus. The **Run option**, which appears near the bottom of the Start menu, can be used to open *any* application on your hard or floppy disks.

Clicking on the Run command displays the following dialog box:

---

*Only those documents whose file extension is recognized by Windows NT are listed on this menu. (We will discuss extensions in Section 3.1.)

To start a program from this dialog box, you must know its file name, and possibly the folder in which that file is located — this is the major drawback of using the Run option. (We will discuss files and folders in Section 3.1.) If you have this required information, you can open the desired application by performing any of the following actions:

- Type the appropriate folder and file names (the program's *path name*) in the Open text box. (If a highlighted name already appears there, just type over it!) Then, click on the OK button or press the Enter key.

- If you have previously started the desired application from the Run dialog box, its name may appear on the Open drop-down list. Display this list (by clicking on the down-triangle), select the program's file name, and activate the OK button.

- Click on the Browse command button to open the Browse dialog box and use it to help you locate the program's file name; then choose the OK button. (This technique requires some familiarity with the Windows NT folder system, discussed in Chapter 3.)

In any case, the Run dialog box will close and the program will start.

Starting a program from a floppy disk

As you can see, using the Run option is usually not the easiest way to start a program. However, there is one case in which Run is especially useful — when the program you want to start is on a floppy disk (diskette). To start a program from a floppy:

1. Insert the diskette in its drive.

2. Select the Run option from the Start menu.

3. Type the characters a: (for the primary floppy drive) followed by the program's file name in the text box; for example, a:big-game.

4. Press the Enter key or click on the OK button. The Run dialog box will close and the program will start.

Other Ways to Start Applications

Typically, Windows NT provides a variety of ways to perform just about any task, and opening applications is no exception. You have already seen several ways in which the Start menu can be used for this purpose. Here are a few additional important techniques for starting programs.

The easiest way   If an icon representing an application or document appears on the Desktop, just *double*-click on it to open that application or document. (In Chapter 1, we used this technique to open the My Computer application.) If you use a particular application frequently, it makes a lot of sense to place an icon (*shortcut*) for it on the Desktop. We will discuss how to do this in Section 3.4.

Using Windows NT Explorer or My Computer   Just about every aspect of your computer system can be accessed using either Windows NT Explorer (on the Start menu's Programs submenu) or My Computer (which is represented by an icon on the Desktop). Both of these applications can locate and start any program on your hard or floppy disks. We will discuss Explorer and My Computer in Chapter 3.

Closing an Application

If you read Chapter 1 carefully (or worked its tutorials), you already know how to close a Windows-based application — just close its window. As usual, this task can be done in several ways. The following techniques are listed (more or less) in order of likely use; take your pick:

Ways to close Windows-based applications

- Click on the application window's close button (on the right end of the title bar). 

- Choose Exit from the application's File menu.

- Right-click on the application's Taskbar button and choose Close from the resulting menu.

- Press Alt+F4 (hold down the Alt key, tap the F4 key, and release Alt).

- Double-click on the application's Control icon (on the left end of the title bar).

- Open the application's Control menu by clicking on its Control icon (right-clicking on the title bar may also work) and choose the Close option.

NOTE

If you have used the application to make changes to a document and did not subsequently save the document to disk, Windows will display a warning message before closing the application. We will discuss this further in Section 2.2.

Closing DOS applications

As we mentioned in the Introduction, Windows NT not only runs applications specifically designed for itself and other versions of Windows, but it also runs most *DOS applications*. Although some DOS applications can be closed by selecting Exit from their File menus (if they have one!), none of the other techniques listed above is likely to work. If you try one of them, you'll probably just get a message that "This program cannot respond to the End Task request."

Unfortunately, DOS applications, especially older ones, are notorious for performing common tasks in their own peculiar ways. So, you'll just have to learn the keystrokes or mouse clicks necessary to exit each DOS application you use. After exiting the program, its window might still remain on the screen, with the word *Inactive* displayed at the left end of the title bar. To close the window, use any of the usual techniques (such as clicking on the close button).

There is another way to exit *any* application, but it should only be used in an emergency; for example, if the application has "locked up", and no longer responds to the keyboard or mouse. In this case:

1. Press the Ctrl+Alt+Del keystroke combination (that is, hold down the Ctrl and Alt keys, tap the Del key, and then release Ctrl and Alt), which opens the Windows NT Security dialog box.

2. Choose the Task Manager command button and, in the resulting dialog box, click on the Applications tab. A list of all programs that are currently running will appear.

3. The offending application should be highlighted on this list. (If it isn't, click on it.) Now, activate the End Task command button and follow the on-screen instructions.

4. Close the Task Manager dialog box.

Using this procedure, you will probably lose all unsaved work in the application that has locked up, but other open programs should survive unscathed.

TUTORIAL

Try the following exercise on your own.

1. Turn on your computer, if necessary, to start up Windows NT.

2. Open the WordPad application from the Start menu:

   - Click on the Start button to open the Start menu.
   - Point at the Programs option (and keep the mouse pointer stationary for a few moments) to open this submenu.
   - Now, point at the Accessories item at the top to display another submenu.
   - Finally, click on the WordPad item to start this application.

3. Close the WordPad application by clicking on its close button.

4. Open the Start menu and point at the Documents option to open this submenu.

5. If any documents are listed, click on one of them, which should open that document within the application that created it. Close this application by choosing Exit from its File menu.

6. Place the Student Disk in its drive.

7. Start the DOSPROG application on this diskette:

   - Open the Start menu and click on the Run option to open the Run dialog box.
   - Type a:dosprog in the Open text box and press the Enter key. The Run dialog box will close and the program will start.

8. Exit the DOSPROG application by following the on-screen instructions. If the application window remains on the screen, close it by clicking on the close button.

2.2   *An Introduction to WordPad; Documents*

In Windows, the word *document* is used to refer to any collection of data that is created by an application. Thus, a document could be a letter written using a word processor, a picture created by a painting program, or a collection of numbers produced by a spreadsheet program. Nevertheless, there are certain operations that are common to almost all documents: they can be created, saved, opened, printed, and closed. The way in which a document is created *does* vary considerably from application to application. However, all Windows documents are opened, saved, printed, and closed in a uniform way. (This is one of the beauties of using Windows!) In this section, we will use the Word-Pad application to illustrate these operations.

An Introduction to WordPad

WordPad is one of the small applications (sometimes called *applets* or *accessories*) that is included as part of the Windows NT package. Word-Pad is a *word processor* — an application used to create text-based documents such as memos, letters, reports, and so on. In this section, we will be viewing WordPad as an example of a typical Windows NT application, but in the process you will learn enough to use it to produce very simple documents. WordPad's features will be discussed in more detail in Chapter 5.

To start WordPad, select Programs from the Start menu and Accessories from the resulting submenu. Then, click on the WordPad item on the Accessories submenu. This action starts WordPad and opens a window similar to the one in Figure 4. (The Toolbar, Format Bar, Ruler, and Status Bar may or may not be displayed.)

Entering text   Once you have started WordPad, type whatever you want at the keyboard; the corresponding text will appear in the *document window* and be stored in the computer's internal memory, RAM. The *insertion point*, the blinking vertical bar, indicates where the next character you type will appear on the screen.

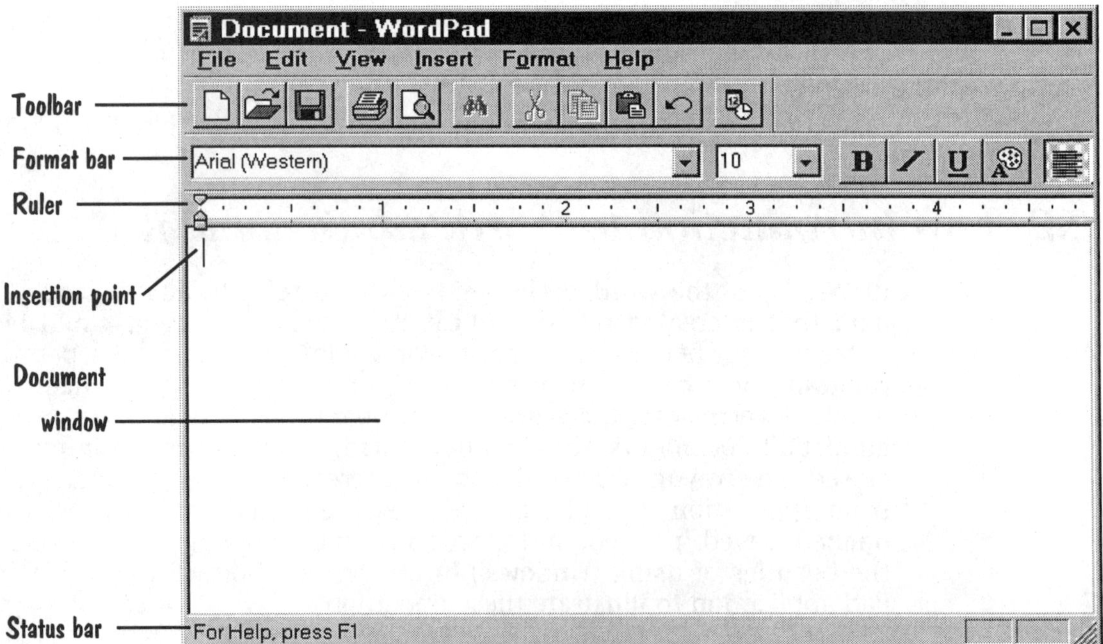

Figure 4   The WordPad Window

When you reach the end of a line, just keep typing; WordPad's *word wrap* feature will automatically continue the text at the beginning of the next line. To start a new line manually, press the Enter key and the insertion point will also move to the beginning of the next line. To skip a line, press Enter again. (When you reach the bottom of the window, moving to the next line will scroll the window down.)

For example, if you type your name, your class, and the date, pressing the Enter key after your name and class, the three entries will appear on separate lines. Moreover, if you press Enter *twice* after the date and then type Homework 1, the screen will look like the one shown in Figure 5.

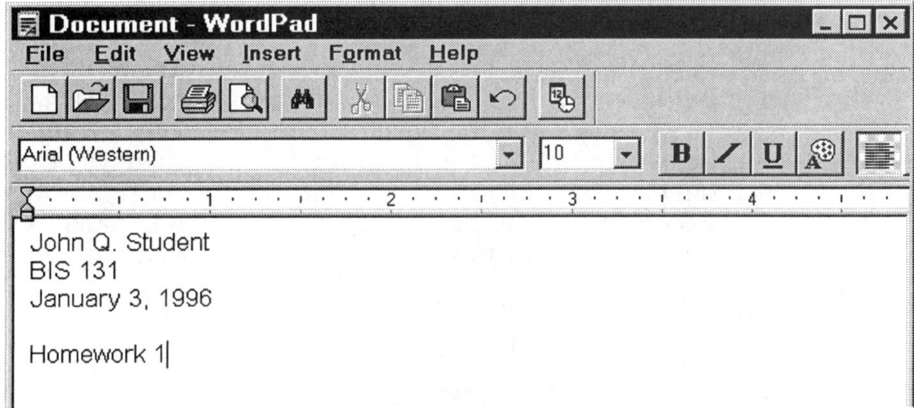

Figure 5   Entering Text into the WordPad Window

Correcting mistakes

It is very easy to correct typing errors. To erase the character just to the *left* of the insertion point, press the Backspace key (which may be labeled ←); to delete the character just to the *right* of the insertion point, press the Delete (Del) key. Holding down either key erases a succession of characters. You can use the mouse or the keyboard to move the insertion point to a mistake anywhere in the document:

- To use the mouse, scroll the document window (Section 1.3), if necessary, until the desired location is visible on the screen. Then, click on this location to move the insertion point there.

- You can also use the Arrow keys (←, →. ↑, ↓) to move the insertion point left, right, up, or down and to scroll the window.

For example, suppose your screen looks like the one in Figure 5, and you realize you've made a mistake: your middle initial is "X", not "Q".

To correct the error:

1. Move the insertion point just before the Q by either mouse-clicking on this location or pressing the Up Arrow key four times and the Left Arrow key six times.

2. Press the Delete key to erase the Q.

3. Type an X.

Saving a Document

The short document we just created (Figure 5) is not only displayed on the screen, but also stored in RAM. If we start a new document, close WordPad, or shut down Windows, the document will be removed from both the screen and RAM. Thus, if we want to retrieve this document in the future, we must store a copy of it on a more permanent medium — we must **save** the document to disk. The save operation, with your help, also provides a name for the document. In this section, we will only discuss how to save a document to a floppy disk (diskette), but once you learn to navigate the Windows NT folder system (Chapter 3), you will see how to save it to a specified location on a hard disk.

The Save command

To save the document that is currently displayed to a floppy disk:

1. Insert the diskette into its drive.

2. Choose Save from the File menu.

   - If this document has been saved before, the current version will be saved under the same name, *replacing the former version on disk.* The File menu will close and you will be returned to the document window.

   - If this document has *not* been saved before, the Save As dialog box (Figure 6) opens and you must carry out all the remaining steps of this procedure.

3. If the *Save in* box does not contain "3½ Floppy", then display its drop-down list (like the one at the right) by clicking on the down-triangle. Now select the appropriate floppy drive by clicking on it.

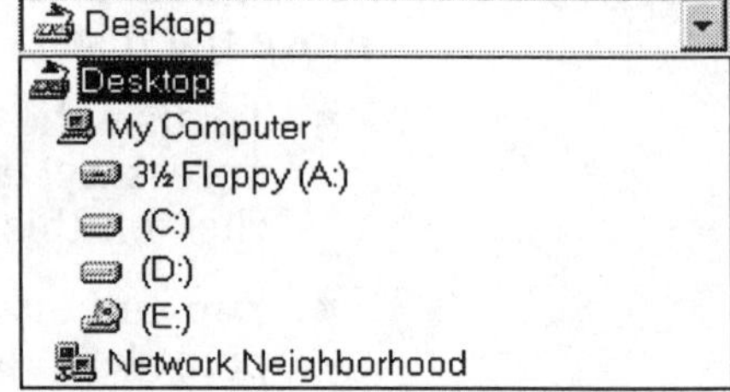

4. Erase the name in the File name text box (click in the box

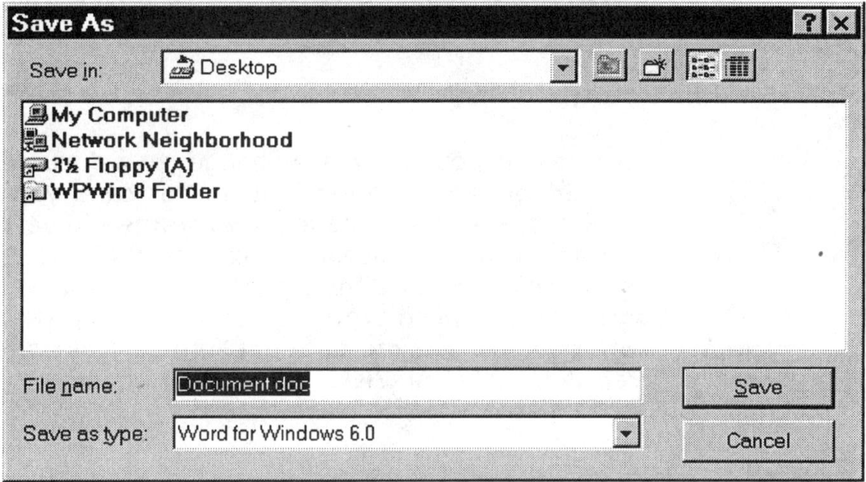

Figure 6   The Save As Dialog Box

and then use the Delete or Backspace key) and type a name[*] for the document. For example, in saving the document displayed in Figure 5, we might use the name Homework 1.

5. To complete the save operation (and close the dialog box), press the Enter key or click on the Save command button.

N O T E

A simpler way to save a document in WordPad and many other Windows NT applications is to use its **Toolbar**, which sits just under the menu bar, as shown in Figure 4. (If the Toolbar is not visible on the screen, choose the Toolbar item from the View menu to display it.) The icons on the Toolbar provide quick access to certain menu commands. When you mouse-point at one of the icons, a **tool tip** appears, indicating the icon's function:

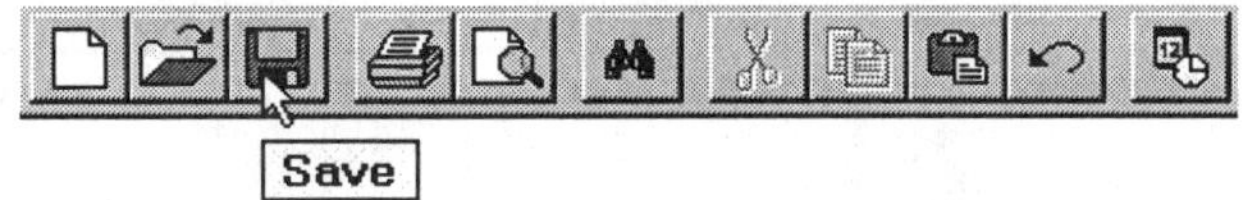

---

[*]If you're using an application, such as WordPad, designed to run under Windows NT 4 or Windows 95, you may choose almost any name. If you're using any other program, the name you choose should be no longer than 8 characters and some characters (such as a blank space) are not allowed. See Section 3.1 for more information.

To activate a Toolbar function, just click on it. For example, clicking on the floppy disk icon has the same effect as choosing Save from the File menu!

The Save As command

On occasion, you may make changes to a document, but want to keep both the old and new versions. In this case, you cannot use the Save command; it will automatically erase the old version while saving the new one. Instead, you should choose the Save As item from the File menu, which displays the Save As dialog box even though the current document has been previously saved. Now, just save the new (current) version under a name different from the old one, and both versions are safely stored on disk.

Closing a Document

To **close** a document means to remove it from both the screen and RAM. When you exit a Windows application, any open documents are closed automatically. You may, however, wish to close a document before exiting your application, perhaps to begin working on another document. To accomplish this in WordPad:

The New command

1. Choose New from the File menu or click on the New icon on the Toolbar. The New dialog box will be displayed.

2. Activate the OK command button to accept the default document type. If you have not saved the latest changes to this document, a message similar to the following one will appear:

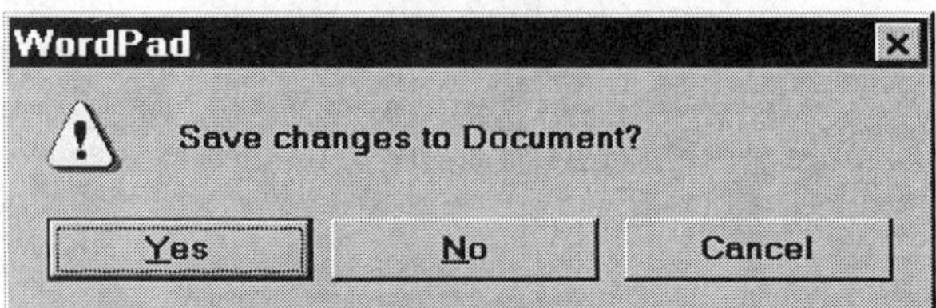

3. Choose the Yes command button and Windows will give you the opportunity to save your changes; choose No and the document will close, but your changes will not be saved to disk. Clicking on the Cancel button (or pressing the Escape key) returns you to the document; in this case, neither the document nor WordPad will close.

N O T E

WordPad only allows one document window to be open at any time. Certain other Windows applications allow multiple open document windows. Choosing New in such a case does not close the current document; it just clears it from the screen. To close a document when multiple open windows are allowed, choose Close from the File menu.

Opening a Document

When you save a document, it is stored on disk under the name you have chosen for it. Saving a document does not remove it from the screen or the computer's RAM, so you *can* continue to work on it. However, once it has been closed, to work on the document again you must have Windows copy it from disk into RAM and display it on the screen. In other words, you must **open** the document. Just as there are many ways to open an application, Windows provides many ways to open a document.

The Open command

To open a document in an application that is on screen, one normally uses the Open command. We will demonstrate how to use this command to open a document that is stored on a floppy disk, but once you learn to navigate the Windows NT folder system, it will be just as easy to open any document. To open a document stored on a diskette:

1. Start the application that created the document.

2. Insert the diskette containing the document into its drive.

3. Choose Open from the File menu or click on the Open icon on the Toolbar. The Open dialog box, like the one in Figure 7 (on the next page), will be displayed. If the floppy drive does not appear in the *Look in* text box, click on the down-triangle and select the floppy drive from the drop-down list.

4. If the name of the document you want to open isn't listed, display the *Files of type* drop-down list and select the entry labeled "All Documents (*.*)". A new, probably longer, list of names will be displayed and the document you are seeking may be one of them.

5. Select the document you want to open from the list. It will become highlighted.

6. Activate the Open command button. The dialog box will close and the specified document will open.

Open programs and documents simultaneously

The Open command works well if the relevant application is already running. If it isn't, you may be able to open a document and the application that created it at the same time using one of the following simple techniques:

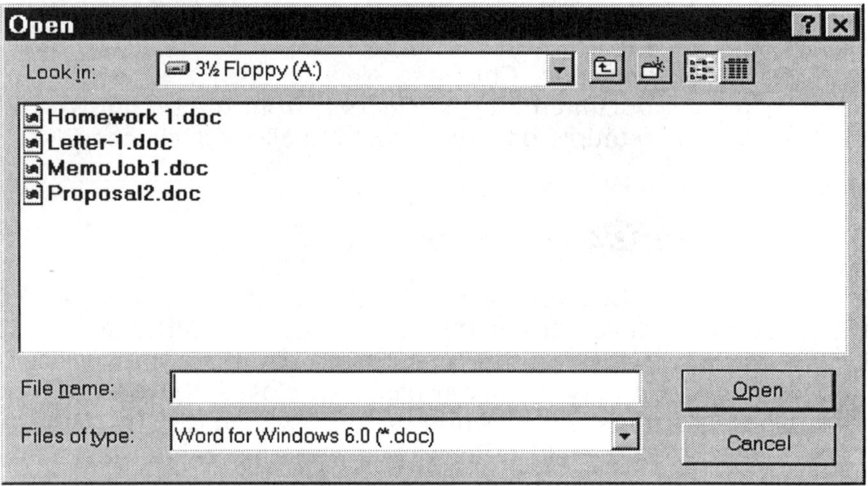

Figure 7   The Open Dialog Box

- If the document to be opened is represented by an icon (a *short-cut*) on the Desktop, just double-click on this icon. The application associated with the document will start running and the document will open within it. (We will discuss how to create shortcuts in Section 3.4.)

The Documents option

- If the document was saved recently, then to open it:

    1. Select the Documents option from the Start menu (by clicking on the Start button and pointing at *Documents*). A submenu of recently saved documents will be displayed.

    2. Click on the desired document. The application associated with it will start and open the document, as well.

NOTE

These simple techniques do not always work as planned. Even though a document was just saved, it may not appear on the Documents submenu. Moreover, when you double-click on a document's icon or select an item from the Documents submenu, Windows may start an application other than the one that created the specified document.

Printing a Document

When you **print** a document, you send a copy of it to a printer. Here is the most straightforward way to print a document:

1. Open the document if it is not already on screen.

2. Choose the Print command from the File menu. The Print dialog box will open, as shown in Figure 8.

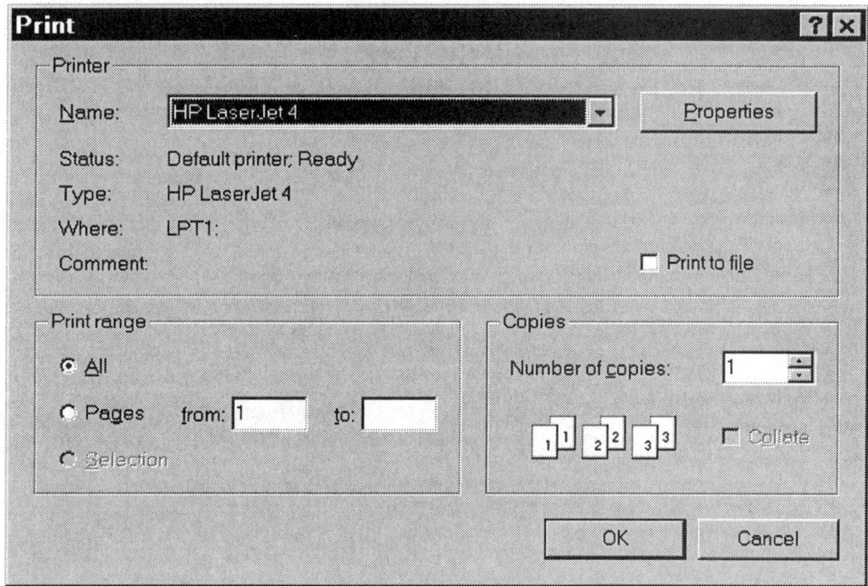

Figure 8   The Print Dialog Box

3. Make the desired selections from this dialog box:

   - If your computer is connected to more than one printer, you can select the one you want to use from the Printer Name drop-down list.

   - If you don't want to print the entire document (indicated by the *All* option button), you can print a range of pages by clicking on the *Pages* option button and then filling in the *from* and *to* text boxes. You can also *select* a portion of your document (as described in Section 2.3) prior to opening the Print dialog box and then print just the selected text by clicking on the Selection option button.

   - If you want to print more than one copy, change the number that appears in the *Number of copies* text box. To collate (sort) the copies, select the Collate check box.

4. Make sure that the selected printer is ready to receive information.

5. Activate the OK command button. The document (or the selected portion of the document) will be printed.

If you want to print a document using the default information in the Print dialog box (for example, all pages and one copy), you need not open this dialog box. Just click on the Print icon on the Toolbar. The dialog box will not be displayed and the print process will begin immediately.

TUTORIAL

Try the following exercise on your own.

1. Turn on your computer (if it's not already on) to start Windows NT.

2. Start the WordPad word processor: Click on the Start button, point at Programs to open this submenu, point at Accessories to open a second submenu, and then click on WordPad on the latter.

3. Insert the Student Disk in its drive and open the Homework 1 document that is stored on it: Choose the Open command from the File menu, select the floppy drive from the *Look in* drop-down list, click on the name "Homework 1", and activate the Open command button.

4. Edit the Homework 1 document so that it gives *your* name and class and the current date. To do so:

   - Repeatedly press the Delete key until the current name is erased.
   - Type in your name.
   - Click the mouse pointer (an "I-beam" symbol) at the beginning of the next line (or press the Right Arrow key once) to move the insertion point to this location.
   - Repeat these steps to correct the class and date.

5. Save the new document under the new name My Homework 1: Choose the Save As (*not* Save) command from the File menu, select the floppy drive from the *Save in* drop-down list, type the new name in the *File name* text box, and activate the Save command button.

6. Print the current document: Either

   - Choose Print from the File menu and activate the OK button.
   or
   - Click on the printer icon on the Toolbar. (If it is currently not visible, choose Toolbar from the View menu to display it.)

7. Clear the current document from the screen: Select New from the

> File menu (or click on the "page" icon on the Toolbar) and then activate the OK command button in the dialog box.
>
> 8. Exit WordPad: Choose Exit from its File menu or click on the close button on the title bar.

2.3   *Running Several Applications at Once*

As you know, Windows allows you to run several applications at the same time, each of which is instantly available. To see how this can be useful, suppose that you are using the WordPad word processor to write a report and you realize that a picture will illustrate your point better than the proverbial thousand words. To create the picture, you start Paint, the painting program supplied with Windows NT and which (like WordPad) is found on the Accessories submenu of the Start menu's Programs option.

Starting Paint does not close WordPad, so these two applications are now both running at the same time (see Figure 9). After completing

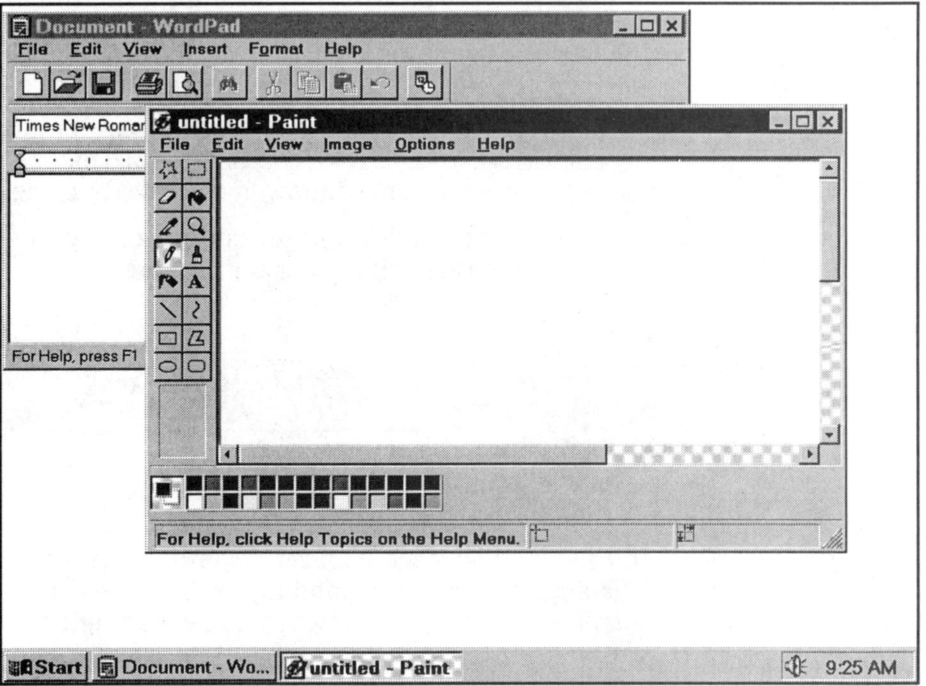

Figure 9   WordPad and Paint Open on the Desktop

your picture, you switch back to WordPad, copy the picture into the word processing document, and continue writing. Before you finish this Windows session, you might use other applications as well, perhaps to make a backup copy of your documents or just to take a break with a computer game.

To make use of the kind of flexibility illustrated in this scenario, you have to be able to quickly and easily switch among several running applications and to transfer information between them. We will discuss these techniques in the remainder of this section.

Switching Among Applications

Each application that is currently running is represented by a button on the Taskbar. The program in which you are currently working is called the **active application**. Its Taskbar button appears to be "brighter" than the others and its title bar is highlighted (see the Paint button and title bar in Figure 9).

Ways to switch applications

To switch from the active application to an inactive one, perform any of the following actions:

- If any portion of the inactive program's window is visible, just click within that window. It becomes the active one and moves to the front.

- Click on the inactive program's Taskbar button. (Remember: If the Taskbar is not visible on the screen, it can be displayed by pressing the Ctrl+Esc keystroke combination.) This application becomes the active one and its window is displayed on the screen.

- Hold down the Alt key and press the Tab key. A window similar to the following one will appear on the screen:

In this window, each icon represents a currently running program. The application corresponding to the "boxed in" icon has its name displayed in the window. To cycle through your running applications, continue to hold down the Alt key, and repeatedly press the Tab key; the "box" will move from icon to icon. When the name of the desired application appears in the window, release the Alt key. Windows activates the named application and displays it on the screen.

Transferring Information between Documents

The process of transferring information — for example, a block of text or a picture — from one document (the *source*) to another (the *target*) usually involves the following steps:

1. In the source document, *select the information* to be transferred. Here's how to select a *block of text* while running any Windows application. Either

   - Position the mouse pointer in front of the first character in the desired block of text and drag the insertion point to the end of the block.

   or

   - Position the insertion point in front of the first character in the desired block of text, hold down the Shift key, move the insertion point to the end of the block (say, by using the Arrow keys), and then release Shift.

   In either case, the selected text will be highlighted. (If you want to *deselect* the text, just click the mouse anywhere else in the document or press an Arrow key.)

2. *Cut* or *copy* the selected information to the Windows **Clipboard**, a temporary storage location in RAM set aside for this purpose. When information is **cut**, it is deleted from the source document and moved to the Clipboard; when information is **copied**, it is also transferred to the Clipboard, but the source document remains unchanged. To perform the cut or copy operation, choose the Cut or Copy command from the source application's Edit menu.

WARNING

The Clipboard can only hold one block of information at a time. Thus, when you cut or copy something to the Clipboard, Windows automatically erases its previous contents. No warning message is issued!

You can examine the current contents of the Clipboard by opening the **Clipboard Viewer** utility. (Some configurations of Windows NT contain **Clip*Book* Viewer** instead.) To start Clipboard Viewer, choose this item from the Accessories submenu of the Start button. The current Clipboard contents will be displayed in the Clipboard Viewer window. (ClipBook is also started from the Accessories submenu, but the contents of the Clipboard are not displayed automatically; you have to choose the Clipboard command from the Window menu.)

3. Start, or switch to, the target application (unless the source and target are the same) and open the target document, if necessary.

4. In the target document, position the cursor where you want to insert the information.

5. **Paste** (insert) the information on the Clipboard into the target document at the cursor position by choosing the Paste command from the target application's Edit menu.

Pictorially, the process looks like this:

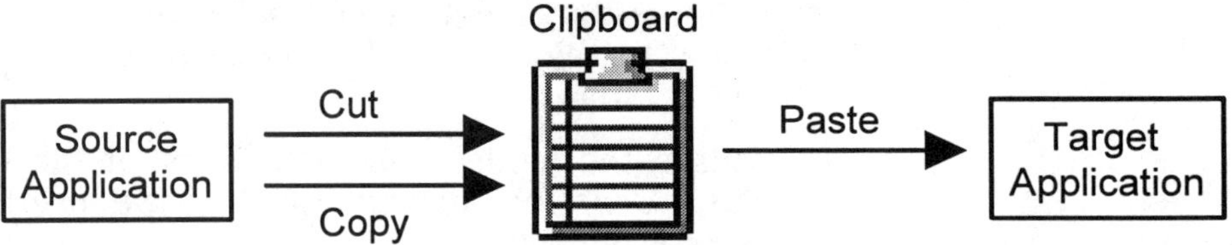

Here are a couple of other ways to issue the cut, copy, or paste commands that work with many Windows applications. After selecting the text to be transferred to the Clipboard, you can *cut or copy* it by either

- Pressing Ctrl+X for cut or Ctrl+C for copy.

or

- Positioning the mouse pointer over the selected text, right-clicking, and choosing Cut or Copy from the resulting menu.

To *paste* text from the Clipboard, position the cursor where you want to insert the text and then, either press Ctrl+V or right-click the mouse and choose Paste from the resulting menu.

NOTE

If you want to copy the *entire current screen* to the Clipboard, press the Print Screen key. To copy the *active window* to the Clipboard, press Alt+Print Screen. In both cases, you can paste these graphics into the target document in the usual way, as described in steps 4 and 5 of the procedure given above.

An Example

Now let's take a look at a specific example of the cut/copy and paste process. We will copy some text from a WordPad document into a Notepad document. (Notepad is a very simple word processor, a *text editor*, supplied with Windows NT.) First we start WordPad and open the Homework 1 document, which can be found on the Student Disk. The resulting WordPad window is shown in Figure 10.

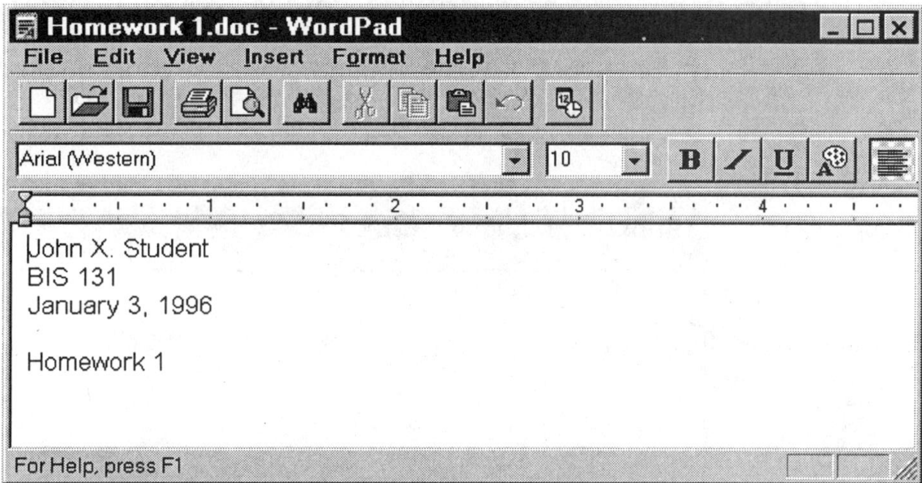

Figure 10   The Text to be Copied

Suppose we want to copy the first three lines (the student's name, his class, and the date). To do so, we must first select the text. Notice that the insertion point in Figure 10 is already positioned at the beginning of this block of text. So, all we need do to select it is

- Hold down the Shift key, tap the Down Arrow key three times, and release Shift.

or

- Position the mouse pointer at the insertion point and drag it down until the first three lines are highlighted.

In either case, the text in the window will look like this:

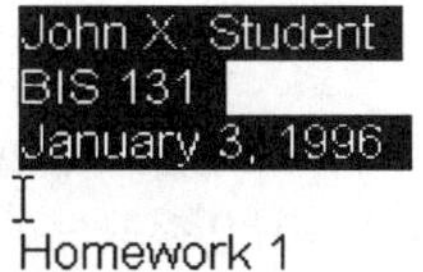

Now, we copy the selected text to the Clipboard by choosing the Copy command from WordPad's Edit menu.

To paste the contents of the Clipboard into Notepad, we start this

application by clicking on its name on the Accessories submenu of the
Start menu's Programs option. (Or, if Notepad is already running, we
switch to it by clicking on its Taskbar button.) Then, we choose the
Paste command from Notepad's Edit menu. The selected text will be
transferred to the beginning of the Notepad document, as pictured in
Figure 11. (Notice that the pasted text has a somewhat different
appearance from the original. This occurs because Notepad only
displays text in the font — typeface — shown here.)

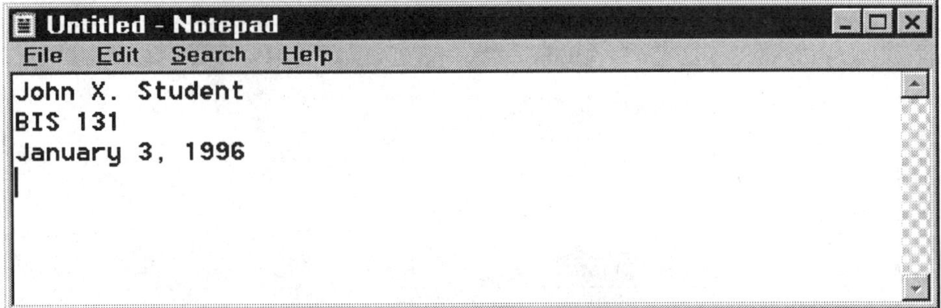

Figure 11   The Original Text Pasted into Notepad

Try the following exercise on your own.

TUTORIAL

1. Turn on your computer (if it's not already on) to start up Windows
   NT. Close any open windows.

2. Start the WordPad word processor (from the Accessories submenu
   of the Start menu's Programs option).

3. Type the text: This is a test.

4. Select this block of text by either:

   - Dragging the insertion point to the beginning of the sen-
     tence.

   or

   - Holding down the Shift key, tapping the Left Arrow key until
     the insertion point is at the beginning of the sentence, and
     releasing Shift.

   In either case, the sentence should now be highlighted.

5. *Cut* the selected text to the Clipboard by choosing Cut from Word-
   Pad's Edit menu or by pressing Ctrl+X.

6. Start the Notepad application by clicking on its name on the Accessories submenu of the Start menu's Programs option.

7. *Paste* the text from the Clipboard into Notepad by choosing Paste from its Edit menu or by pressing Ctrl+V.

8. Switch to WordPad by clicking on its Taskbar button.

9. Paste the sentence into the WordPad document by right-clicking the mouse and selecting Paste from the resulting menu.

10. Close WordPad and then close Notepad, answering No to the "Save changes?" warning message in both cases.

2.4   Installing and Removing Applications

From time to time, you will probably want to use software that is not yet installed on your system or perhaps to remove old, no longer needed programs from your hard disk. In this section, we will discuss how to install and remove applications. We will also describe the process of adding Windows components, such as games and accessories, to your system from the Windows NT CD-ROM.

Installing New Programs

When you buy application software for use on your computer, it comes on a CD-ROM or a set of floppy disks. Before you can use an application, it must be **installed** on your hard disk. The installation process copies files from the distribution disks to the hard disk and supplies Windows with information about how the program operates. The mechanics of the process differ somewhat from application to application depending on the media (floppy disk or CD-ROM) used and whether or not the software was designed to run under Windows NT.

Windows NT CD-ROMs   If your new application was designed to run under Windows NT or Windows 95 and comes on a CD-ROM, the installation process may be very simple.

1. Start Windows and insert the CD in its drive. A dialog box, typically entitled "Install New Program Wizard", will open.

2. You will then be presented with a sequence of screens (or "pages") that provide information or ask you to state your preferences concerning various aspects of the installation process. To move to

the next page, activate the Next command button.

3. When the process is complete, activate the Finish button.

Installing other applications

For applications that come on floppy disks (or on CDs, but do not install as described above), the installation process is usually almost as easy. With Windows running:

1. Insert the floppy disk labeled "Install" or "Setup", or the application's CD-ROM, in its drive.

Add/Remove Programs

2. Click on the Start button, point at the Settings option on the Start menu, and choose Control Panel from the resulting submenu.

3. In the Control Panel window, double-click on the Add/Remove Programs icon to open the dialog box shown in Figure 12.

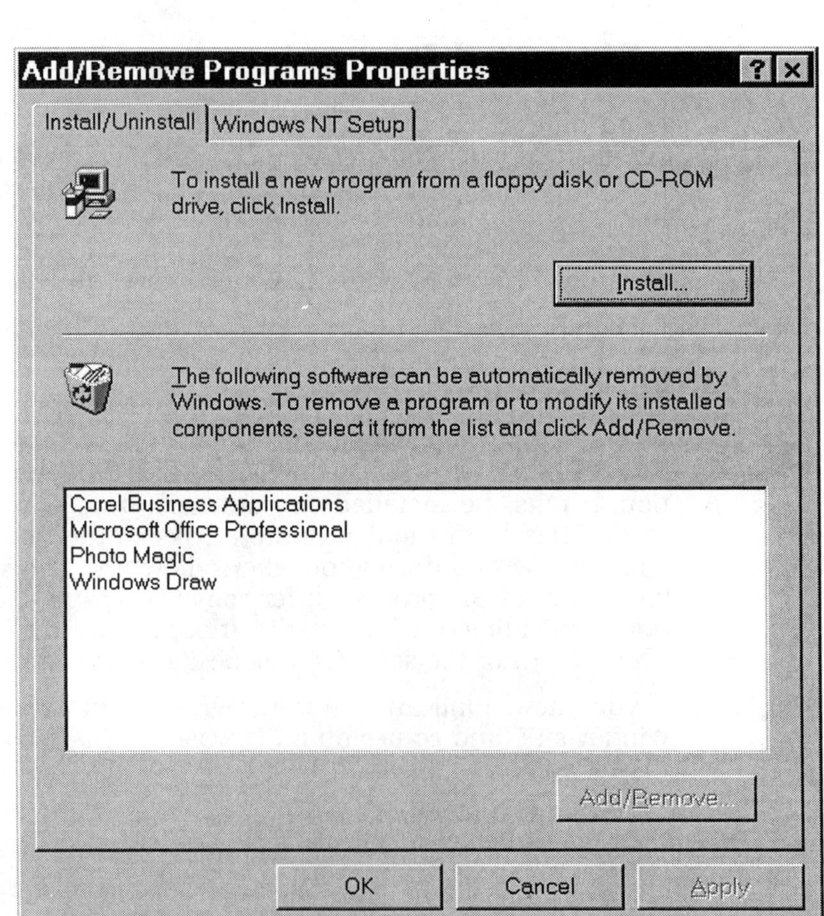

Figure 12   Add/Remove Programs Properties Dialog Box

4. Choose the Install command button. The Install Program dialog box will appear.

5. Choose the Next command button. Windows will automatically search the floppy disk or CD for an installation program and, if found, display its name.

6. If Windows is unable to locate the installation program (or if you are certain it has not found the right one), type this program's name in the text box. (You will find this information in the application's documentation or on the installation disk itself.)

7. Choose the Finish command button. The new application's installation program will then begin to run.

8. Respond to any on-screen queries until the installation process is complete. A menu item for the new application is usually placed on one of the Start button's submenus during the process to make it easy to run the newly-installed software.

Uninstalling Applications

If you no longer use a certain application, you might want to remove (or **uninstall**) it from your hard disk. This process entails deleting all of its program files, as well as removing any references to the application in Windows NT itself (such as the Start button submenu item that opens the application). Although deleting most of the program files is not difficult once you understand how to navigate the Windows folder system (see Chapter 3), manually removing *all* files and references to the program is next to impossible.

Fortunately, for applications designed to run under Windows NT or Windows 95, you can use the Add/Remove Programs utility to perform this task. To uninstall such an application:

1. Start Control Panel from the Settings option of the Start menu, as described above.

2. Double-click on the Add/Remove Programs icon in the Control Panel window to open this utility (Figure 12).

3. Click on the desired application in the list box. It will become highlighted. (If the program you want to remove does not appear on the list, it cannot be automatically removed by Windows.)

4. Click on the Add/Remove command button. A dialog box will open asking if you really want to remove this program.

5. Click on the Yes command button unless you've changed your mind about uninstalling the application.

Adding Windows Components

When Windows NT was set up on your computer, it is likely that some of the *components* (programs and other files) on the Windows CD-ROM were not installed on your hard disk. As a result, as you read this text, you might occasionally see a reference to a feature that is not present on your system. To install such a Windows component:

1. Start Control Panel from the Settings option of the Start menu, as described above.

2. Double-click on the Add/Remove Programs icon in the Control Panel window and click on the Windows NT Setup tab in the resulting dialog box to display the page shown in Figure 13.

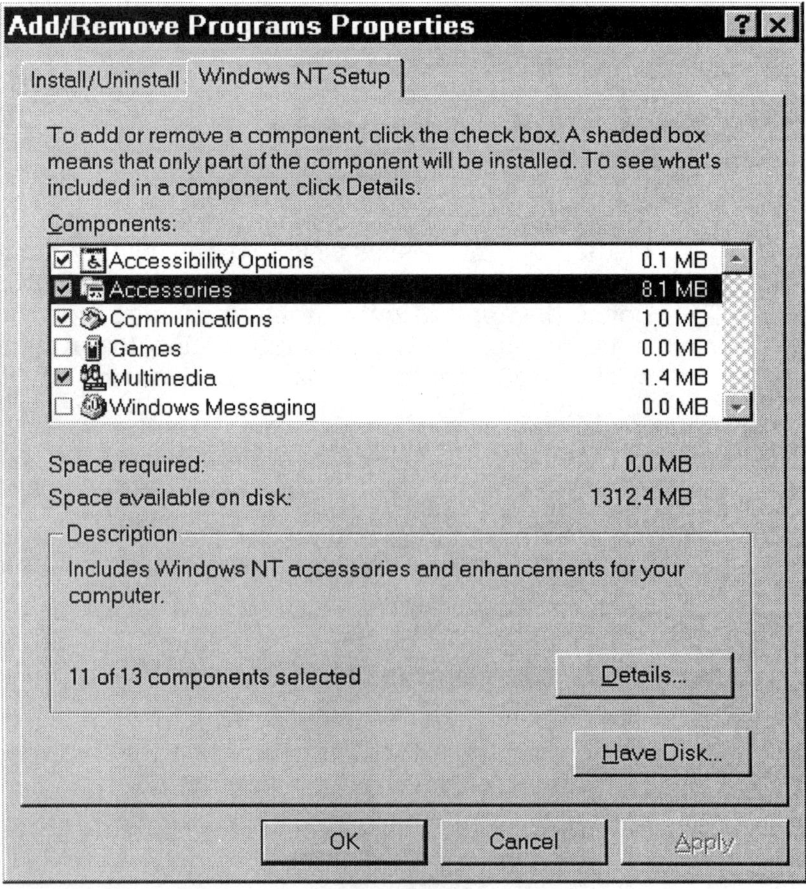

Figure 13   Adding Windows Components

The types of components you can add are displayed in the Components list box. The check box to the left of a component type indicates whether or not components of that type are already installed on your hard disk.

- If a check mark appears against a white background (see Accessibility Options in Figure 13), then all the components of this type are installed.

- If a check mark appears against a gray background (see Accessories in Figure 13), then some of the components of this type are installed. (To see which ones, choose the Details command button.)

- If no check mark appears (see Games in Figure 13), then none of the components of this type is already installed.

3. To install Windows components of a particular type, click on that item in the list and choose the Details command button. A list of components of that type will appear.

4. Select the check box for each component you want to add.

5. Insert the Windows NT CD-ROM into its drive and choose the OK command button twice. Windows will copy the selected components to your hard disk.

6. Close the Windows NT CD-ROM and Control Panel windows.

2.5   Getting On-screen Help

No matter how experienced you become at using Windows and its applications, there will be times when you'll need some help in performing a particular task. At such a time, you might find the answer to your questions in this book, but it may be more convenient to use the Windows NT **online help** system. This powerful feature provides immediate on-screen information about Windows itself and the Windows application that is currently active on your Desktop.

Accessing Online Help

Types of help available   The Windows NT Help system provides access to several kinds of online help:

1. Extensive help is available for Windows itself and can be accessed at any time. This kind of help includes general information about

using Windows, procedures for performing specific tasks, and troubleshooting advice when things go wrong.

2. Application-specific help is provided by the publisher of each program you use. It can be accessed when that application is running.

3. *Context-sensitive* help provides help with the task at hand. It is available for Windows NT and for most Windows applications.

Starting the Help system

How you access the Windows Help system depends on the kind of help you need:

- To access help with Windows NT, click on the Start button and then choose the Help option from the Start menu. The dialog box shown in Figure 14 will open.

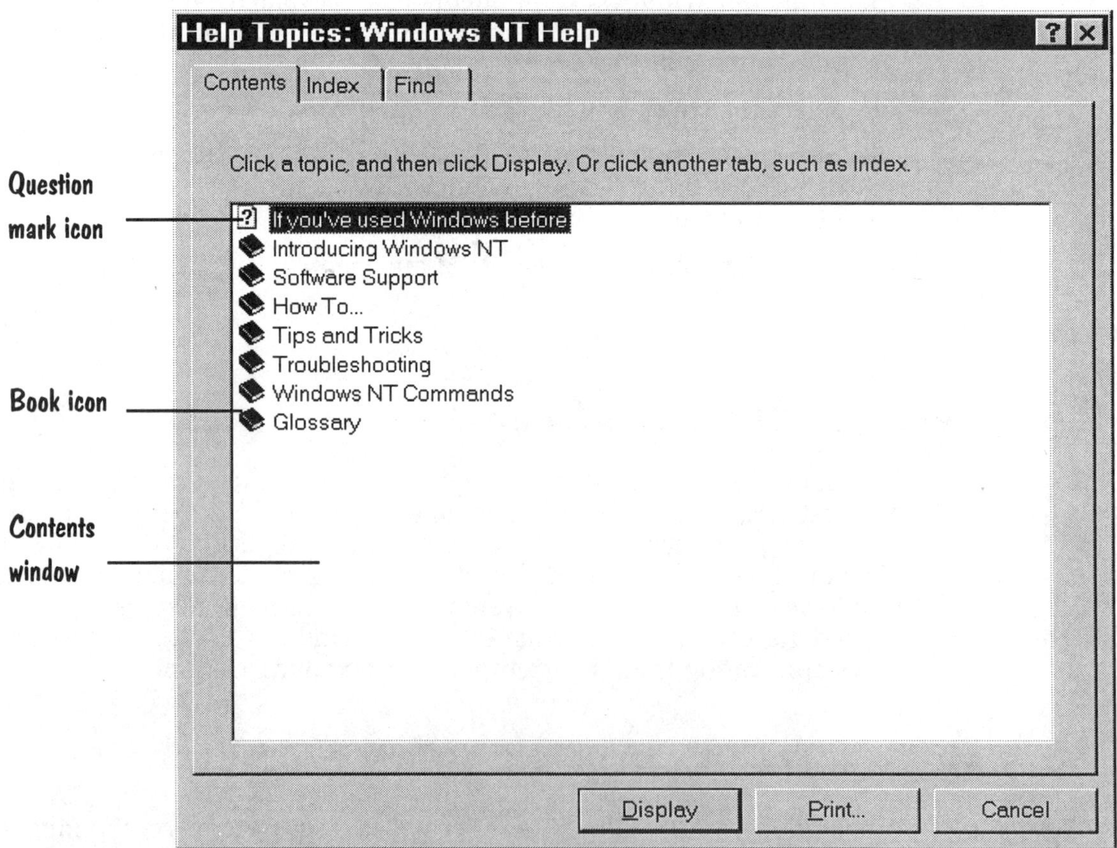

Figure 14   The Windows Help Topics Dialog Box

- Help for the active Windows application can be accessed by displaying that program's Help menu and choosing the option entitled Help Topics or Help Contents. If this application was designed to run under Windows NT, a dialog box similar to the one in Figure 14 will open; if not, a Help dialog box will open, but it may look different from the one in Figure 14.

- There are a couple of ways to access context-sensitive help. We will discuss them at the end of this section.

Locating the Information You Need

Notice that the Help Topics dialog box in Figure 14 has three tabs: Contents, Index, and Find. The corresponding pages of this dialog box provide different ways to locate the information you need.

The Contents Page   Clicking on the Contents tab (if this page is not already displayed) provides access to information of a general nature. For example, as you can see in Figure 14, the Windows Help Contents topics include an introduction to Windows NT, procedures for performing some common tasks, and help with troubleshooting.

If a topic in the Contents window is preceded by a book icon (such as "Introducing Windows NT" in Figure 14), double-clicking on this topic will "open the book" and display a list of subtopics. For example, Figure 15 shows the Contents window after double-clicking on Introducing Windows NT and then double-clicking on Network Services.

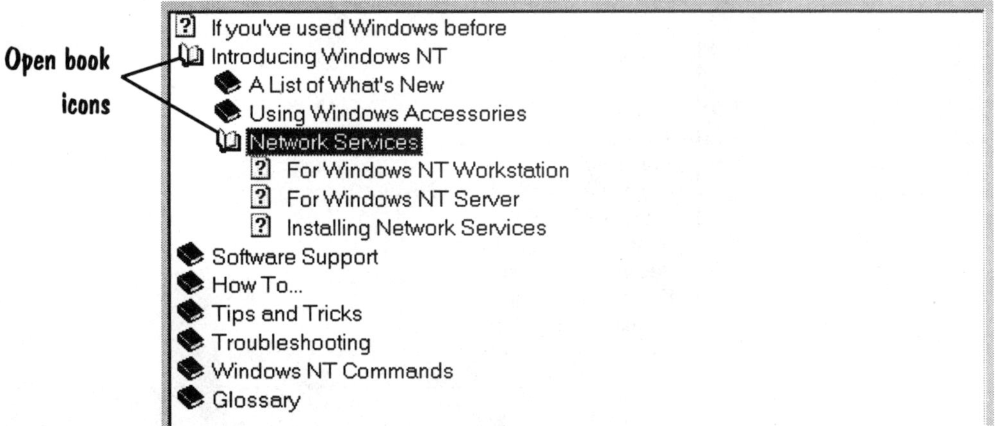

Figure 15   Displaying Subtopics in the Contents Window

If a topic on the Contents list is preceded by a question-mark icon (such as "If you've used Windows before" in Figure 15), double-clicking on that item will open a Help window supplying information about the topic. (You can also open a topic's Help window by clicking on the topic, which highlights it, and then activating the Display command button.) We will discuss these Help windows later in this section.

Instead of viewing information about a topic on-screen, you can print this material by clicking on the desired topic and activating the Print command button. The Print dialog box, like the one shown in Figure 8 of Section 2.2, will appear on the screen. To begin printing, choose the OK command button.

The Index Page   Clicking on the Index tab of the Help Topics dialog box displays a much more detailed list of items than Contents (see Figure 16).

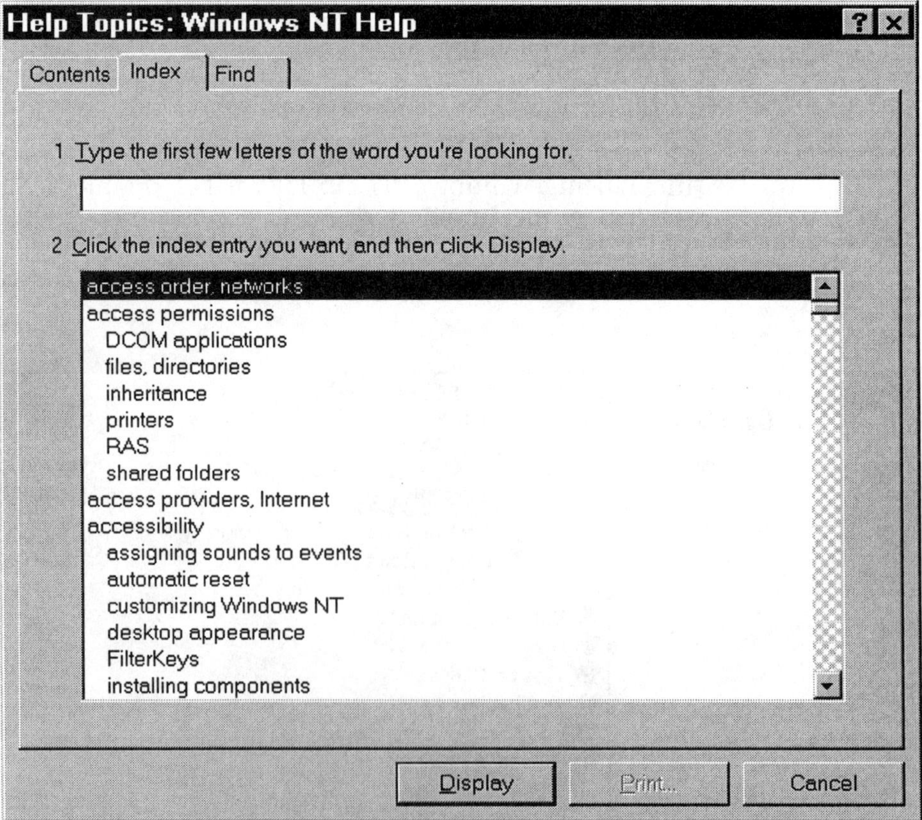

Figure 16   The Index Page of the Help Topics Dialog Box

To use Index to open a Help window for a particular topic:

1. Double-click on the desired item, or click on it and then click on the Display button.

2. If there is more than one topic associated with the item you have chosen in step 1, a Topics Found dialog box will open, displaying a list of subtopics. Double-click on the desired topic (or click on it and then on Display).

The Find Page   Windows NT and applications designed to run under it contain a *Find utility* that enables you to search Help for a specific word or phrase. When Help's Find utility is first accessed for Windows or an application, it searches the relevant Help files and creates a database of the words it finds. Once the database is set up, you can use Find by clicking on its tab in the Help Topics dialog box (the result is shown in Figure 17) and carrying out these three steps:

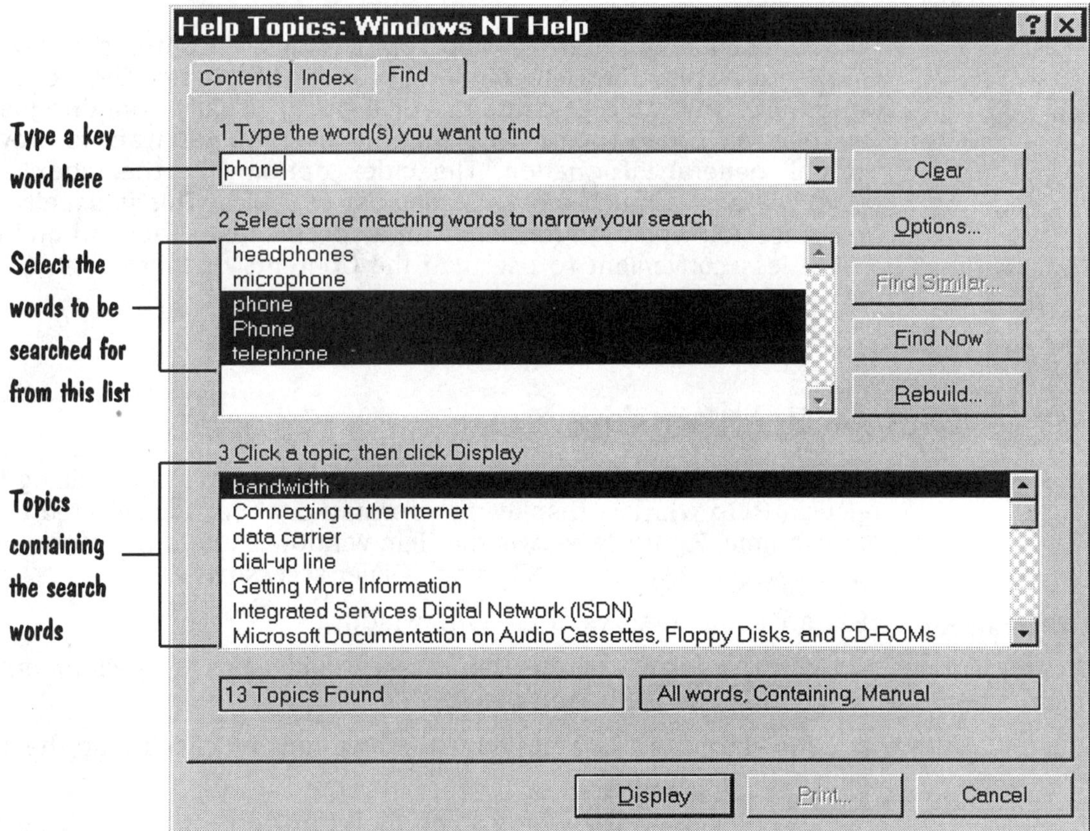

Figure 17   The Find Page of the Help Topics Dialog Box

1. Type a key word in the text box at the top of the Find page. For example, if you are trying to determine how to use your modem with Windows to place a phone call, you might type *phone*. Now click on the Find Now command button, and a list of words in the Find database that match your key word will appear in the middle window. (If Find Now is dimmed, the list of words will appear as you type.)

2. From the list in the middle window, select the words in which you are interested. To select words, click on the first, then hold down the Ctrl key as you click on the others. For example, if you're interested in phone calls, select *phone*, *Phone*, and *telephone* in this manner. The topics that contain these words then appear in the bottom window.

3. Select a topic from the bottom window by clicking on it and choosing the Display button (or by just double-clicking on the topic). The Help window for this topic will open.

You can use any of the three Help Topics pages — Contents, Index, or Find — to display the Help window for a specific topic. The Contents option (like the table of contents for a book) usually contains just a few relatively broad topics. This option is useful if you want to browse through general information. The Index option (like the index of a book) contains a much more detailed list of topics. This is usually the first place you would go for help with a specific task. The Find utility is a little less convenient to use than the Contents or Index, but it may locate information that the other two cannot.

Using a Help Window

Activating the Display command button in the Help Topics dialog box opens a **Help window** displaying information about the selected topic. For example, Figure 18 shows the Help window containing information about using the Windows NT Phone Dialer accessory.

Features of a Help window

Here are some features of the Help window:

- You can return to the Help Topics dialog box by clicking on the Help Topics command button.

- You can return to a previous Help window by clicking on the Back command button.

- If you click on the Options command button (or right-click in the window) a menu is displayed that allows you to:

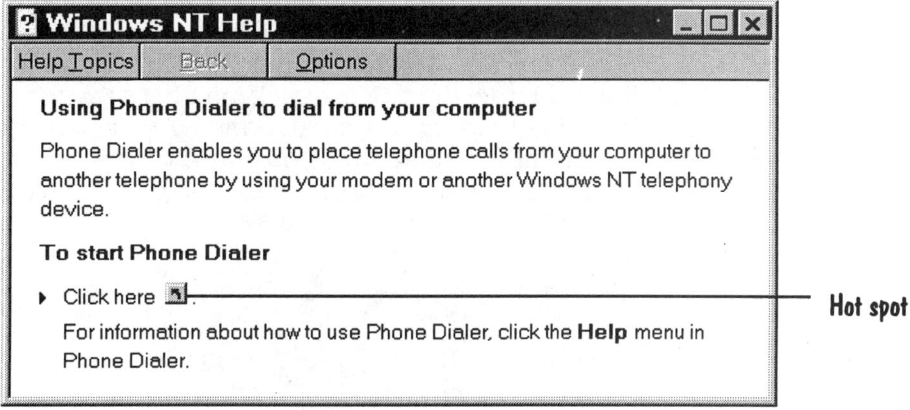

Figure 18   A Typical Help Window

Annotate the topic; that is, associate additional information with it. Once the topic is annotated, a paper clip icon appears next to its title; clicking on this icon opens a dialog box that displays your annotation.

Copy the contents of the Help window to the Clipboard.

Print the contents of the Help window on a printer.

Choose from three *font* sizes for the Help window's text.

Choose to keep the Help window *on top* so that it doesn't disappear from view when you switch to an application.

- Some windows contain **hot spots**, represented by small square buttons. If you mouse-point at one of these, the pointer becomes a hand icon. Clicking on a hot spot opens a new window with related information or, if the hot spot contains an arrow, clicking on it opens an application.

Context-Sensitive Help

Context-sensitive help provides information about some aspect of the task at hand. For example, suppose you've opened the Run dialog box (see Section 2.1) but forgotten the purpose of the Browse command button. You can use Windows online context-sensitive help to explain its function without bringing up the entire Help system. Context-sensitive help, when it's available, can be accessed in several ways:

- If the active window contains a question-mark button on the title bar, click on this button. The cursor will become an arrow with the question-mark attached, as shown at the right. Now click on the item for which you want help, and a small window will pop up, displaying information about this object. For example, if you click on the question-mark icon in the Run dialog box and then on the Browse command button, the following window will pop-up:

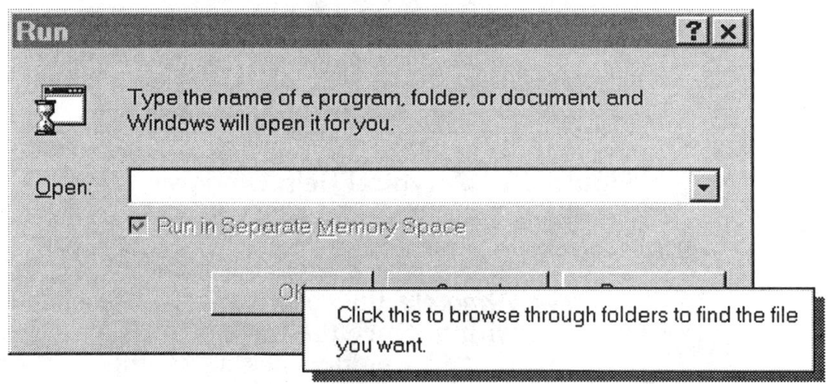

To close the pop up window, click anywhere on the screen.

- With Windows NT and most applications designed for it, you can right-click on an object to access context-sensitive help. Right-clicking displays a one-item *What's This?* menu:

Click on this menu item to open an explanatory pop-up window.

- When using older Windows applications, you won't see a question-mark button and right-clicking on an object won't work either. However, the application's dialog boxes may contain a Help command button. If not, try pressing the F1 function key or the Shift+ F1 keystroke combination to get help with the dialog box.

Try the following exercise on your own.

1. Turn on your computer (if necessary) to start Windows NT.

2. Start Windows NT Help by clicking on the Start button and then

clicking on the Start menu's Help option. The Windows Help Topics dialog box will open.

3. Let's locate information about the Calculator accessory that is supplied with Windows NT:

   - Click on the Index tab to display the Index page.
   - Type the word *calculator* in the text box.
   - In the topics window, double-click on the "Calculator" entry.

   A Help window entitled "Using Calculator to make calculations" will open.

4. Click on the *hot spot* — the small gray button with a curved arrow on it — to start Calculator. Its window will appear on the screen. Close the Windows NT Help window.

5. Now let's get some general information about Calculator:

   - Choose Help Topics from the Help menu. The Calculator Help Topics window will open.
   - Click on the Contents tab (if necessary) to display this page.
   - Display the list of subtopics under *Performing Calculations* by double-clicking on its "book" icon. Then, click on *Performing a simple calculation* and click on the Display command button. A Help window with information about this topic will open.

6. Click on the Options command button to display the Options menu and successively choose each option to see what it does.

7. Click on the Help Topics command button to return to the Calculator Help Topics dialog box.

8. Click on the Find tab to display the Find page. (If the Find Setup Wizard dialog box appears, click on the Next command button, then on the Finish button.)

9. Let's search for information on clearing the calculator's memory:

   - Type *clear* in the text box and choose the Find Now button, if it's not dimmed. One or two words will appear in the middle window and one or two topics in the bottom window.
   - Select (click on) the topic "To work with numbers stored in memory" and activate the Display command button. A Help window with information on this topic will open.

10. Click on the Back command button to return to the first Calculator Help window. Close this window.

11. Notice that one of the calculator keys is labeled *Back*. To determine the function of this key:

- Right-click on it. The one-item *What's This?* menu will be displayed.
- Click on the *What's This?* command. A window will pop up explaining the function of the Back key. Click anywhere in the Calculator window to close the pop-up window.

12. Close the Calculator application.

Review Exercises

Section 2.1

1. You can open the Start menu by clicking on the Start button or by pressing the ___________ keystroke combination.

2. Positioning the mouse pointer over the ___________ item on the Start menu displays a menu of programs and groups of programs.

3. To close an application, you can choose ___________ from its File menu.

4. True or false: You can start an application that is represented by an icon on the Desktop by double-clicking on that icon.

5. True or false: To start a program named MyProg that is located on the floppy disk in the A: drive, choose Run from the Start menu, type A:MyProg in the dialog box, and press the Enter key.

6. True or false: All DOS applications are exited in the same way as a Windows application.

7. Which of the following items on the Start menu can never be used to start your word processor?

    a. Programs
    b. Documents
    c. Settings
    d. Run

8. Which of the following will not exit a Windows application?

    a. Clicking on its close button.
    b. Clicking on its minimize button.
    c. Right-clicking on its Taskbar button and choosing Close from the resulting menu.
    d. Pressing the Alt+F4 keystroke combination.

Section 2.2

9. WordPad is listed on the ___________ submenu, which contains a group of small applications built into Windows NT.

10. To ___________ a document means to copy it from the computer's RAM onto disk.

11. To ___________ a document means to copy it from disk into RAM and simultaneously display it on the screen.

12. The ___________ option on the Start menu displays a list of recently-saved documents.

13. True or false: Choosing New from WordPad's File menu closes the current document and clears the document window.

14. True or false: If you create but never save a document, you will not be able to open it once it has been closed.

15. True or false: You can open, close, save, and print a WordPad document by using its Toolbar.

16. True or false: If you click on the print icon on the WordPad Toolbar, one copy of the entire on-screen document will be printed.

17. WordPad's File menu contains two different commands for

    a. Saving a document.
    b. Opening a document.
    c. Printing a document.
    d. Exiting the application.

18. To save a document that is not yet named:

    a. You can use the Open command.
    b. You can use the Save command.
    c. You can use the New command.
    d. None of the above commands can do the job.

Section 2.3 19. To switch to an inactive application, you can click on its button located on the ___________.

20. You can select a block of text by positioning the insertion point at the beginning of the block and holding down the ___________ key as you move the insertion point to the end of the block.

21. When information is cut or copied from a document, it is transferred to the Windows ___________.

22. True or false: Windows NT allows you to have more than one application window open on the screen.

23. True or false: When information is transferred to the Clipboard, its previous contents (if any) are erased.

24. True or false: Pressing the Print Screen key copies the entire screen to the Clipboard.

25. Which of the following techniques cannot be used to switch to an inactive application?

    a. Click on the inactive application's window.
    b. Click on the inactive application's Taskbar button.
    c. Press the Ctrl+Esc keystroke combination.
    d. Press the Alt+Tab keystroke combination.

26. To transfer selected information to the Clipboard and simultaneously delete it from a document:

    a. Choose Cut from the application's Edit menu.
    b. Choose Copy from the application's Edit menu.
    c. Choose Paste from the application's Edit menu.
    d. Choose Delete from the application's Edit menu.

Section 2.4 27. To ____________ an application means to copy its files from the distribution disks to the computer's hard disk and set up the application for use in Windows.

28. To add Windows components, such as Accessories or Games, use Control Panel's ____________ utility.

29. True or false: Some applications that are distributed on CD-ROMs can be installed without starting Control Panel.

30. True or false: The Add/Remove Programs uninstall utility can be used to uninstall *any* application.

31. To start Control Panel, from the Start menu, choose the

    a. Programs option.
    b. Documents option.
    c. Settings option.
    d. Run option.

32. Using the Add/Remove Programs utility in Control Panel

    a. You can install applications to your hard disk.
    b. You can uninstall applications present on your hard disk.
    c. You can add Windows components to your hard disk.
    d. You can perform all the above tasks.

Section 2.5 33. To obtain online help for Windows itself, click on the Help item on the ____________ menu.

34. To obtain online help for the active application, click on the Help Topics item on the ____________ menu.

35. If a topic on the Contents page of the Help Topics dialog box is preceded by a ____________ icon, it contains a list of subtopics.

36. If you would like to change the font size of the text in a Help window, begin by clicking on the ___________ command button.

37. True or false: If a window has a question-mark button on the title bar, you can click on this button to access context-sensitive help.

38. True or false: Clicking on a hot spot in a Help window displays a new window or starts an application.

39. True or false: If you can't locate the topic you're seeking in the Help Topics Index, you should try the Help Topics Find utility.

40. Which of the following is not a tab in a Help Topics dialog box:

    a. Contents
    b. Glossary
    c. Index
    d. Find

41. The Options menu in a Help window allows you to

    a. Return to the Help Topics dialog box.
    b. Return to a previous Help window.
    c. Print the contents of the window.
    d. Change the size of the Help window.

42. To obtain context-sensitive help in a Windows NT dialog box:

    a. Click on an object in the box.
    b Double-click on an object in the box.
    c. Right-click on an object in the box.
    d. Drag the *What's This?* button onto an object.

Build Your Own Glossary

43. The following words and phrases are important terms that were introduced in this chapter. (They appear within the text in bold-face type.) Use WordPad (see Section 2.2) to enter a definition for each term, preserving alphabetical order, into the Glossary file on the Student Disk.

Active application	Document	Programs option
Application	Documents option	(on Start menu)
Clipboard	(on Start menu)	Run option
Clipboard Viewer	Help window	(on Start menu)
Clipbook Viewer	Hot spot	Save a document
Close a document	Install a program	Toolbar
Context-sensitive	Online help	Tool tip
help	Open a document	Uninstall a program
Copy to Clipboard	Paste from Clipboard	WordPad
Cut to Clipboard	Print a document	

Lab Exercises

Work each of the following exercises at your computer. Begin by turning the machine on (if necessary) to start Windows NT. Then, close all open windows.

**Lab Exercise 1
(Section 2.1)**

a. Start Command Prompt, which is a DOS application that appears on the Programs submenu of the Start menu. If, once Command Prompt is open, you don't see a title bar, press Alt+Enter to run Command Prompt in a window.

b. Try to close Command Prompt by pressing Alt+F4. Does this work? If not, try to close its window by clicking on the close button. If this doesn't work, type Exit and press the Enter key to close Command Prompt.

c. Insert the Student Disk in its drive. Then, display its contents by choosing the Run command from the Start menu, entering A: in the text box, and choosing the OK button. Now, start the Dosprog program by double-clicking on the Shortcut to Dosprog item in the new window.

d. If Dosprog is not running in a window, press Alt+Enter. Try to close this application by clicking on its close button. What does the resulting dialog box tell you? (Click on the Cancel button to close the dialog box.)

e. Exit Dosprog by pressing the Enter key. Notice that its window remains on the screen, but the title bar has changed. What word now appears on it?

f. Click on the close button again to close the Dosprog window, close the "A:\" window, and remove the Student Disk from its drive.

g. Repeatedly open and close the Windows NT Explorer application, which can be found on the Programs submenu of the Start menu. Try the following methods for closing it:

>   Click on its close button.
>   Right-click on its Taskbar button and choose Close from the resulting menu, if one appears.
>   Press Alt+F4.
>   Right-click the title bar and choose Close from the resulting menu, if one appears.

Which techniques worked?

Lab Exercise 2
(Section 2.2)

a. Start the WordPad word processor.

b. Type your name, your class, and the date on separate lines. Then, skip a line and type: Chapter 2, Lab Exercise 2

c. Insert the Student Disk in its drive.

d. Save your document to this diskette; use the name Ch 2, LabEx 1. What name appears on the title bar?

e. Print the document.

f. Type the current time on the same line as the date.

g. Save the revised document using the Save command on the File menu. Did the name on the title bar change?

h. Print the revised document.

i. Exit WordPad and remove the diskette from its drive.

Lab Exercise 3
(Section 2.2)

a. Start the WordPad word processor and insert the Student Disk in its drive.

b. Open the document named Memo on this diskette.

c. Change the date to the current date, the *From* entry to your name, and the *Re* entry to Windows NT.

d. Move the insertion point to the end of the document (two lines below *Re*) and type a short description of Windows NT.

e. Save the document to the floppy disk under the new name WinNT Memo (using the Save *As* command).

f. Print the revised document.

g. Exit WordPad and remove the diskette from its drive.

Lab Exercise 4
(Section 2.3)

a. Start the WordPad word processor and insert the Student Disk in its drive.

b. Open the document named Preamble on this diskette.

c. Select all the text in this document except for the title.

d. Copy the selected text to the Clipboard.

e. Move the insertion point to the end of the document (deselecting the block of text in the process) and then move the insertion point down two lines by pressing the Enter key twice.

f. Paste the contents of the Clipboard into the document.

g.   Repeat steps *e* and *f.* (The preamble should now appear three times.)

h.   Print the current document.

i.   Exit WordPad, answering No to the "Save changes?" message, and remove the diskette from its drive.

Lab Exercise 5 (Section 2.3)

a.   Start the WordPad word processor and then start the Calculator application by clicking on Calculator on the Accessories submenu of the Start menu's Programs option.

b.   Open Calculator's View menu. If Standard is not checked, choose this item; otherwise, press the Escape key to close the View menu.

c.   Click successively on the 1, 2, and 3 calculator keys (which enters the number 123 into the calculator's "display").

d.   Copy the contents of the display to the Clipboard by choosing Copy from the Edit menu. (Notice that in the Calculator application, you need not select the number before copying it.)

e.   Switch to WordPad and paste the Clipboard contents into the document.

f.   Switch back to Calculator and copy its window to the Clipboard (using *Alt*+Print Screen, not Print Screen).

g.   Exit Calculator, which makes WordPad active.

h.   Skip a couple of lines and paste the contents of the Clipboard (the captured window) into the WordPad document.

i.   Print the document and exit WordPad (saving the document to a floppy disk if you want).

Lab Exercise 6 (Section 2.5)

a.   Start Windows NT Help by choosing Help from the Start menu (which opens the Windows NT Help Topics dialog box).

b.   If the Contents page is not displayed, click on its tab.

c.   Right-click within the Contents topics window and click on the *What's This?* command. What is the title of this pop-up window? Close the pop-up window.

d.   Click on the question-mark button on the title bar; then on the Contents tab. What message is displayed? Close the pop-up window.

e.   Display the topic entitled "If you've used Windows before". What is the title of the resulting Help window?

f.   In the Help window, click on the "How do I start programs?" hot spot. Which technique for starting programs is described?

g.   Open the Options menu for this Help window and point at the Font item. What choices do you have for font size?

h.   Close the Help window to exit Help.

Lab Exercise 7 (Section 2.5)

a.   Start WordPad and choose Help Topics from the Help menu to open the WordPad Help Topics dialog box.

b.   Let's locate information about the WordPad Ruler. Click on the Index tab (if this page is currently not displayed).

c.   Type *ruler* in the text box. What is the name of the topic that is highlighted? Select the topic "To show or hide the ruler".

d.   Activate the Display command button to open the Help window corresponding to this topic. On which WordPad menu does the command that shows or hides the Ruler appear?

e.   Return to the Help Topics dialog box and click on the Find tab. (If the Find Setup Wizard dialog box appears, click on Next, then on Finish.)

f.   Type *ruler* in the text box. How many topics are listed in the bottom window?

g.   Display the topic entitled "To set tabs in paragraphs". On which WordPad menu is the Tabs command located?

h.   Choose the Tabs command from the appropriate WordPad menu. The Tabs dialog box will open. Now, using either the *setting tabs* Help window or context-sensitive help in the Tabs dialog box, answer the following questions:

- What is the difference between the Clear and Clear All commands?
- What is the purpose of the Set command button in the Tabs dialog box?
- How does one delete a tab using the Ruler?

i.   Close the Help window and exit WordPad.

CHAPTER 3

Managing Files, Folders, and Disks

In Chapter 2 we discussed, in a general way, how to use applications (programs) and documents. Both applications and documents are stored in files, which in turn are located in folders on a disk. This chapter describes how to use Windows NT Explorer and My Computer to perform basic operations on files, folders, and disks. To be more specific, you will learn:

1. How files and folders are organized on a disk.

2. The rules for creating valid file and folder names.

3. How to select files and folders in Windows NT Explorer.

4. How to use Windows NT Explorer to

   - Move or copy files and folders.

   - Create, rename, and delete files and folders.

   - Create shortcuts.

5. How to use My Computer to locate and manipulate files and folders.

6. How to use Explorer or My Computer to format and copy floppy disks.

3.1   Files and Folders

Computer disks are capable of storing a lot of information — both data and programs. In order to facilitate access to this information, Windows NT, with your help, organizes it into files and folders. In this section, we will provide some useful information about these concepts.

What are Files and Folders?

Files   A **file** is a collection of information that has been generated by the computer and stored (saved) on disk. A file may contain an application, in which case it's called a *program file*, or data created by an application, which is a *data file*. For example, recall that when you save a document for the first time in the WordPad word processor (itself a collection of files stored on your hard disk), you choose a name for that document. When you issue the Save (or Save As) command, Windows creates a file by copying the document from internal memory (RAM) to disk and assigning the name you chose to it.

Folders   Since a hard disk can contain thousands of files, it is necessary to organize them into **folders** (or **directories**[*]). Each folder is a collection of related files that you (or a program) have grouped together and given a name. For example, you might place all the letters you've written in one folder called Letters and all your reports in another folder called (you guessed it) Reports.

Sometimes it makes sense to place a related group of folders within a larger folder. In this case, the bigger folder is called the **parent folder** and each of the folders within it is a **subfolder** (or *child folder*) of the parent. For example, your disk might have several folders that contain word processing data files: Letters, Reports, and so on. To better organize the disk, you could place all of these in a (parent) folder called, say, Word Processing. (A parent folder can contain files as well as subfolders. For example, the Word Processing folder might hold the *program* files for your word processing application.)

The folders on a disk form a tree-like structure with subfolders branching out from their parents, which in turn may be subfolders themselves. On each disk there is one folder, called the **root folder**, that contains all the others. Figure 1 shows a *folder tree* — a graphical

---

[*]The Windows NT 4 documentation uses the term *folder* instead of *directory*. If you are familiar with DOS, Windows 3.1, or Windows NT 3.51, just think *directory* whenever you see *folder*. Don't worry; you'll soon get used to the new terminology.

way of representing the folder structure of a disk. Notice that in a folder tree, the root is at the top!

In Figure 1, the root folder is designated by "3½ Floppy (A:)" and its three subfolders (Drawing Files, Word Processing, and Zingers) are shown connected to it by dotted lines. Notice that the Drawing Files and Word Processing folders have subfolders of their own (each connected to its parent by dotted lines), and one of these subfolders (Letters) also has subfolders. Each folder, including the root, may contain files as well.

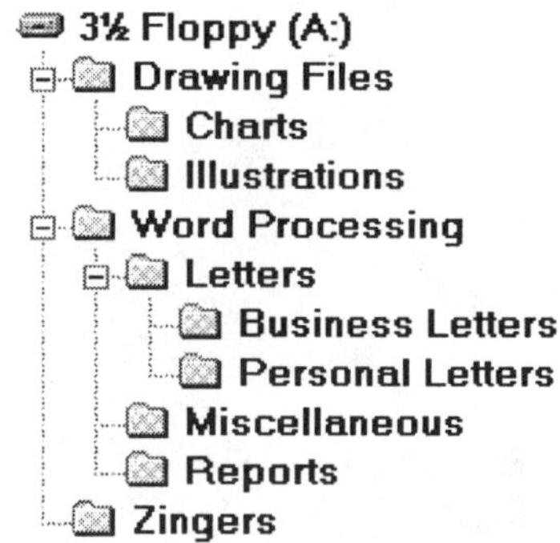

Figure 1   A Folder Tree

Naming Files and Folders

Disk drive designations
Every drive, folder, and file used by your computer must have a name. Drive designations (for hard and floppy disk drives, CD-ROM drives, network drives, and the like) are assigned by the operating system. They consist of a single letter followed by a colon; for example, A: and B: are reserved for the computer's floppy drives, and its primary hard disk is designated C:, even if there is only one floppy drive. Other drives (D:, E:, etc.) may be present as well.

DOS file names
Naming files can get complicated. There are different rules for what constitutes a valid file name depending on whether the program that created the file was designed to run under DOS or Windows 3.1 on the one hand, or under Windows NT or 95 on the other. If the program that created the file is a DOS or Windows 3.1 application, the resulting name is known as a **DOS file name**, and must follow these rules:

- The name may consist of two parts: A required *filename* containing from one to eight characters, possibly followed by an *extension* consisting of up to three characters. If the extension is present, it must be separated from the filename by a period (.). For example, for the file Joe.Ltr, Joe is the filename and Ltr is the extension.

- The filename and extension may contain any characters *except*

period (.)	comma (,)	colon (:)
semicolon (;)	quotation mark (")	brackets ([ ])
slash (/)	backslash (\)	equals sign (=)
vertical bar (|)	question mark (?)	asterisk (*)

Moreover, *no spaces* are permitted in a DOS file name.

- Lowercase letters are not distinguished from uppercase letters. So, the names MyFile, myfile, and MYFILE are considered identical.

For example, the following names are all valid:

    Ch1   Ch1.Txt   Ch-1.{   history.rpt   X   1(#$%).n1

However, the following names are *invalid* DOS file names:

    inventory.dat   (Filename is too long.)
    Top Gun   (Spaces are not allowed.)
    File:1   (The colon is an illegal character.)

Windows NT file and folder names

Windows NT frees us from many of the restrictions imposed by DOS file names. Most importantly, in naming a file created by a Windows NT-based application or *any* Windows NT folder, you may use up to 255 characters, including spaces. (For this reason, these names are called **long file names**.) Moreover, all punctuation marks *except* for the following ones are permitted in long file names:

    colon (:)   vertical bar (|)   quotation mark (")
    slash (/)   backslash (\)   question mark (?)
    asterisk (*)

As a result, the following names are valid for a folder or for a file created by an application designed to run under Windows NT:

    J. Gomez - Letter 1   (but *not*   J. Gomez: Letter 1)
    BIS HW #7 1-5-98   (but *not*   BIS HW #7 1/5/968)
    Annual Report - 1997   (but *not*   "Annual Report - 1997")

Long file names may have extensions, but they are usually assigned by Windows, not the user.

NOTE

Long file names can only be created and used by Windows 95 and NT and applications designed to run under them. So, when you are running a DOS or Windows 3.1 program, you have to follow the stricter rules for DOS file names.

This situation raises an interesting question: What happens if you try to open a document with a long file name in an application that doesn't support long file names? In this case, Windows NT supplies a "DOS alias", a related DOS file name, for use in this application. To form the alias, Windows truncates the original file name to six characters and inserts two special symbols followed by the file's extension. In addition, any blank spaces are deleted and illegal characters are replaced by underscores. For example, suppose you create documents named Assignment #5, Assignment #6, and Asg [7] in WordPad and then open each of these documents in a Windows 3.1-based word processor. Here, the document file names become assign~1.doc, assign~2.doc, and asg_7_~1.doc.

Path Names

When you start an application, Windows automatically specifies a certain folder as the current (or default) folder for that application. (To see which folder is the current one, just open the Save As or Open dialog box; it will be displayed in the *Save in* or *Look in* text box.) If you want to refer to any file in the current folder, you need only give its file name. For example, if you save a file, naming it Sam.doc, it is automatically placed in the current folder.

To refer to a file that is not in the current folder, you must change folders or give the file's **path name**, a kind of road map that tells Windows how to find the file. The path name for a file begins with the drive designation (for example, C:), followed by the names of the root folder (which is \, a backslash) and all subfolders, from largest to smallest, that contain the file, and ends with the name of the file itself. All subfolder names must be followed by backslashes. Thus, the complete path name for a file called Sam.doc in the Personal Letters folder in the folder tree shown in Figure 1 is:

A:\Word Processing\Letters\Personal Letters\Sam.doc

3.2   *An Introduction to Windows NT Explorer*

When you use Windows on a regular basis, you will frequently find it convenient to delete, move, copy, or rename files and folders. Windows' primary tool for performing these kinds of operations is the **Explorer** application. In this section, we will provide some basic information about Explorer; its capabilities will be discussed in more detail in Sections 3.3 and 3.4.

The Explorer Window

To start Explorer:

1. Click on the Start button (or press Ctrl+Esc) to open the Start menu.

2. Point at the Programs option and click on Windows NT Explorer

on the resulting submenu. A window similar to the one in Figure 2 will open.

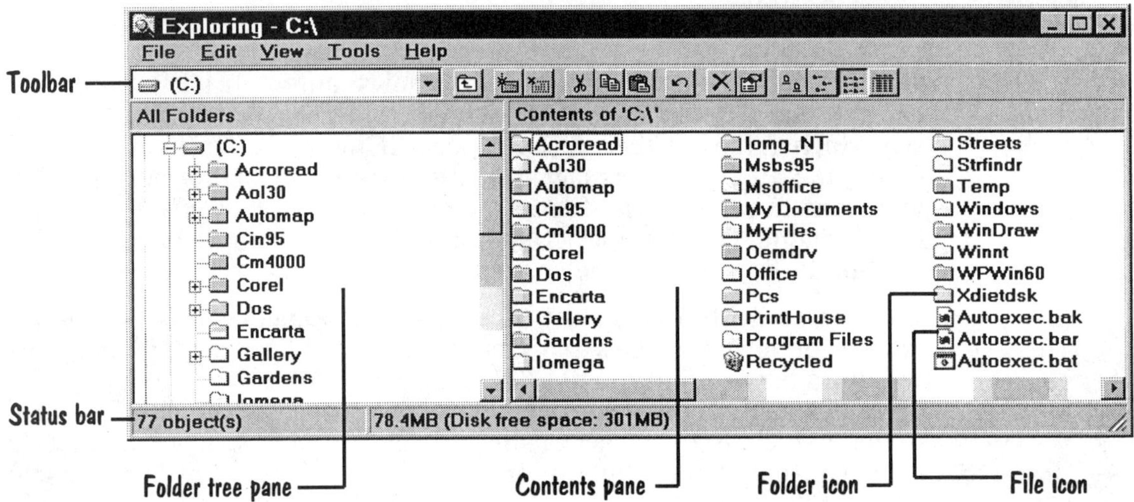

Figure 2   The Explorer Window

The Explorer window has a title bar, menu bar, and toolbar at the top and a status bar at the bottom. The toolbar and status bar can be hidden. To hide either bar (or display it if it's currently hidden), choose the item bearing its name from the View menu. Most of the Explorer window is divided into two large subwindows or *panes*: the *folder tree pane* on the left and the *contents pane* on the right. The remainder of this section describes these parts of the Explorer window.

The Folder Tree Pane

The **folder tree pane** lists all folders on all drives connected to your computer and also provides access to other objects on the Desktop, such as My Computer and the Recycle Bin. In fact, if you scroll up the folder tree pane, you'll see that all objects listed in this window, including drives, are considered subfolders of the Desktop folder!

When you start Explorer, the drive containing the Winnt folder is displayed at the top of the folder tree pane and all immediate (*child*) subfolders are listed in alphabetical order beneath it. The files and folders contained within the current (or *open*) folder are shown in the contents pane. For example, in Figure 2, the contents pane displays the subfolders and some of the files in the C:\ folder. If you want to view the contents of another object in the folder tree pane, just scroll the folder tree up or down until that object is visible and click on it. Its name will become highlighted and, if it is represented by a folder icon, that icon will "open", as shown at the right. 

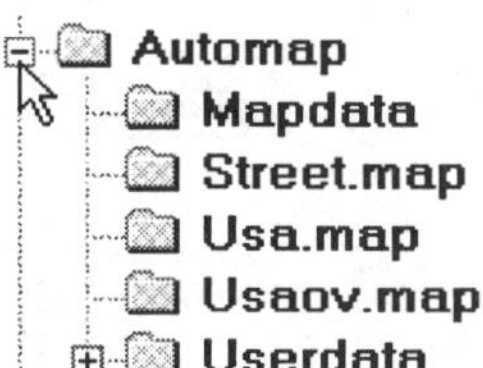

NOTE

Opening a folder displays an up-to-the-moment list of its contents, even if they have changed in the current session. You should be aware, however, that there are situations in which the contents pane does not accurately reflect the contents of the open folder. The most common of these occurs if you change the disk in a floppy drive when its folder is open; in this case, Windows will continue to display the contents of the previous disk. To view the contents of the new disk, either click again on the floppy drive icon in the folder tree pane or choose the Refresh command from the View menu.

Expanding the folder tree

To see subfolders that are hidden from view (even after scrolling), you have to *expand* a branch of the folder tree. When a folder contains hidden subfolders, its name and icon are preceded by a plus (+) symbol (see, for example, the Automap folder in Figure 2). To view these subfolders, expanding this branch of the folder tree, either

- Click on the plus symbol.

or

- Double-click on the folder name or icon.

In either case, the subfolders will be displayed and the plus symbol will become a minus (-) symbol. (If you double-click on the folder's name, that folder also becomes the current folder and its contents are displayed in the contents pane.) Clicking on the minus symbol *collapses* the branch, hiding the subfolders.

For example, if we click on the plus symbol next to the Automap folder icon, a list of subfolders will be displayed, as shown at the right. Notice that there is a plus symbol attached to the Userdata subfolder, indicating that this folder has subfolders of its own. Now, if we click on the minus sign preceding Automap, this branch collapses, returning the folder tree to its original look, as in Figure 2.

The Contents Pane

As you know, the **contents pane** of the Explorer window lists all folders and files contained in the current folder. The word *folder* in this context refers to any folder, drive, or other object (such as My Computer) that can be accessed through Explorer.

Just as in the folder tree pane, clicking on an object in the contents pane selects that object, highlighting its name and icon. (We will have more to say about selecting objects in Section 3.3.) If you *double*-click on an object, what happens next depends on the nature of the object:

Double-clicking an object in the contents pane

- Double-clicking on a folder icon opens that folder, displaying its contents in the contents pane. (In other words, double-clicking on a folder icon in the contents pane has the same effect as clicking on the corresponding icon in the folder tree pane.)

- Double-clicking on a program file icon opens the corresponding application. This technique provides an effective way to start any application on your hard or floppy disks.

- Double-clicking on a document file that is associated with an application starts that application and opens the given document within it.

- Double-clicking on any other kind of file icon displays the Open With dialog box. This dialog box allows you to select an application to be used with the given file. Choosing the OK command button starts that application and opens the file within it.

The Tools menu

On a well-used hard disk, there may be hundreds of folders, with a correspondingly intricate folder tree. It's not surprising that finding a particular folder may be difficult. To help you in this regard, Explorer provides easy access to the Windows Find utility. You can open this utility by pointing at the Find item on the Tools menu and then choosing Files and Folders from the submenu. (We will discuss Find in Appendix B.)

Contents Pane View Options

Explorer displays the contents pane in one of four ways, depending on your preference. These options are described below; to select one of them, choose the corresponding item from the View menu. The selected view option will remain in effect, even in future Windows sessions, until you change it again.

The Large Icons and Small Icons View Options   Here, each object in the contents pane is represented by an icon (either large or small) labeled with the name of the object (Figures 3 and 4). You can move these icons one by one to a prominent position in the window (say, the upper left corner) by dragging them with the mouse. To be more specific:

Moving icons

1. Select the icon that you want to move by clicking on it.

2. Position the mouse pointer over this icon, hold down the left mouse button, and move the pointer to the icon's new location. An outline of the icon (and its label) will move with the pointer, as shown at the right.

3. When the icon is positioned where you want it, release the mouse button.

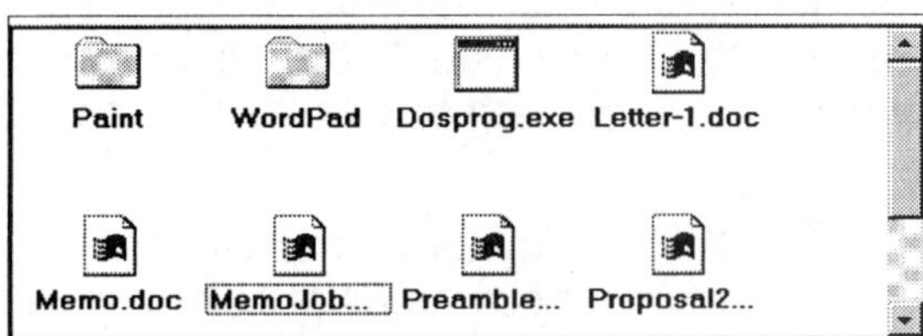

Figure 3 Contents Pane — Large Icons

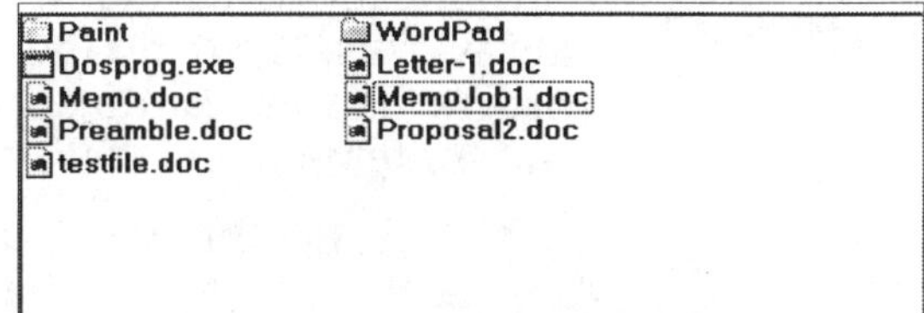

Figure 4 Contents Pane — Small Icons

Lining up the icons

To display the new arrangement of icons in neatly ordered rows and columns (as illustrated in Figures 3 and 4), choose Line Up Icons from the View menu. Or, to have Windows automatically line up the icons whenever they are moved, turn on the Auto Arrange option from the Arrange Icons submenu of the View menu. (Turning *off* this option before rearranging icons may make it easier to carry out the process.)

The List and Details View Options   Choosing the List option (Figure 5) from the View menu displays the icons and their names in the contents pane in a similar way to that of the Small Icons option. (With the List option, the icons are displayed in columns instead of rows and cannot be individually moved about.) The Details option (Figure 6) lists the objects in the contents pane, one per line, together with the information specified on the buttons at the top of this pane:

- *Size* refers to the size of a file in kilobytes (KB) or megabytes (MB).

- *Type* refers to the kind of object; for a file, Windows determines its type (for example, *application*) from the file name extension.

- *Modified* provides the most recent date and time that a file was saved; for folders, it is the time it was created.

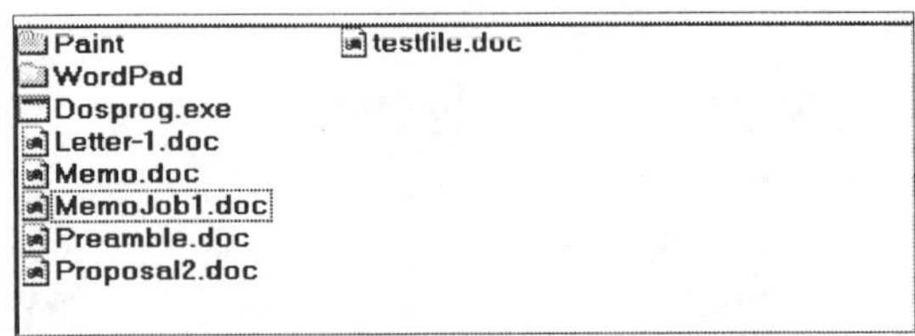

Figure 5   Contents Pane — List Option

Figure 6   Contents Pane — Details

Ordering files in the Details view

By default, the Details view displays the files in the contents pane in the alphabetical order of their names. (Folders in the contents pane are always displayed at the top of the list.) You can list files in other orders, as well. To do so, click on the appropriate button at the top of the contents pane; that is:

- Click on the Size button to list files in order of increasing size; click again on this button to list them in decreasing size order.

- Click on the Type button to list files in alphabetical order by type; click again on this button to list them in reverse alphabetical order by type.

- Click on the Modified button to list files in order of their last modification date; most recently modified files are listed first. Clicking again on this button lists recently modified files last.

- Click on the Name button to restore alphabetical ordering by name; clicking again on this button lists files in reverse alphabetical order.

The icons in *all* the view options (Large Icons, Small Icons, List, and Details) can be ordered by either name, file size, type, or modification date. Just choose the appropriate item from the Arrange Icons submenu of the View menu. However, "reverse orders" are not possible using the Arrange Icons submenu. For example, selecting *by Size* from this menu lists the icons in order of

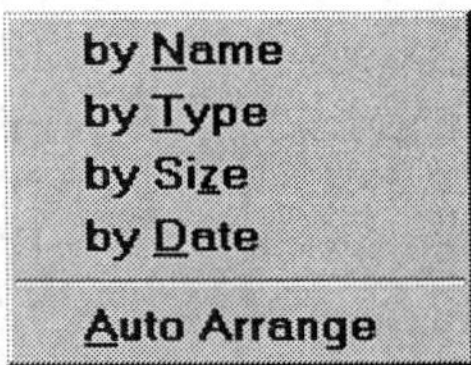

increasing file size; icons cannot be listed in order of *decreasing* size using the Arrange Icons menu.

You can use Explorer's toolbar to quickly select a different contents pane view option. Just click on the appropriate button, as indicated below. (The "List" button is shown selected.)

In any view, you may want to make the contents pane as large as possible. To do so, first maximize the Explorer window. Then, move the mouse pointer over the vertical bar sepa-rating the folder tree and contents panes (the pointer be-comes a double-headed arrow, as pictured at the right). Now, drag the bar to the left, and the contents pane will expand accordingly. 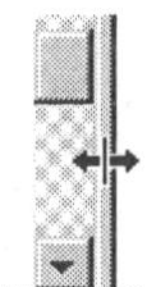

NOTE

As you can see, the toolbar contains several other buttons and a drop-down list, as well. The drop-down list and the Up One Level button next to it provide alternate ways to navigate the Windows folder system. They are of more benefit in My Computer than in Explorer, and will be described when we discuss the former in Section 3.5. Some of the other buttons on the toolbar are helpful in performing operations on files and folders; they will be discussed in Sections 3.3 and 3.4.

TUTORIAL

Try the following exercise on your own.

1. Turn on your computer, if necessary, to start up Windows NT and close any open windows.

2. Start Explorer: Click on the Start button, then point at the Pro-grams option on the Start menu, and finally click on Windows NT Explorer on the resulting submenu. The Explorer window will open. Maximize this window.

3. Insert the Student Disk in its drive and select this drive in the folder tree (left) pane of the Explorer window. For example, if the Student Disk is in the A: drive, scroll the folder tree pane up until the "3½ Floppy (A:)" folder appears; then, click on this item.

The files and folders in the root folder of the floppy disk will be displayed in the contents (right) pane of the window.

4. Expand the "3½ Floppy (A:)" branch of the folder tree by clicking on the plus symbol to the left of this item. (You can also do this by double-clicking on the name "3½ Floppy (A:)".)

5. Choose the Large Icons option from the View menu. Now, drag the Paint folder icon to a new position in the contents pane: Position the mouse pointer over it, then hold down the left mouse button while moving the pointer (and icon) to a new location in the contents pane, and finally release the mouse button.

6. Arrange the icons in the contents pane neatly by choosing Line Up Icons from the View menu.

7. Point at the Arrange Icons command on the View menu and then choose *by Size* from the submenu to sort the files in order of increasing size. Take note of the other sorting options available on the submenu!

8. If the Toolbar is not visible in the Explorer window, choose Toolbar from the View menu to display it.

9. Successively click on the Small Icons, List, and Details Toolbar buttons. (To determine which ones they are, hold the mouse over each Toolbar button until the identifying *Tool Tip* appears.) Notice the effect of each view option.

10. With the Details view in effect, sort the files in order of the last date they were saved by clicking on the button labeled *Modified* at the top of the contents pane. Click on this button again to reverse the order. Also try the other buttons (Name, Size, and Type) to see their effect.

11. Exit Explorer (as you would any application) and remove the Student Disk from its drive.

3.3   *Moving and Copying Files and Folders*

An application like WordPad allows you to modify the content of *files*; Explorer, on the other hand, allows you to manipulate the contents of *folders*. Using Explorer, you can move, copy, rename, delete, and create files and folders. In Sections 3.3 and 3.4, we will describe how to accomplish each of these tasks.

Selecting Files and Folders

The first step in using Explorer to manipulate a file, a folder, or a group of files or folders is to identify or *select* the objects[*] in which you are interested. A selected object is displayed with a highlighted name and icon, as illustrated below.

▪**Memo.doc**

Selected object

▪ **Memo.doc**

Object not selected

How to select an object

To select an object from the *folder tree pane*:

1. If necessary, scroll the pane or expand the tree (see Section 3.2) until the name of the object appears.

2. Click on the object to select it. (The selected folder will open, displaying its contents in the contents pane.)

To select an object from the *contents pane*.

1. Scroll the pane, if necessary, until the name of the object appears.

2. Click on the object to select it. (If the selected object is a folder, it will *not* open; the current folder remains unchanged. However, *double*-clicking on a folder in the contents pane *does* open it, making it the current folder.)

Selecting multiple objects

To save time in performing operations on files and folders, it is often useful to manipulate several of them at once. For example, if you want to delete ten files from disk, it is faster to select all ten and then perform the delete operation, rather than selecting and deleting them one at a time. Selecting *multiple* (more than one) objects can only be done in the contents pane, but it can be done in several ways:

- Click on one of the objects to be selected; then, hold down the Ctrl key and click on the others; finally, release Ctrl.

- If the objects to be selected are *in consecutive order*. click on the first object; then, hold down the Shift key and click on the last object in the group; finally, release Shift.

---

[*]Recall that, in this context, an *object* is any item listed in Explorer's folder tree or contents pane. Any Explorer object (including My Computer, a floppy drive, and the Desktop itself!) that is not a file is considered to be a *folder*.

- If the objects to be selected are *adjacent to one another*, drag a box around them, as illustrated at the right. To be more specific, position the mouse pointer to the upper left of the objects to be selected, hold down the left mouse button, move the pointer to the lower right of the desired objects, and release the button.

- To select *all* objects in the contents pane, choose Select All from Explorer's Edit menu. To select *almost all* the objects in the contents pane, select those objects you do *not* want and choose Invert Selection from the Edit menu.

As an example of the selection process, here's one way to select the objects shown highlighted in Figure 7:

1. The files Memo.doc, MemoJob1.doc, and Preamble.doc are in consecutive order, so we click on the first, hold down the Shift key, click on the last, and release Shift.

2. To select the remaining files, Dosprog.exe and testfile.doc, we hold down the Ctrl key, click on each file, and release Ctrl.

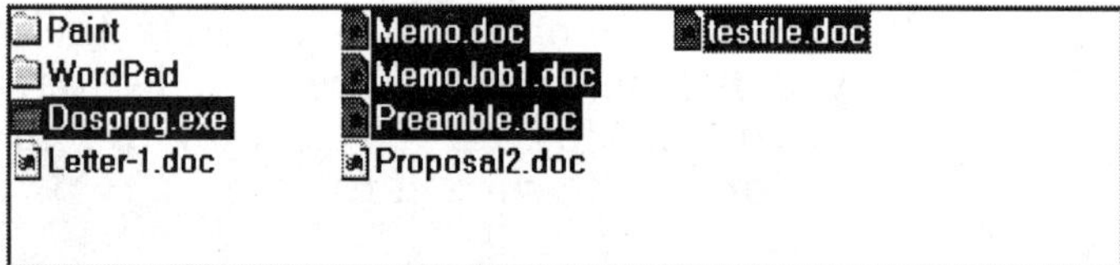

Figure 7   Selection Process Example

To select additional objects after at least one has been selected, be sure to hold down the Ctrl key while clicking. If you forget to press this key, all previously selected objects will be deselected!

If you want to deselect an object after some have been selected, hold down the Ctrl key while clicking on the object. Here, too, don't forget to hold down Ctrl. Otherwise, all objects *except* the one you click on will be deselected!

Moving and Copying Objects

When you **move** an object, it is deleted from its original location and placed in a new location. When you **copy** an object, a duplicate of that object is placed in the new location, but it is not deleted from the original. If the object being moved or copied is a folder, then it and all its contents (files and subfolders alike) are moved or copied to the new location. With one exception (which we will mention later), the move and copy operations are performed in analogous ways, so we will discuss them together.

You can move or copy an object from one folder (the *source*) to another (the *destination*) in two fundamental ways:

- Drag the object from the source and drop it onto the destination.

- Cut or copy the object from the source and paste it into the destination.

Drag-and-Drop Move or Copy   To move or copy objects using the **drag-and-drop** method sometimes takes a little preparation, but the actual operation is very simple. It involves the following steps:

1. Select the objects to be moved or copied.

2. Arrange the Explorer window so that at least one of the selected objects as well as the destination folder are both visible. To do this, you may have to scroll or expand the folder tree to display the destination folder.

3. Position the mouse pointer over any selected object and:

   - If you want to *move* the object, hold down the Shift key and drag the pointer to the destination.

   - If you want to *copy* the object, hold down the Ctrl key and drag the pointer to the destination.

   As you drag the mouse pointer, it seems to pull the objects' icons and names with it (see Figure 8, on the next page). The plus symbol below the pointer arrow in Figure 8 indicates that this is a copy operation. When *moving* objects, the plus symbol will not appear.

4. As the mouse pointer approaches the destination folder, the latter will become highlighted (see the Backup folder in Figure 8) to let you know that you're on target. Now, release the mouse button (and the Ctrl or Shift key) and the *Moving...* or *Copying...* animated dialog box will appear, confirming that the operation is taking place. (If you change your mind and want to abort the process, press the Escape key before releasing the mouse button.)

If you try to move or copy an object into a folder that already contains an object with the same name, the Confirm File Replace (or Confirm

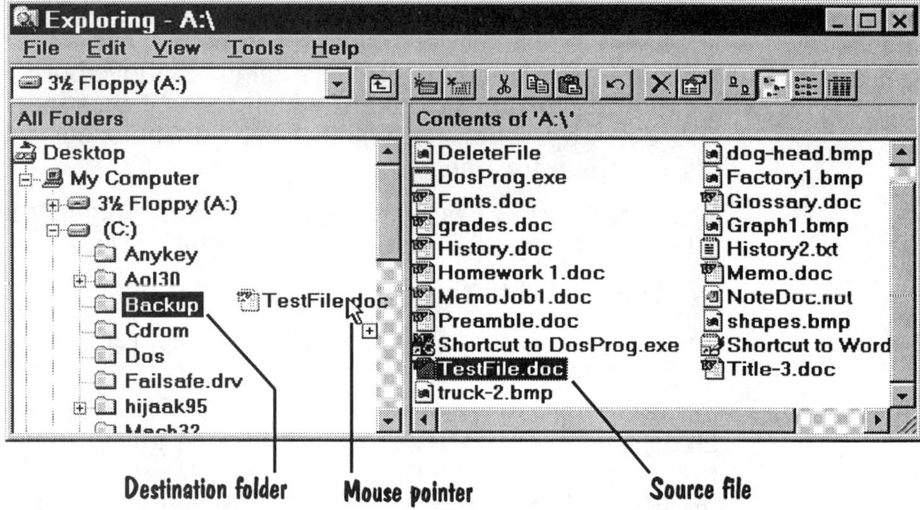

Figure 8   Drag-and-Drop Copying

Folder Replace) dialog box (Figure 9) will appear. Choose the Yes command button if you want the source file to replace the destination file in this folder, *deleting the destination file* in the process. Otherwise, click on the No button. (If you are moving or copying multiple objects, this dialog box will also contain Yes to All and Cancel buttons. Choos-

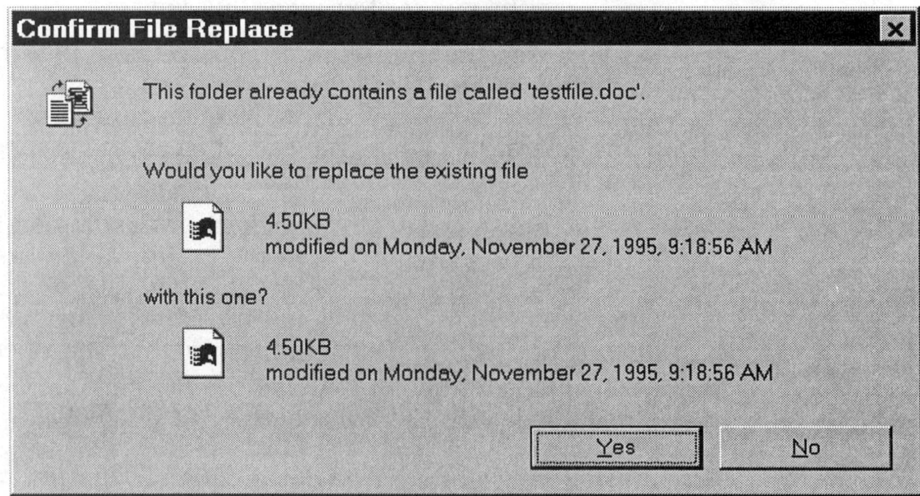

Figure 9   The Confirm File Replace Dialog Box

ing Yes to All indicates that you want to replace all destination files that have the same name as a source file; choosing Cancel aborts the Move or Copy operation.)

When *moving* objects between folders on the *same drive*, you do not have to hold down the Shift key while performing the drag-and-drop. When *copying* objects between folders on *different drives*, you do not have to hold down the Ctrl key.

If you don't want to memorize the Shift/Ctrl rules, Windows NT provides an alternative: just *right-drag* a selected object from the source to the destination. In this case, when you release the mouse 

button, the menu shown here will appear. To *move* the file to the destination, choose the Move Here command; to *copy* the file, choose the Copy Here command.

Both the left-drag and right-drag techniques work when the destination is an icon on the Desktop or the Desktop itself. For example, to copy a file to the My Computer folder, select the file in Explorer and either

- Drag it onto the My Computer icon on the Desktop (you need not hold down the Ctrl key).

or

- Right-drag it onto the My Computer icon and choose Copy Here from the menu that pops up when you release the mouse button.

Cut/Copy and Paste Move or Copy   The second basic method for moving or copying objects resembles the process for transferring information from one document to another (see Section 2.3). It involves the following steps:

1. Select the objects to be moved or copied.

2. Choose Cut (if you're moving the objects) or Copy (if you're copying the objects) from any of the following:

   - Explorer's Edit menu.

   - Explorer's toolbar.

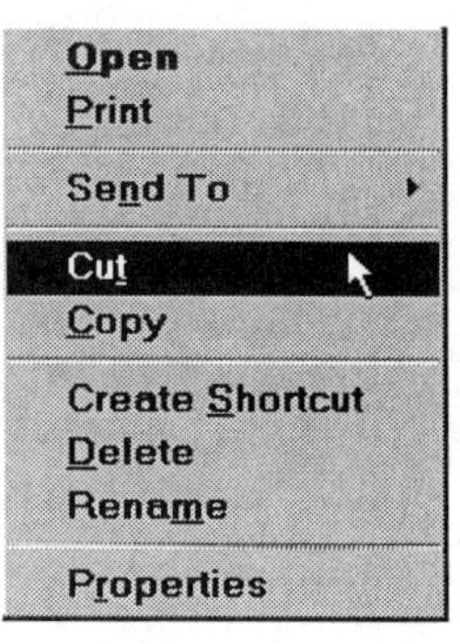

- The menu (pictured at the right) that pops up when you right-click on one of the selected files.

3. Select the destination folder in the folder tree pane.

4. Choose Paste from Explorer's Edit menu, toolbar, or the menu that pops up when you right-click the destination folder.

If there is an object in the destination folder with the same name as one of the objects being moved or copied, a Confirm File Replace or Confirm Folder Replace dialog box will be displayed (see Figure 9). Choose the Yes or No command buttons, as you wish.

Suppose you move or copy an object (using any method) and then decide that this wasn't such a good idea. You could move the object back to the source folder or delete it from the destination, but there is an easier way. Windows supplies an Undo command that cancels the last move or copy. This command is located on Explorer's Edit menu. It can also be executed by clicking on the Undo Toolbar button (shown at the right).

The Send To Command

Perhaps the most common use of the copy operation in Windows is to copy a file or group of files to a floppy disk. This action is usually taken for one of two reasons:

- To *back up* files on the hard disk (to make copies in case the hard disk becomes damaged or its files cannot be accessed for some other reason).

- To transfer files to another computer.

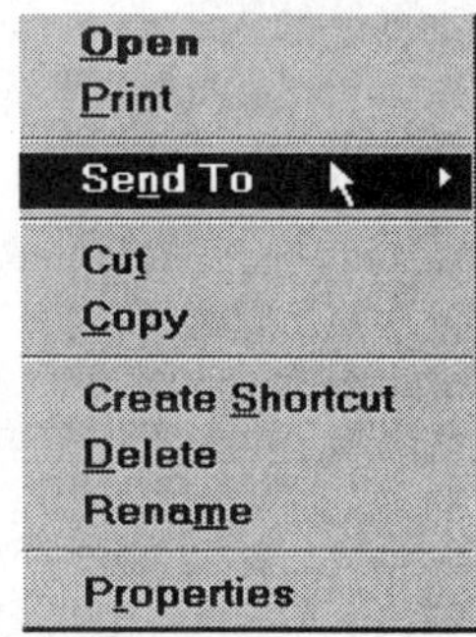

Windows NT makes it very easy to copy files or entire folders to a floppy disk. To do so:

1. Select the objects you want to copy.

2. Right-click on one of them, which opens the menu shown at the right.

3. Point at the Send To command on this menu.

4. Choose the appropriate floppy disk drive from the resulting sub-menu.

TUTORIAL

Try the following exercise on your own.

1. Turn on your computer, if necessary, to start up Windows NT, and close any open windows.

2. Start Explorer, maximize its window, and select the List view option from the View menu or toolbar.

3. Insert the Student Disk in its drive and select this drive (for example, "3½ Floppy (A:)") in the folder tree pane.

4. Select the last five (consecutive) files listed by clicking on the first of them, then holding down the Shift key while clicking on the last.

5. Deselect the selected files by clicking on an empty part of the contents pane.

6. Select the files Fonts, Preamble, and Testfile by clicking on the first of these, then holding down the Ctrl key as you click on the other two.

7. Deselect the Fonts file by holding down the Ctrl key while clicking on it.

8. Move the two remaining selected files to the Paint subfolder using the (right-) drag-and-drop method:

   - Move the mouse pointer over either file name and press, but do not release, the *right* mouse button.
   - Reposition the pointer so that the Paint folder name and icon become highlighted and release the mouse button.
   - Choose Move Here from the resulting pop-up menu.

9. Move the Testfile and Preamble files back to the root folder of the Student Disk using the cut and paste method:

   - Open the Paint folder by double-clicking on its icon in the contents pane.
   - Select Testfile and Preamble.
   - Choose Cut from Explorer's Edit menu or click on the Cut toolbar button.
   - Open the diskette's root folder by clicking on its drive icon (for example, "3½ Floppy (A:)") in the folder tree pane.
   - Choose Paste from Explorer's Edit menu or click on the Paste toolbar button.

10. Copy the Fonts file from the root folder to the Paint subfolder using (left-) drag-and-drop:

    - Select the Fonts file.
    - Position the mouse pointer over the selected file name, hold down the left mouse button and the Ctrl key (Ctrl is for *copy*, Shift is for *move*).
    - Reposition the pointer so that the Paint folder name and icon become highlighted, and release the mouse button and Ctrl key.

11. Undo the last copy operation by choosing Undo Copy from the Edit menu or by clicking on the Undo toolbar button. 

12. Exit Explorer and remove the Student Disk from its drive.

3.4 Other Operations on Files and Folders

In Section 3.3, we described how to select, move, and copy objects (files and folders). In this section we will continue this discussion, describing how to use Explorer to delete, rename, and create files and folders. We will also introduce the concept of a *shortcut*.

Deleting Files and Folders

Deleting objects from disk is a common operation, often used to create additional free disk space or just to reduce clutter. In the usual sense of the word, to **delete** a file or folder means to remove it and all its contents from disk. When you use Explorer to delete an object, however, that object is normally (but not necessarily always) just copied to a special folder called the **Recycle Bin**. To remove the object from disk, you then have to delete it from the Recycle Bin.

Ways to delete objects

To delete files or folders, start Explorer and select the objects to be deleted (see Section 3.3). Then, perform any of the following actions:

- Press the Delete (Del) key.

- Drag any of the selected objects onto the Recycle Bin icon on the Desktop. 

- Click on the Delete button (shown at the right) on Explorer's toolbar. 

- Choose the Delete command from Explorer's File menu.

- Right-click on any of the selected objects and choose the Delete command from the resulting pop-up menu.

After performing one of these actions, the Confirm File Delete or Confirm Folder Delete dialog box shown in Figure 10 may appear. Choose the Yes or No command button, as appropriate.

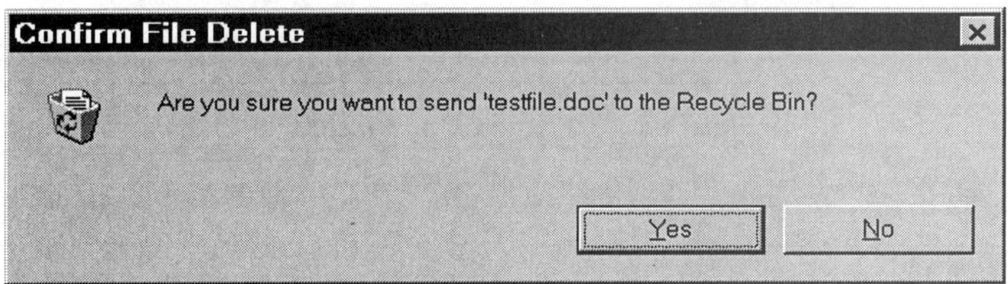

Figure 10   The Confirm File Delete Dialog Box

WARNING

By default, Windows NT does not send files deleted from floppy disks to the Recycle Bin. In this case, the message in the Confirm Delete dialog box will read "Are you sure you want to delete ..." and, if you activate the Yes button, the selected objects will immediately be removed from disk. If one of these objects is a folder, all its contents — files and subfolders alike — will be removed from disk. So, before you give the command to delete files or folders, think about what you are doing and whether you really want to do it!

The Recycle Bin   The Recycle Bin is simply a Windows NT folder. When files or folders are "deleted" by sending them to the Recycle Bin, these objects still take up disk space and can still be retrieved (or *restored*). If you are sure you no longer need an object in the Recycle Bin, you should permanently delete that object to increase your free disk space. The safest way to accomplish this is to:

1. Open the Recycle Bin by double-clicking on its Desktop icon. The Recycle Bin window will be displayed (see Figure 11 on the next page).

2. Select the objects you want to delete.

3. Delete the selected objects: Press the Delete key, or choose Delete from the File menu, or click on the toolbar's Delete button, or right-click on a selected object and choose Delete from the pop-up menu.

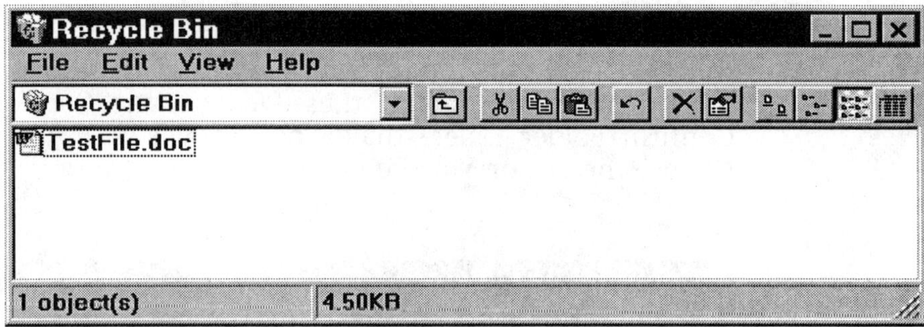

Figure 11   Recycle Bin Window — List View

4. If a Confirm Delete dialog box appears, asking whether you're sure you want to delete the objects, choose the Yes button (unless you've changed your mind). The selected objects are now removed from disk.

NOTE

As you can see in Figure 11, the Recycle Bin window strongly resembles the Explorer window. In fact, the Recycle Bin window is just Explorer's view of the Recycle Bin folder without the folder tree pane. There are, however, two menu options available for the Recycle Bin that are not available for a typical folder:

1. You can choose Empty Recycle Bin from the File menu to delete *all* objects in the Recycle Bin. (You can also accomplish this task by right-clicking on the Recycle Bin's Desktop icon and then choosing Empty Recycle Bin from the pop-up menu.)

2. You can choose Restore from the File menu to move selected objects back to their original location.

Renaming Files and Folders

To **rename** (change the name of) a file or folder:

1. Start Explorer and select the object to be renamed.

2. Perform any of the following actions:

   - Choose Rename from Explorer's File menu.

   - Right-click on the selected object and choose Rename from the pop-up menu.

   - Click again on the selected object.

In any case, Windows places a box around the selected object's name (as shown at the right) to let you know that this object can now be renamed.

3. Type a new name for the object and press the Enter key.

If an object in the current folder has the same name as the one you are trying to assign to the selected object, the following dialog box will be displayed:

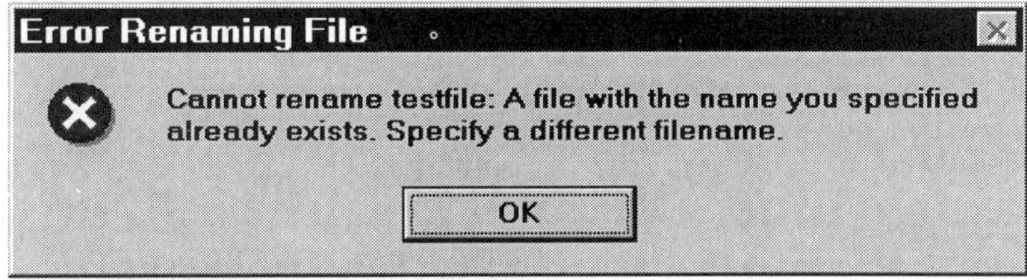

Click on the OK button (or press the Enter key) and this message will be cleared from the screen. If you want to give the selected object the same name as an existing object in that folder, you have to first rename or delete the existing one.

NOTE

You can rename objects on the Desktop in a similar way:

1. Select the object to be renamed by clicking on it.

2. Either click on the object again; or right-click on the object and choose Rename from the pop-up menu. Windows will place a box around the object's name.

3. Type a new name and press the Enter key.

Creating New Files and Folders

As you know, data files (documents) are normally created within a specific application. For example, if you start WordPad, type some text, and save the resulting document (assigning it a name in the process), a file with that name is created on disk. Most of the folders on your hard disk were also created "automatically"— usually when Windows NT or an application was installed.

You can also use Explorer to create both files and folders. (Creating a file this way is not terribly useful, but creating a new folder — say, to hold certain related documents — is an important operation.) To create a file or folder:

1. Start Explorer and select (in the folder tree pane) the folder in which you want the new object to reside.

2. Take either of the following actions:

   - Point at the New item on the File menu.

   or

   - Right-click on an empty part of the contents pane and point at the New item on the resulting pop-up menu.

   In either case, a submenu, similar to the one in Figure 12, will be displayed.

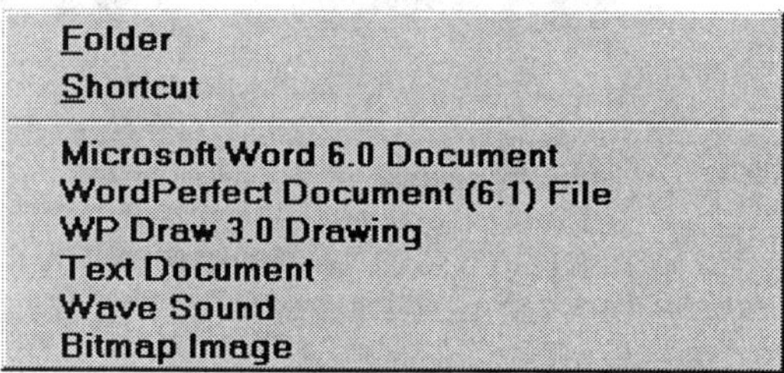

Figure 12   The New Menu

3. Choose either Folder or one of the file types listed at the bottom of this menu. A new object will appear in the contents pane named, for example, New Folder, New Text Document, or New Bitmap Image. The name of the object will be highlighted and boxed-in, ready for renaming.

4. Rename the object whatever you want by typing a new name and pressing the Enter key.

As an example, we will create a new subfolder of the Winnt folder and name it Data Files. To do so, we:

1. Start Explorer.

2. Scroll the folder tree pane until the Winnt folder comes into view.

3. Click on the Winnt folder to select it. (The word *Winnt* becomes highlighted.)

4. Point at the New command on Explorer's File menu and choose Folder from the resulting submenu. (A highlighted object called *New Folder* appears in the contents pane; the "box" around its name indicates that the folder is ready to be renamed.)

5. To rename the folder, type Data Files and press the Enter key.

Creating Shortcuts

Recall (from Section 2.1) that one of the easiest ways to start an application is to double-click on its Desktop icon. Consequently, it would certainly be convenient to have an icon on the Desktop for each of your favorite programs. As you will see, Windows makes this easy to do.

What's a shortcut? Most Desktop icons actually represent **shortcuts** to objects (files or folders); when you double-click on such an icon, the shortcut provides Windows NT with the location and name (the path name) of the corresponding object. Thus, a shortcut is not a copy of an object, just a small file called a *pointer* (or *link*) that tells Windows where to find the relevant file or folder. For this reason, you can create shortcuts to your heart's content with very little adverse effect on your free disk space.

There are several methods for creating Desktop shortcuts. Here are a couple of ways you can use Explorer to accomplish this task. The first of these makes use of the drag-and-drop technique described in Section 3.3 for copying and moving files and folders.

Creating a shortcut by drag-and-drop

1. Start Explorer and open the folder that contains the object for which you want to create a shortcut.

2. Select the desired object and right-drag it onto an empty part of the Desktop.

3. When you release the right mouse button, the menu at the right will pop up.

Shortcut "arrow"

4. Choose Create Shortcut(s) Here from this menu. The shortcut will now appear on the Desktop as an icon. (Icons for shortcuts contain a small arrow in the lower left corner, as shown here for the WordPad shortcut icon.)

If dragging icons around is not your favorite thing, you can use a cut-and-paste technique to place a shortcut on the Desktop:

Creating a shortcut by cut-and-paste

1. Start Explorer and open the folder that contains the object for which you want to create a shortcut.

2. Select the desired object.

3. Choose the Create Shortcut item from either the File menu or the menu that pops up when you right-click on the selected object. A new object entitled "Shortcut to ..." will appear (highlighted) in the contents pane.

4. Move the new shortcut to the Desktop, as follows:

- Cut it to the Clipboard by clicking on the *Cut* Edit menu command or toolbar button.

- Paste it onto the Desktop by right-clicking on an empty part of the Desktop and choosing Paste from the pop-up menu.

Once a shortcut has been placed on the Desktop (using any method), you can:

- Move the shortcut to another location by dragging it with the mouse.

- Rename the shortcut by right-clicking on it and choosing Rename from the pop-up menu. A "box" will appear around the shortcut's name. Now, type a new name and press the Enter key.

NOTE

You can also create shortcuts directly on the Desktop without starting Explorer. This technique makes use of the Create Shortcut "wizard", which is started in the following way:

1. Right-click on an empty part of the Desktop. A menu will pop up.

2. Point at New on this menu and then choose the Shortcut option on the resulting submenu. The Create Shortcut wizard, a series of dialog boxes that guides you through the process, will start.

3. Follow the instructions in each dialog box and then choose the Next command button to move to the next dialog box.

4. Choose the Finish command button to complete the process. The new shortcut will appear on the Desktop.

TUTORIAL

Try the following exercise on your own.

1. Turn on your computer, if necessary, to start up Windows NT, and close any open windows.

2. Start Explorer and select the List view option from the View menu or toolbar.

3. Insert the Student Disk in its drive and select this drive (for example, "3½ Floppy (A:)") in the folder tree pane.

4. Select the file named DeleteFile from the contents pane.

5. Size and move the Explorer window so that the selected file, the Recycle Bin icon (on the Desktop), and an empty part of the Desktop are all visible.

6. Create a shortcut for the selected file and place it on the Desktop:

   - Right-drag the file onto an empty part of the Desktop.
   - Choose Create Shortcut(s) Here from the menu that pops up when you release the mouse button.
   - Rename the shortcut icon "DelFile" by clicking on it, typing the new name, and pressing the Enter key.

7. Delete the new DelFile icon by dragging it (using the left mouse button) onto the Recycle Bin icon.

8. Restore the DelFile shortcut: Open the Recycle Bin (by double-clicking on its icon), select the DelFile shortcut, and choose the Restore command from the File menu. Now, close the Recycle Bin.

9. Delete the DelFile shortcut again, this time by selecting it and pressing the Del key. Answer Yes to the Confirm Delete query.

10. Rename the DeleteFile object in the root folder of the floppy disk: Right-click on this file in the contents pane, choose Rename from the pop-up menu, type a new name, and press the Enter key.

11. Delete this newly-renamed file by choosing Delete from Explorer's File menu. Answer Yes to the Confirm Delete query.

12. Exit Explorer and remove the Student Disk from its drive.

3.5   My Computer

As you know, the Desktop contains an icon called **My Computer** that provides access to virtually all aspects of your computer system. In particular, from the My Computer window you can carry out all the operations on files and folders that we have discussed in this chapter. This is not surprising because the My Computer icon is simply a built-in shortcut that starts Explorer and opens the My Computer folder within it! If you keep this fact in mind, it will be easier to understand the workings of My Computer.

Starting My Computer

My Computer

You can open the My Computer window, which is shown in Figure 13 on the next page, by double-clicking on its Desktop icon. Notice that this window is similar in appearance to the Explorer window, but My Computer lacks a folder tree pane; it uses a single subwindow, a contents pane, to display information.

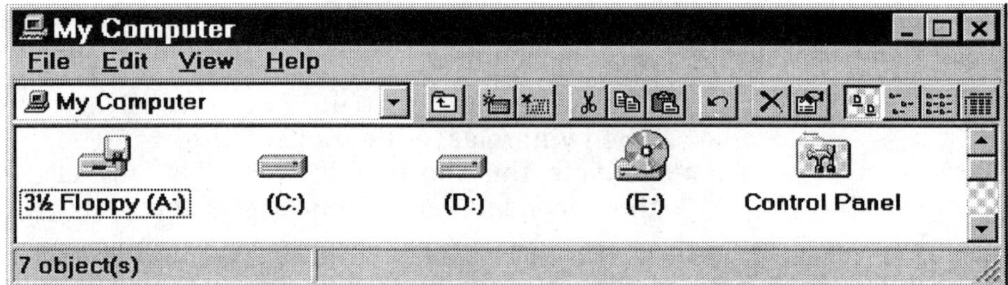

Figure 13   The My Computer Window — Large Icons View

NOTE

You can also start My Computer by right-clicking on its icon and choosing Open from the resulting pop-up menu. Interestingly enough, if you choose Explore instead of Open from this menu, Explorer will start and display a dual-pane view of the My Computer folder.

The fact that the My Computer window lacks a folder tree pane results in two basic differences between the way My Computer and Explorer are used to locate and manipulate objects:

1. My Computer provides less flexibility than Explorer in navigating (or **browsing**) the Windows file system. For example, it is often more difficult to locate a particular folder in My Computer.

2. Certain drag-and-drop operations are not carried out as easily in My Computer as in Explorer. For example, it is usually more difficult to drag a given file onto a certain folder in My Computer.[*]

We will now examine the consequences of each of these differences.

Using My Computer to Browse Folders

Opening a subfolder

Once you have started My Computer, you can easily access its subfolders: your computer's drives, the Printers folder, and so on (see Figure 13). Just double-click on an icon to open one of these folders, and its contents will be displayed in a new window. For example, if you double-click on the "(C:)" icon, a window will open displaying all the

---

[*]In light of these deficiencies, you might be wondering why Microsoft chose to give My Computer such prominence in the Windows NT interface. One reason for this approach is to provide easy access, especially for the novice user, to all aspects of the computer system — its drives, files, printers, settings, and so on.

files and subfolders in the root folder of the C: drive. A subfolder of *any* folder is opened in the same way — by double-clicking on its icon.

NOTE

The previous My Computer window may or may not close when a new one opens. You can control whether or not a separate window opens whenever you change folders by choosing the Options command from the View menu, selecting the appropriate option button in the resulting dialog box, and choosing the OK command button. We will further discuss this feature later in this section.

Opening a parent folder

If you want to open the parent folder of the current folder (going up one level in the folder tree), take any of the following actions:

- Press the Backspace key.

- Click on the Up One Level button on the current window's toolbar (Figure 14). Remember: If the toolbar is not displayed, choose Toolbar from the View menu to display it.

- If the parent window is visible on the screen, click on it; or, if the parent window's button appears on the Taskbar, click on that.

Figure 14   The My Computer Toolbar

Using the Go to Folder drop-down list

The Go to Folder drop-down list on the toolbar (see Figure 14) provides a way to change folders more quickly in certain situations. When you open this drop-down list (by clicking on the down-triangle), a "mini-tree" is displayed, showing the immediate (child) subfolders of the Desktop and My Computer, as well as the chain of subfolders forming the path to the current folder (Figure 15). The current folder is shown in the text box at the top of the list.

To display the contents of one of the

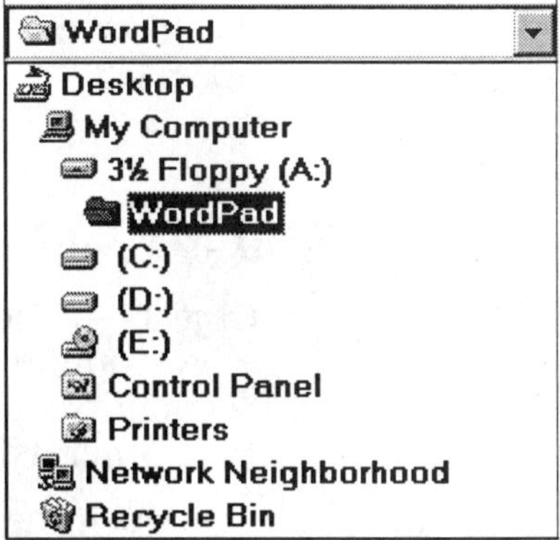

Figure 15   A Typical Go to Folder Drop-down List

listed folders, just click on it. The Go to Folder drop-down list can be a great time-saving convenience. For example, suppose the current folder is WordPad, as in Figure 15. To display the contents of the root folder of the C: drive, just open the drop-down list and click on the "(C:)" object.

The following tips make it easier to use My Computer to browse folders:

- The default view option for My Computer is Large Icons. It's much easier to see what's in the current folder if you use the View menu or the toolbar buttons to switch to the Small Icons or List view option (see Section 3.2).

- Display the *path* of the current folder on its window's title bar (if it is not already displayed there) by choosing the Options command from the View menu, clicking on the View tab in the resulting dialog box, selecting the *Display the full path in the title bar* check box, and choosing the OK command button.

- If each change of folder has opened a separate window, you can close all these windows at the same time by holding down the Shift key while clicking on the last window's close button.

Some Windows dialog boxes (such as Run, Save As, and Open) allow you to browse folders as you do in My Computer. For example, if you activate the Browse command button in the Run dialog box (see Section 2.1), a dialog box like the one in Figure 16 will open. Using the toolbar buttons, you can select a List or Details view option or go Up One Level. You can also Go to Folder via the toolbar drop-down list. In addition, if you're looking for a file of a particular type, you can restrict the kinds of files that are displayed by using the *Files of type* drop-down list.

Using My Computer to Operate on Files and Folders

Objects — files, folders and shortcuts — are manipulated from within a My Computer window in essentially the same way as in Explorer (see Sections 3.3 and 3.4). For example, you can copy a file from one folder to another using the Copy and Paste commands, as follows:

1. Open the folder containing the file to be copied.

2. Right-click on the desired file, which selects it and displays a pop-up menu.

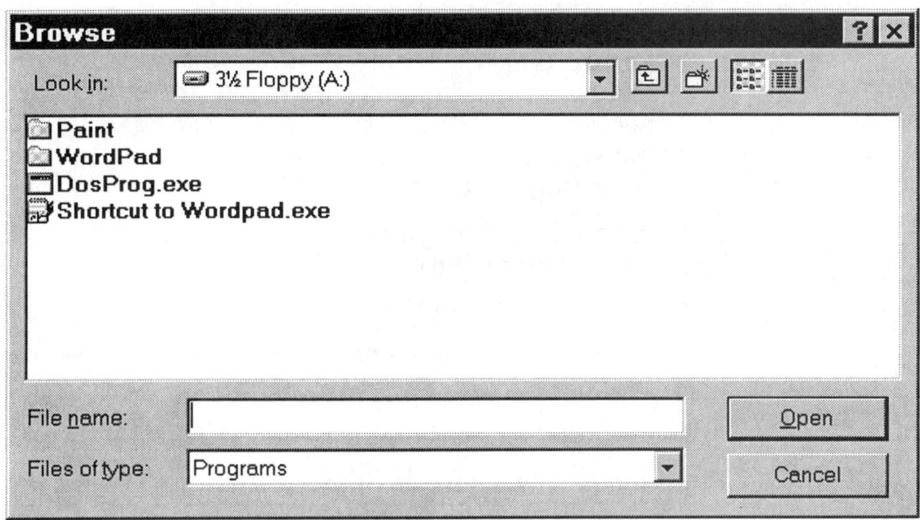

Figure 16   A Browse Dialog Box

3. Choose the Copy command from the pop-up menu.

4. Right-click on the destination folder's name, which displays a pop-up menu.

5. Choose the Paste command from this pop-up menu and the process is complete.

Notice that this procedure could be used without change in Explorer, but there is one subtle difference in its execution here. To carry out steps 1 and 4 in Explorer, you would most likely just scroll and expand the folder tree pane (if necessary) until the name of the desired folder appeared; then click on it. In My Computer, on the other hand, you might have to open several windows in each of steps 1 and 4 before the desired folder became visible!

Drag-and-drop in My Computer   The difference just described causes the greatest trouble if you want to perform a drag-and-drop move or copy (see Section 3.3). The problem here is that the object to be moved or copied *and* the destination folder must be visible at the same time. This is not much of a problem in Explorer, but requires some preparation in My Computer.

The trick to drag-and-drop moving or copying in My Computer is to open both the source and destination folders and arrange them so that both are visible on the screen. For example, suppose we want to copy a file named Testfile.doc on a floppy disk to the My Documents folder on the C: drive. To do this using drag-and-drop in My Computer:

1. Insert the floppy disk into the A: drive and start My Computer.

2. Ensure that a separate window will open for each new folder by choosing the Options command from the View menu and (if necessary) selecting the *Browse folders using a separate window for each folder* option button in the resulting dialog box before activating the OK command button.

3. Back in My Computer, double-click on the (C:) icon to open the root folder of the C: drive, C:\.

4. Scroll the C:\ window until the My Documents folder appears.

5. Switch back to the My Computer window by clicking on it or its Taskbar button.

6. Double-click on the A: drive icon to open its window.

7. Scroll this window (if necessary) until Testfile.doc appears and click on this file to select it. The current arrangement of windows is shown in Figure 17.

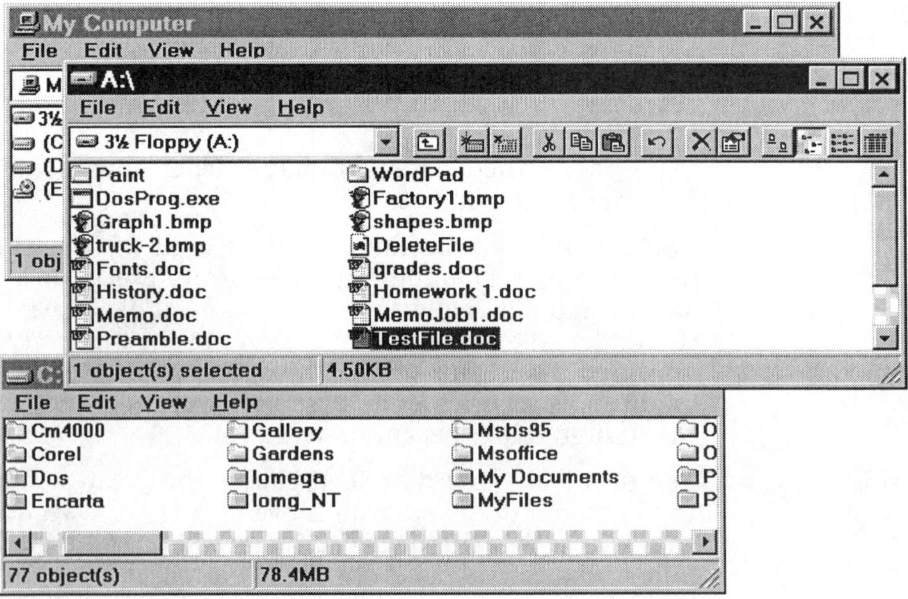

Figure 17   Preparing to Copy with My Computer

8. If necessary, resize or move the floppy drive window and the C:\ window so that the names Testfile.doc and My Documents are

both visible.

9. Drag the Testfile.doc file onto the My Documents folder. The Copying animated dialog box will confirm that the copy operation is taking place.

TUTORIAL

Try the following exercise on your own.

1. Turn on your computer, if necessary, to start up Windows NT, and close any open windows.

2. Start My Computer by double-clicking on its Desktop icon.

3. Elect to use a single My Computer window to display all folders:

   ▪ Choose Options from the View menu to open the Options dialog box.
   ▪ Select the "Browse folders by using a single window that changes as you open each folder." option button.
   ▪ Choose the OK command button.

4. Insert the Student Disk in its drive and then select this drive by double-clicking on the appropriate icon (for example, "3½ Floppy (A:)").

5. Open the WordPad subfolder by double-clicking on it.

6. Right-click on the Fonts file in the WordPad subfolder and copy it to the Clipboard by choosing the Copy command from the pop-up menu.

7. Open the root folder on the A: drive (A:\), the parent of the WordPad folder, by either clicking on the Up One Level toolbar button or pressing the Backspace key.

8. Paste the Fonts file into the A:\ folder by choosing the Paste command from the Edit menu. If the Confirm File Replace dialog box appears, choose the No command button.

9. If the toolbar is not visible in the My Computer window, display it by choosing Toolbar from the View menu. Open the root folder on the C: drive:

   ▪ Open the toolbar's Go to Folder drop-down list (see Figure 14 on page 105).
   ▪ Click on the "(C:)" item in the drop-down list.

10. Close the My Computer window and remove the Student Disk from its drive.

3.6   *Formatting and Copying Floppy Disks*

All the procedures we have discussed in this chapter apply to files and folders on floppy disks (diskettes) as well as hard disks. Two additional operations are useful with floppies: formatting and copying disks. In this section, we will discuss these procedures.

Formatting a Floppy Disk

Before information can be stored on a disk, the disk must be **formatted**. This process prepares the disk to store information, dividing it into sectors and creating a file allocation table on it, and also erases any data that had been stored on the disk prior to formatting. Hard disks are usually formatted by the manufacturer or dealer, and most floppies are also sold already formatted. (In the latter case, the word "formatted" will appear on the box and on each individual disk.) Nevertheless, from time to time, you will have to format a diskette for one of the following reasons:

- To prepare an unformatted diskette for use.

- To reformat a Macintosh disk for use on your IBM-compatible computer.

- To quickly erase all files on a disk.

WARNING

Keep in mind that the format procedure erases all information on the disk being formatted! So, never format a disk unless you are sure there is nothing stored on it or (if there is data on the disk) that you no longer need its contents. Unless the disk is fresh out of the box, it's wise to use Explorer or My Computer to check its contents before formatting it.

If you format a disk and then realize you made a mistake — it did contain some information you need — immediately inform your instructor or lab coordinator. It *might* be possible to recover the desired files if you have not yet used the newly-formatted diskette.

To format a floppy disk:

1. Insert the diskette to be formatted in its drive.

2. Start My Computer or Explorer and select this drive.

3. Right-click on the selected drive and choose Format from the resulting pop-up menu (Figure 18). Or, in My Computer, choose Format from the File menu. A Format dialog box, like the one in Figure 19, will be displayed.

4. Select the proper Capacity for the diskette from the drop-down list — *1.44 MB* if the disk is a high density one (with an "HD" on its label); *720 KB*, otherwise.

5. Leave the *File System* and *Allocation Unit Size* at their current settings.

6. Type a name for the diskette in the Volume Label text box if you want to associate a name with this diskette. (The *volume label* for a diskette is displayed by certain applications.)

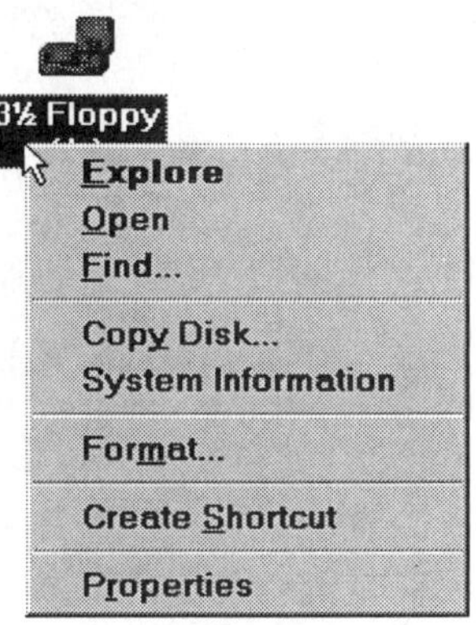

Figure 18
Floppy Disk Menu

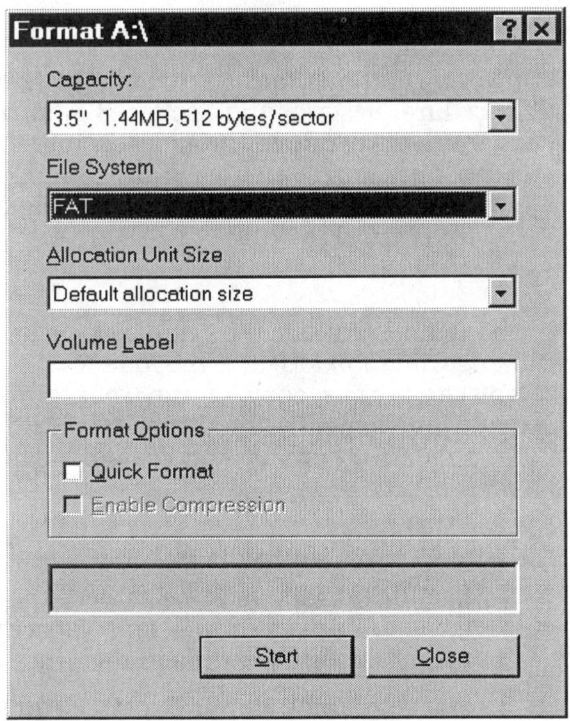

Figure 19   The Format Dialog Box

7. The Quick Format option can only be used with diskettes that have already been formatted. Selecting this check box will "erase" all information on the disk (by removing the file allocation table and other system information). This option provides a convenient way to erase old, unneeded disks so they can be used again. Quick Format is much faster than the normal (or *full*) format process.

8. Choose the Start command button to begin the formatting process. A dialog box will appear, warning you that formatting the disk will erase all information on it.

9. Choose the OK command button to proceed (or the Cancel button to abort the process). A bar graph showing the progress of the process will appear at the bottom of the "Formatting" dialog box.

10. After a couple of minutes, a Format Complete dialog box will be displayed. Click on its OK button and then choose the Close button in the Format dialog box to remove these dialog boxes from the screen.

Copying an Entire Diskette

If your computer has two floppy disk drives, you can use the copy procedure, described in Section 3.3, to copy all files from one diskette to another. Windows provides a more direct way — the Copy Disk menu command — to perform this operation (even if your machine only has one floppy disk drive), as long as the diskettes have the *same size and capacity*.

WARNING

When you carry out the copy disk process, all existing information on the *destination disk* — the one you're copying to — is erased and replaced with a copy of the *source disk* — the one you're copying from. Consequently, before beginning the process, be sure that there are no files of any value on the destination disk.

Here's how the copy disk process works:

1. Insert the diskette to be copied (the *source disk*) in its drive. If you have two drives of the same capacity, insert the disk to be copied to (the *destination disk*) in the other drive.

2. Start My Computer or Explorer and select the source drive.

3. Right-click on this drive and choose Copy Disk from the pop-up menu (see Figure 18). Or, in My Computer, choose Copy Disk from

the File menu. A Copy Disk dialog box, similar to the one in Figure 20, will be displayed.

4. Choose the Start command button to begin the copying process. Messages and a bar graph at the bottom of the Copy Disk dialog box will indicate the progress of the operation.

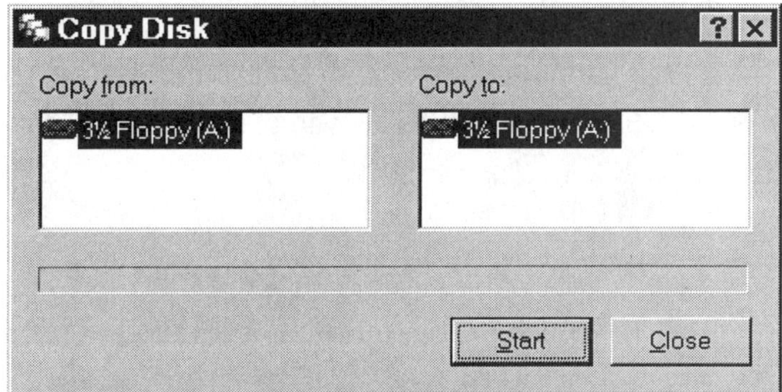

Figure 20   The Copy Disk Dialog Box

5. If you have only one floppy drive, the following dialog box will appear halfway through the copy process:

Insert the destination disk in its drive and choose the OK command button. Remember that the copy process will *erase all information* on the destination disk!

6. When the copy process is complete, a message to this effect will appear at the bottom of the Copy Disk dialog box. When it does, choose the Close command button; the Copy Disk dialog box will be removed from the screen.

Review Exercises

Section 3.1

1. A ____________ is a collection of information generated by a program and saved on disk.

2. A ____________ is a collection of files that have been grouped together and given a name.

3. True or false: A folder may contain files and/or subfolders.

4. True or false: If the path name for a file is A:\Paint\Truck.bmp, then it is located in the Paint folder on the disk in the A: drive.

5. Which of the following is a valid DOS file name?

    a. Homework 1
    b. Homework.1
    c. HomeworkOne
    d. All of these names are valid DOS file names.

6. Which of the following is a valid long file name?

    a. Homework 1
    b. Homework.1
    c. HomeworkOne
    d. All of these names are valid long file names.

Section 3.2

7. In the Windows NT Explorer window, the ____________ pane can contain both files and folders.

8. To see the subfolders of a given folder in Explorer's left pane (if they are not currently displayed), click on the ____________ symbol that precedes the name of the folder.

9. If you want to display the size of a file shown in Explorer's contents pane, click on the ____________ item on the View menu.

10. True or false: Explorer's left pane only shows the folders present on the C: drive.

11. True or false: In Explorer, you can use the toolbar to select one of four view options (Large Icons, Small Icons, List, or Details).

12. True or false: In Small Icons view in Explorer, it is possible to order the icons in alphabetical order by file type.

13. The only Explorer view option in which you can display files in decreasing size order is:

    a. Large Icons
    b. Small Icons
    c. List
    d. Details

14. In which of the following view options can file names and icons be moved, one by one, around Explorer's contents pane?

    a. Large Icons only
    b. Small icons only
    c. Both Large Icons and Small Icons
    d. Neither Large Icons nor Small Icons

Section 3.3   15. To select two nonconsecutive files in Explorer, click on the first and hold down the ____________ key while clicking on the second.

16. To copy a file from one folder to another on the C: drive, hold down the ____________ key and drag the file to its destination.

17. A simple way to copy a selected file to the disk in the A: drive is to right-click on the file, point at the ____________ command on the pop-up menu, and choose 3½ Floppy (A) from the submenu.

18. True or false: To select a group of objects that are in consecutive order in Explorer's contents pane, click on the first and then hold down the Shift key while clicking on the last.

19. True or false: When you right-drag an object in Explorer and release the mouse button, the pop-up menu allows you to move *or* copy it to the new location.

20. True or false: The Cut and Paste buttons on Explorer's toolbar can be used to move text, but not files.

21. If one object in Explorer's contents pane is selected and you click on another (without holding down any key), then

    a. The first object is deselected; the second is selected.
    b. The first object remains selected; the second is not selected.
    c. Both objects are selected.
    d. Neither object is selected.

22. To *move* a file from the Winnt folder to the disk in the A: drive, you can

    a. Use the Cut and Paste commands on Explorer's Edit menu.
    b. Drag the file from the Winnt folder and drop it on the A: drive icon.
    c. Use the Send To command.
    d. None of these techniques can be used to move the file.

Section 3.4   23. If you select an object in Explorer and press the Delete key, that object is normally moved to a folder called the ____________.

24. To create a subfolder of the current folder using Explorer, right-click in the contents pane and point at the ____________ command on the resulting pop-up menu.

25. Windows places a ____________ around an object's name to let you know that this object can now be renamed.

26. True or false: If you choose the Empty Recycle Bin command from its File menu, all objects in the Recycle Bin are removed from disk.

27. True or false: Shortcuts on the Desktop cannot be renamed.

28. True or false: A shortcut to a file is actually a copy of that file.

29. In Explorer, to delete the currently selected object, you can

    a. Press the Delete key.
    b. Choose the Delete command from the File menu.
    c. Click on the toolbar's Delete button.
    d. Perform any of the above actions.

30. Suppose you have just created a shortcut in Explorer. To place this shortcut on the Desktop, you can

    a. Drag it onto the Desktop.
    b. Cut it to the Clipboard and Paste in onto the Desktop.
    c. Copy it to the Clipboard and Paste it onto the Desktop.
    d. Perform any of the above actions.

Section 3.5   31. To start My Computer, ____________ on its Desktop icon.

32. In My Computer, to open the parent folder of the one currently open, press the ____________ key on the keyboard.

33. True or false: In My Computer, you can control whether or not a separate window is displayed when you open a new folder.

34. True or false: You can use My Computer to move, copy, delete, rename, and create files, but not folders.

35. Suppose My Computer is displaying the contents of the Winnt folder, which is a subfolder of the root folder on the C: drive. Opening the Go to Folder drop-down list, you will see

    a. Every subfolder of the Winnt folder.
    b. Every subfolder of the root folder on the A: drive.
    c. Every subfolder of the My Computer folder.
    d. None of the above folders.

36. In My Computer, which view options are available?

    a. Large Icons and Small Icons, but not List or Details.
    b. List and Details, but not Large Icons or Small Icons.
    c. Large Icons, Small Icons, List, and Details.
    d. Only the default view is available.

Section 3.6   37. To format a floppy disk using Explorer, begin by ____________ on the appropriate drive icon in the folder tree pane.

38. The Copy Disk command can only be used with floppy disks of the same ___________ and ___________.

39. True or false: After formatting a disk, you will not be able to access the information that had previously been stored on it.

40. True or false: When you use the Copy Disk command, all information on the source disk is erased.

41. To format a floppy disk that has never been formatted, before choosing the Start command in the Format dialog box, you must

    a. Select the Quick Format check box.
    b. Deselect the Quick Format check box.
    c. Enter text in the Volume Label text box.
    d. None of the above actions will work.

42. To copy the contents of one floppy disk to another of the same size and capacity, you can

    a. Use the Copy Disk command on My Computer's File menu.
    b. Use the Copy Disk command located on the right-click menu for the floppy drive.
    c. Copy all the files on the first diskette to the Clipboard and paste them onto the second diskette.
    d. All of the above techniques will work.

Build Your Own Glossary

43. The following words and phrases are important terms that were introduced in this chapter. (They appear within the text in boldface type.) Use WordPad (see Section 2.2) to enter a definition for each term, preserving alphabetical order, into the Glossary file on the Student Disk.

Browse folders	File	Parent folder
Contents pane	Folder	Path name
Copy file or folder	Folder tree pane	Recycle Bin
Delete file or folder	Format a diskette	Rename file or folder
Directory	Long file name	Root folder
DOS file name	Move file or folder	Shortcut
Drag-and-drop	My Computer	Subfolder
Explorer		

Lab Exercises

Work each of the following exercises at your computer. Begin by turning the machine on (if necessary) to start Windows NT. If you want to produce a written record of your answers, review the material on WordPad and capturing screens in Sections 2.2 and 2.3.

Lab Exercise 1
(Section 3.2)

a. Start Windows NT Explorer and maximize its window.

b. Insert the Student Disk in its drive and select this drive in the folder tree pane.

c. Display, *in the folder tree pane*, the subfolders of the floppy disk drive's (root) folder. How did you do this?

d. Select the Details view option. In what year was the Dosprog application created?

e. Sort the files by modification date. Which *object* is at the top of the list? Which *file* is highest on the list?

f. Select the Large Icons view.

g. Interchange the positions of the Paint and Memo icons. Use the View menu to line up the icons. Did the icons return to their original positions?

h. Restore the Explorer window and resize it so that the Paint and Memo icons are visible, but the window is as small as possible. Which scroll bars appeared? *Optional*: Capture this Explorer window.

i. Close Explorer and remove the diskette from its drive.

Lab Exercise 2
(Section 3.3)

a. Start Explorer and maximize its window.

b. Insert the Student Disk in its drive and select this drive in the folder tree pane.

c. Select Small Icons view. In what order are the files listed?

d. Select all files (but no folders). How did you do this?

e. *Copy* the selected files to the Paint folder on the floppy disk by dragging them onto the Paint icon. Is it *necessary* to hold down the Ctrl key while dragging the files?

f. Open the Paint folder and select the Details option. How many of the listed files are *not* of the "Bitmap Image" type?

g. *Move* (by drag-and-drop) the copied files back to the root folder of the floppy disk. (Answer "Yes to All" to the Confirm Replace message.) Is it *necessary* to hold down the Shift key while dragging the files?

     h.   Close Explorer and remove the diskette from its drive.

Lab Exercise 3
(Section 3.3)

a.   Start Explorer, maximize its window, and select the Small Icons view option.

b.   Insert the Student Disk in its drive and select this drive in the folder tree pane.

c.   Select the file MemoJob1 and *cut* it to the Clipboard. Then, select the file Memo and *copy* it to the Clipboard. Was either file deleted from the contents pane?

d.   Minimize Explorer and any other open windows.

e.   Right-click on the Desktop and choose Paste from the pop-up menu. Which file has appeared on the Desktop?

f.   Restore the Explorer window and resize and move it so that the copied file is visible on the Desktop. Now, using the right-drag technique, *move* the file back to the contents pane. (Answer "Yes" to the Confirm File Replace message.) Where in the contents pane were the file name and icon placed?

g.   Close Explorer and remove the diskette from its drive.

Lab Exercise 4
(Section 3.4)

a.   Start Explorer, maximize its window, and select the Small Icons view option.

b.   Insert the Student Disk in its drive and select this drive in the folder tree pane.

c.   Create a new subfolder of the (root) floppy drive folder. It appears highlighted in the contents pane. What is it called?

d.   Rename the new folder My Folder. How did you accomplish this?

e.   Size the Explorer window so that an empty part of the Desktop is visible. Then, right-drag My Folder to the Desktop, release the mouse button, and choose Create Shortcut(s) Here from the pop-up menu. How would one know, just by looking at the *icon*, that it represents a shortcut?

f.   Open My Folder by double-clicking on its Desktop shortcut. Does its window have both a left and right pane? *Optional:* Reduce the window to a small size and capture it.

g.   Delete the My Folder *folder* from the floppy drive. Did the My Folder *window* close when the folder was deleted?

h.   Close the My Folder window, if necessary, and delete its shortcut.

i.   Open the Recycle Bin and delete any references to My Folder. Was a Confirm Delete message displayed?

j.   Close Explorer and remove the diskette from its drive.

Lab Exercise 5
(Section 3.5)

a.   Start My Computer, maximize its window, and select the List view option.

b.   Choose the Options command from the View menu. In the resulting dialog box, select the lower of the two option buttons and choose OK. What is the selected option called?

c.   Select the drive that contains the Winnt folder by double-clicking on it. Try C: first, then others. On which drive is the Winnt folder located?

d.   Open the Winnt folder. How many immediate subfolders (child folders) does it have?

e.   Successively open the following subfolders: Profiles, All Users, Start Menu, and Programs. What are the immediate subfolders of Programs?

f.   Display the Go to Folder drop-down list. Are all the folders you've opened in this exercise listed there? *Optional:* Close the drop-down list and size the current window so that it's not much larger than this list. Then, capture the active window and reopen the drop-down list.

g.   Select Recycle Bin from the Go to Folder list. In the new window, open the Go to Folder list again. Is the Programs folder still listed there?

h.   Close the Recycle Bin window.

Lab Exercise 6
(Section 3.5)

Repeat Exercise 2, replacing every occurrence of *Explorer* by *My Computer* and *folder tree pane* or *contents pane* by *My Computer window*.

Lab Exercise 7
(Section 3.6)

[This exercise requires a blank floppy disk.]

a.   Start Windows NT Explorer and insert a blank diskette in its drive.

b.   Check the contents of the diskette by selecting the appropriate drive from the folder tree. What is displayed in the contents pane?

c.   If the diskette contains any files or folders, do *not* continue this exercise! Otherwise, format the diskette, deselecting the Quick Format check box. When you choose the Start command button and click on OK in the resulting warning dialog box, what message appears at the bottom of the Formatting dialog box?

d. Again use Explorer to check the contents of the diskette. Are any files or folders listed now?

e. Open the Format dialog box again. This time, select the Quick Format check box and then activate the format process. Approximately how much time did it take to complete the process?

f. Close Explorer and remove the diskette from its drive.

CHAPTER 4

Control Panel: Customizing Windows

People use computers in different ways and for different reasons. With this in mind, the designers of Windows NT provided many ways to customize its user interface. When this capability is used properly, the result is a more pleasant and productive environment. In Section 3.4, we described one way that Windows can be customized — by placing shortcuts for frequently used applications, documents, or folders right on the Desktop. In this chapter, we will discuss how to use the Control Panel utility to further customize windows. To be more specific, you will learn:

1. How to start, use, and close Control Panel.

2. How to choose a repeating pattern or wallpaper to decorate the Desktop.

3. How to select a screen saver.

4. How to change the color and size of various objects in the Windows NT interface.

5. How to adjust the keyboard repeat rate and delay.

6. How to modify the operation of the mouse.

7. How to set the computer's clock, view fonts, and change some of the sounds produced by Windows.

4.1   *An Introduction to Control Panel*

Control Panel is a collection of small programs (*utilities*) that help you customize the Windows user interface — its colors, sounds, mouse operation, etc. — so that it looks and acts the way you want. In this section, we will provide an overview of the workings of Control Panel.

The Control Panel Window

To open the Control Panel window:

Starting Control Panel

1. Click on the Start button (or press Ctrl+Esc) to open the Start menu.

2. Point at the Settings option and hold the mouse steady for a second or two; the Settings submenu will open.

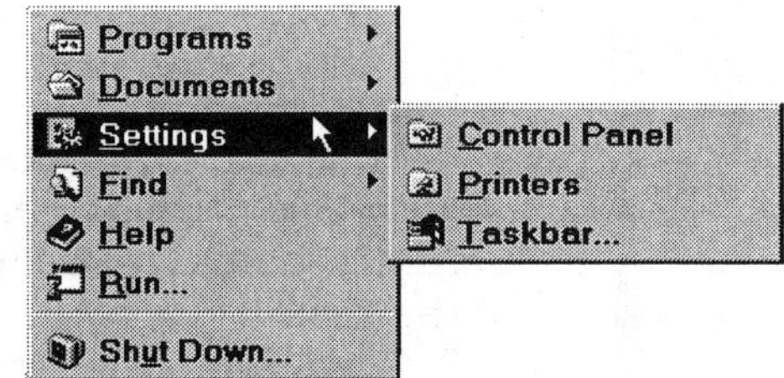

3. Click on the Control Panel item on this submenu. A window, similar to the one shown in Figure 1, will open.

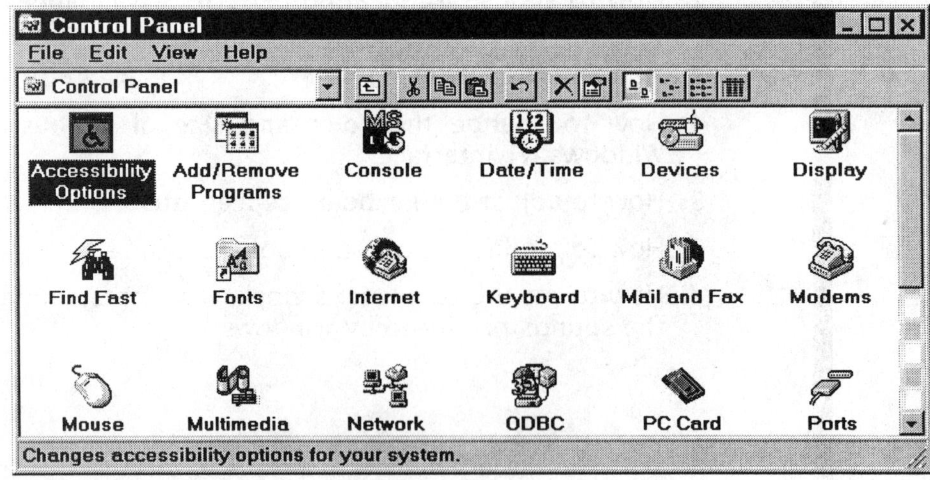

Figure 1   The Control Panel Window

At the top of the window are the usual title and menu bars. Directly below the menu bar is a toolbar, which, as you will see, allows us to quickly access some Control Panel features. (If the toolbar does not appear in your Control Panel window, choose the Toolbar command from the View menu; this command toggles the toolbar on or off.) At the bottom of the window is a status bar (which can also be turned on or off from the View menu). The status bar provides a brief description of the currently selected icon (which, in Figure 1, is *Accessibility Options*).

Control Panel display options

The window shown in Figure 1 represents each of the Control Panel functions as a "large icon". If you want, you can display the various functions in other ways. For example, if we choose the List option from the View menu, the window will look like this:

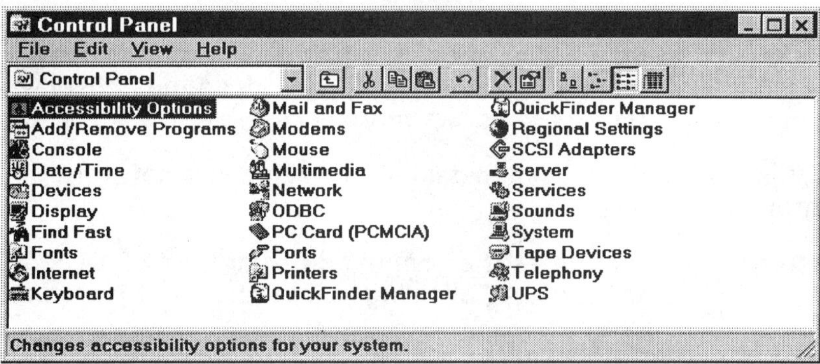

Two other display options are available on the View menu:

- Small Icons view looks similar to List view, but the icons are arranged in a different order.

- Details view lists each function on a separate line, which also contains a brief description of that function.

NOTE

The four display options (Large Icons, Small Icons, List, and Details) can also be accessed from the toolbar. Just click on the appropriate button, as illustrated below:

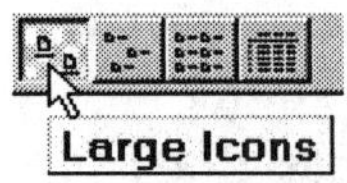

If you forget the function of a toolbar button, point at it with the mouse; a *tool tip* will appear, as shown at the left, identifying it!

Control Panel Functions

Each of the icons displayed in the Control Panel window represents a utility that allows you to customize one aspect of Windows. The number, the type, and sometimes even the names of the available Control Panel functions depend on your system's configuration. The following table describes the most common utilities.

Name	Description
Accessibility Options	Changes the way the keyboard, sounds, display, or mouse behave to make Windows more accessible to people with disabilities.
Add/Remove Programs	Aids you in installing and removing software on your system.
Console	Configures the command prompt, or MS-DOS prompt, window (see Appendix A), allowing you to change, for example, the colors and font size.
Date/Time	Changes the date and time on your computer's clock.
Devices	Configures *device drivers* (the software that allows the computer to communicate with installed devices such as a modem or sound card).
Display	Changes screen colors, type appearance, the Desktop background, the size of objects, and screen resolution; installs screen savers.
Fonts	Adds, removes, and allows you to view the fonts on your system.
Internet	Changes settings that relate to an Internet connection.
Keyboard	Changes the keyboard type, layout, and repeat rate and delay; changes the cursor blink rate.
Mail and Fax	Sets up and edits profiles that determine how incoming and outgoing mail and faxes are handled.
Modems	Installs a new modem and changes a modem's properties.

Mouse	Installs or removes a mouse and allows you to modify aspects of its operation, such as pointer shape or speed.
Multimedia	Changes properties for audio, video, and MIDI (Musical Instrument Digital Interface) devices, and the playing of audio compact discs.
Network	Adds, removes, and configures network connections; aids you in accessing an installed network.
PC Card (PCMCIA)	Configures *PC Cards*, credit card-sized plug-in devices, such as modems, that are normally used with portable computers.
Ports	Configures the system's serial ports, which provide a connection between the computer and devices such as external modems.
Printers	Adds, removes, and changes settings (such as resolution and paper type) for printers.
Regional Settings	Changes international settings such as the format of numbers, currencies, dates, and times.
SCSI Adapters	Configures device drivers for SCSI (Small Computer Systems Interface) devices, such as Zip drives and certain CD-ROM drives.
Services	Stops, pauses, restarts, and configures system *services*, such as the Event Log and Plug-and-Play.
Sounds	Changes Windows and system sounds, such as the sounds heard when Windows is started and exited.
System	Provides system information and allows you to change settings that affect system performance.
Tape Devices	Adds, removes, and configures drivers for backup tape drives.
Telephony	Installs and configures drivers for computer simulated telephone devices, such as answering machines.
UPS	Allows you to control and communicate with an Uninterruptible Power Supply (UPS), a device that provides immediate short-term power for your system should the electrical power to it be cut off.

Choosing a function   To choose one of the available Control Panel utilities, perform any of the following actions:

- Double-click on the appropriate icon.

- Click on the appropriate icon to select it and choose the Open command from the File menu.

- Right-click on the appropriate icon, which selects it and pops up a menu, and choose Open from this menu.

When you modify a Control Panel utility's setting, the new setting remains in effect (every time you use Windows) until it is changed again.

Closing Control Panel

You can close (or exit) Control Panel in any of the following ways:

- Click on the close button on the right end of the title bar.

- Choose Close from the File menu.

- Press the Alt+F4 keystroke combination.

TUTORIAL

Try the following exercise on your own.

1. Turn on your computer, if necessary, to start up Windows and close any open windows.

2. Start Control Panel:

   - Click on the Start button (or press Ctrl+Esc) to display the Start menu.
   - Point at the Settings option to open its submenu.
   - Click on the Control Panel item.

3. Maximize the Control Panel window.

4. If the status bar is not visible at the bottom of the Control Panel window, choose Status Bar from the View menu. Then, successively select (click on) each icon in the window and take note of its function, which is displayed on the status bar.

5. If the toolbar is not visible in the Control Panel window, choose Toolbar from the View menu. Click on each of the four view option buttons on 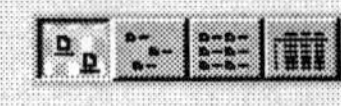 the toolbar and note its effect on the window.

6. Close the Control Panel window by clicking on its close button or choosing the Close command on the File menu.

4.2 *Changing the Desktop Background*

The default Windows NT Desktop has a solid, dark-colored background. In Section 4.3, we will describe how you can change the background color. This section discusses how to change the look of the Desktop in another way: by decorating it with a picture (graphic) and/or a repeating pattern. We will also describe how to have Windows display an animated image — a *screen saver* — when your system has been idle for a specified period of time.

Display

All the changes just described can be accomplished using Control Panel's **Display** function. To start the Display utility, open Control Panel and choose the Display icon from its window (as described in Section 4.1). The Display Properties dialog box, shown in Figure 2, will then open.

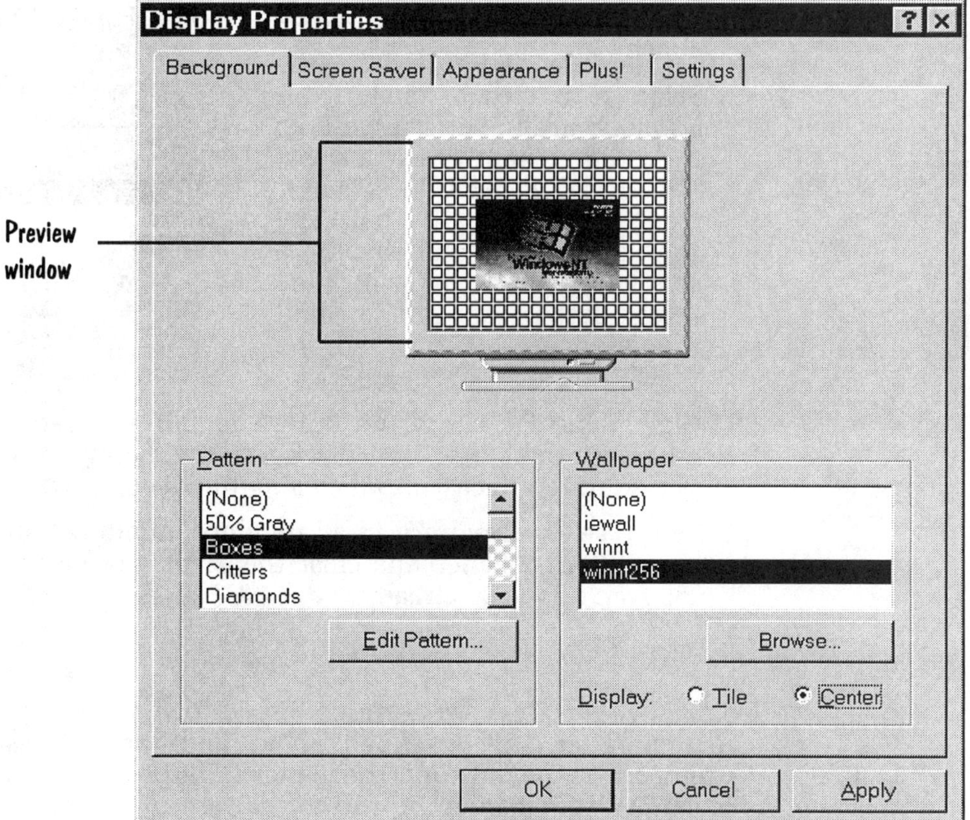

Figure 2 The Display Properties Dialog Box — Background Page

You can also open the Display Properties dialog box without starting Control Panel. First, right-click on an empty part of the Desktop, which pops up the menu shown at the right. Then, choose the Properties item from this menu. The Display Properties dialog box will now appear on the screen.

Choosing a Desktop Pattern

As you can see in Figure 2, the Display Properties dialog box contains five tabs. The first of these, *Background*, allows you to decorate the Desktop with a repeating pattern or a graphic image (*wallpaper*). To use one of the supplied Desktop patterns:

1. Open the Display Properties dialog box (Figure 2) as described above.

2. Select a pattern by clicking on its name in the Pattern list box. If you don't want to use a Desktop pattern, select "(None)" from the top of the list. The preview window will display a sample of that pattern. (The Boxes pattern appears, behind the Windows NT logo, in the preview window of Figure 2.)

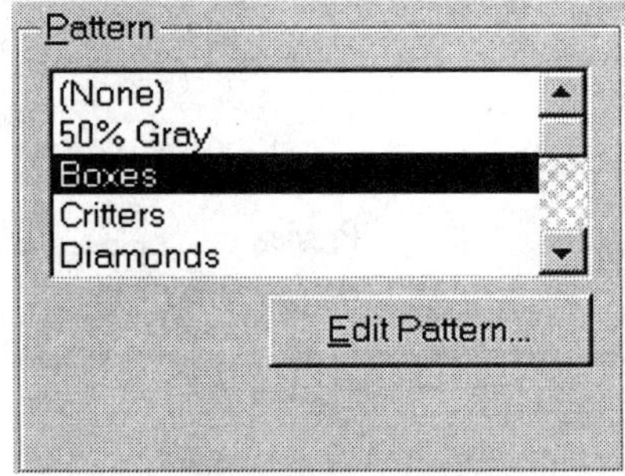

3. Choose the OK command button to put the pattern into effect and close the dialog box, or choose the Apply button to put the pattern into effect without closing the dialog box.

To see the selected pattern in all its glory, minimize all applications (including Control Panel) and close the Display Properties dialog box, if you haven't done so already.

N O T E

You can create Desktop patterns of your own design by selecting an existing pattern as described above and then choosing the Edit Pattern command button. The Pattern Editor dialog box will open, allowing you to change the current pattern or create a new one. The Pattern Editor is fun to play with; if you try it out, click on the close button to close its window when you're done.

Choosing Wallpaper

Instead of using a solid color or patterned Desktop, you can decorate it with a graphic image, commonly known as **wallpaper**. (Yes, using wallpaper to decorate a desktop does sound a little strange!) Choosing wallpaper is easy:

1. Open the Display Properties dialog box (Figure 2).

2. Select a particular wallpaper by clicking on its name in the Wallpaper list box. If you don't want to use wallpaper, select "(None)" from the top of the list. The preview window shows how the wallpaper will look on your Desktop.

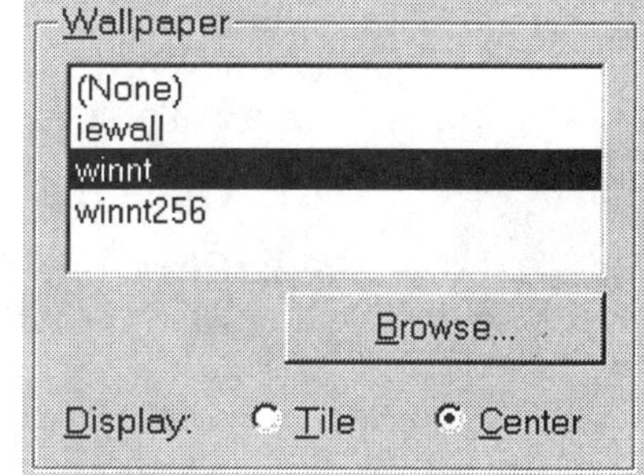

3. Select either the Center or Tile option button.

   - Selecting Center positions the graphic in the center of the screen. If it does not cover the entire screen, the solid or patterned Desktop will be visible around it (see Figure 3a).

   - Selecting Tile repeats the graphic as many times as necessary to cover the entire screen (as in Figure 3b). With small graphics, including most of those supplied with Windows, you will probably want to choose the Tile option.

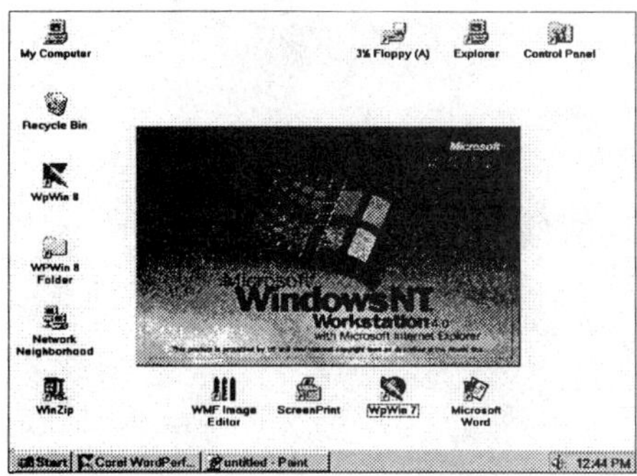

Figure 3a   Centered Wallpaper   **Figure 3b**   Tiled Wallpaper

4. Choose the OK command button to put the selected wallpaper into effect and close the dialog box, or choose the Apply button to put the wallpaper into effect without closing the dialog box.

Choosing a Screen Saver

When a **screen saver** is in effect and neither the mouse nor the keyboard is used for a specified period of time, the screen will go blank or an animated graphic will be displayed. Screen savers are used just for fun or to deter others from viewing your work while you are away from the computer. They may also prevent damage to the screen from an unchanging image being "burned" into it over time.

Using the Display Properties dialog box, you can select and customize a Windows-supplied screen saver, or choose not to use a screen saver. To select a screen saver:

1. Open the Display Properties dialog box (Figure 2).

2. Click on the Screen Saver tab to display the corresponding page of the dialog box, shown in Figure 4.

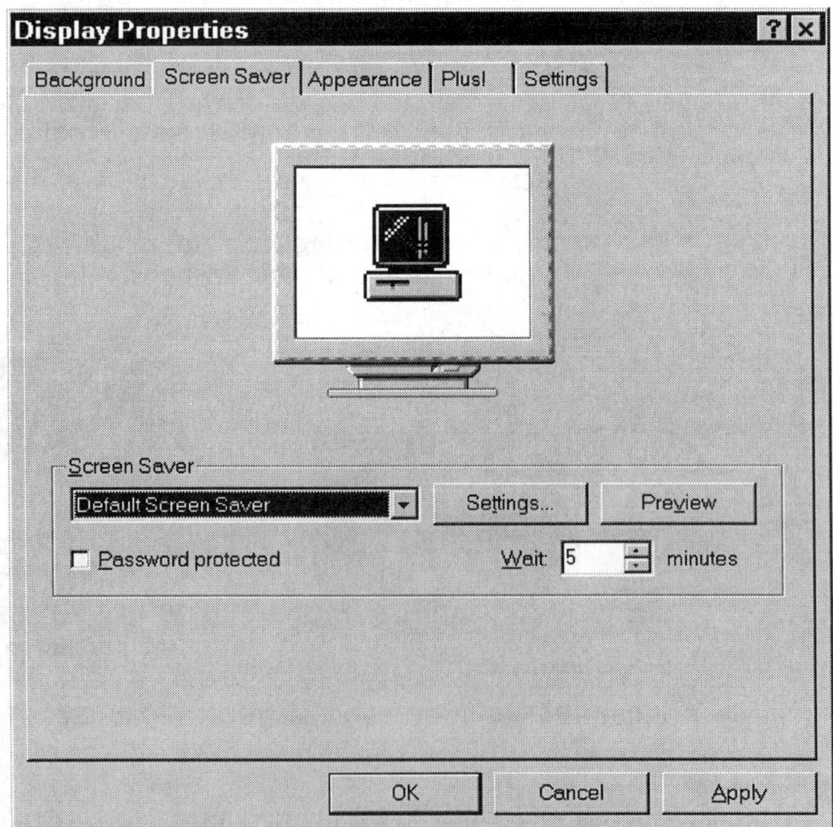

Figure 4   Display Properties — Screen Saver Page

3. Select a screen saver by clicking on its name in the Screen Saver drop-down list. Select "(None)" if you don't want to use a screen saver. With some screen savers, you will then see a simulation of their action in the preview window.

4. To customize the selected screen saver, click on the Settings command button. A dialog box will open allowing you to make certain changes in the way that screen saver works.

5. To see what the screen saver looks like full-screen, click on the Preview command button. The selected screen saver will be activated for a few seconds. (You may have to click the mouse to deactivate it.)

6. To set the *delay time* — how long the system must be inactive before the screen saver appears — type a number in the Wait text box (or make use of the up and down arrows in this box to set the time).

7. Select the *Password protected* check box if you want to require that a valid NT password be entered to remove the screen saver's image from the screen once it has been activated.

8. Choose the OK command button to complete the process and close the dialog box, or choose the Apply button to record your changes without closing the dialog box.

If a screen saver has been selected, it will be activated after the specified delay time. To have the active application reappear on the screen, press any key or move or click the mouse.

TUTORIAL

Try the following exercise on your own.

1. Turn on your computer, if necessary, to start up Windows and close any open windows.

2. Start Control Panel and open the Display utility by double-clicking on its icon.

3. Select several successive Desktop patterns from the Pattern drop-down list and notice their effect in the preview window of the Display Properties dialog box.

4. Select a wallpaper (your choice) from the Wallpaper drop-down list and select the Tile option button. Notice the effect in the preview window. Now, select the Center option button and notice the change in the preview window.

5. Choose the OK command button to close the Display Properties

dialog box and put the pattern and wallpaper into effect.

6. Close the Control Panel window to see the full effect of the changes you have made.

7. Right-click on the Desktop and choose Properties from the pop-up menu to reopen the Display Properties dialog box.

8. Return the Pattern and Wallpaper to their original settings.

9. Click on the Screen Saver tab to open a new page of the Display Properties dialog box.

10. Select 3D Flying Objects from the Screen Saver drop-down list and notice the effect on the preview window.

11. Choose the Preview command button to activate the screen saver (full-screen). Click the mouse to deactivate it.

12. Click on the Wait text box, erase the current number, type 1, and choose the Apply button. This puts the screen saver into effect without closing the Display Properties dialog box.

13. Do not use the mouse or keyboard for one minute. The screen saver will then be activated. Deactivate it by clicking the mouse or pressing a key.

14. Return the Screen Saver drop-down list and Wait time to their original settings and choose the OK command button to close the Display Properties dialog box.

4.3   Changing the Appearance of a Window

In Windows NT, a typical window contains a number of different elements: a title and menu bar, buttons of various sorts, text, icons, scroll bars, and so on. Through Control Panel's Display utility, Windows allows you to create a **window scheme** — to choose the color and size of such elements. This feature is not only fun to play with, but can also make for a more pleasant working environment.

Windows supplies you with two basic levels of control in customizing the appearance of a window:

1. You can choose a *predefined* (built-in) window scheme.

2. You can create a *custom* window scheme (one of your own design) by:

   ■ Choosing a color for each of the window elements.

- Choosing a size for certain elements, such as title, menu, and scroll bars.

- Choosing a *font* (a type style and size) for identifying text within the window, such as titles and button captions.

All these operations are carried out from the Appearance Page of the Display Properties dialog box. To open this dialog box, either

- Start Control Panel (if it's not already open) and choose the Display icon from its window, as described in Section 4.1.

or

- Right-click on an empty part of the Desktop and choose the Properties option from the resulting pop-up menu.

Then, to display the Appearance page of this dialog box, click on the Appearance tab. The resulting window is shown in Figure 5.

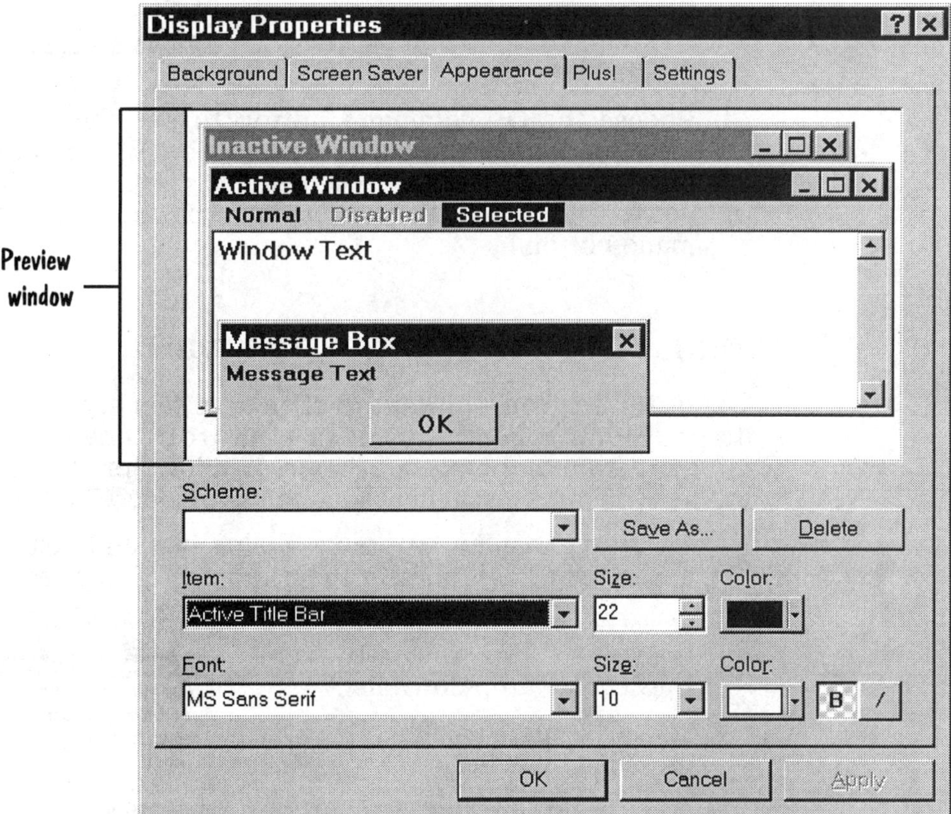

Figure 5   Display Properties Dialog Box — Appearance Page

Choosing a Predefined Window Scheme

Windows comes with a wide variety of built-in schemes that consist of a combination of colors, sizes, and fonts for the various window elements. To select one of these predefined schemes:

1. Open the Display Properties dialog box and select the Appearance page as described above.

2. Open the Scheme drop-down list (by clicking on its down triangle). A list of available schemes will be displayed.

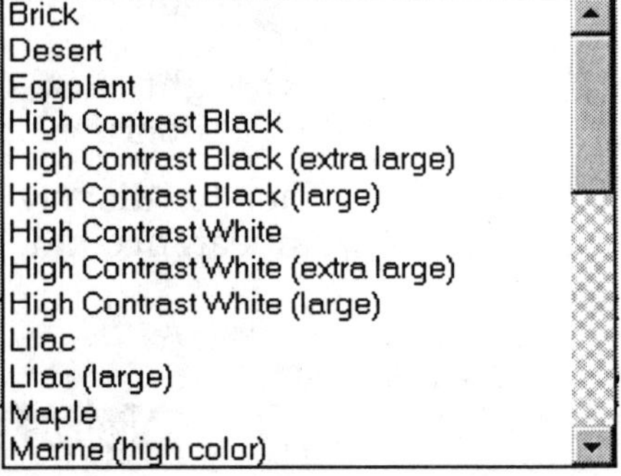

3. Select a scheme from the list. The preview window in the dialog box (see Figure 5) will show the way various screen elements (active and inactive title bars, command buttons, text, and so on) will look under this scheme.

4. Choose the OK command button to put the new scheme into effect and close the dialog box, or choose the Apply button to put the scheme into effect without closing the dialog box. (If you'd rather keep the previous scheme, choose the Cancel command button.)

Creating a Custom Window Scheme

It is likely that you will want to change certain aspects of your favorite predefined window scheme or even create one that is completely different from any built-in scheme. Windows provides you with the tools to fine-tune a scheme as much as you like. Here's how to do it:

1. Open the Display Properties dialog box and select the Appearance page as described at the beginning of this section.

2. Select a predefined scheme that is close to what you want from the Scheme drop-down list.

3. Select a screen element to be modified by either

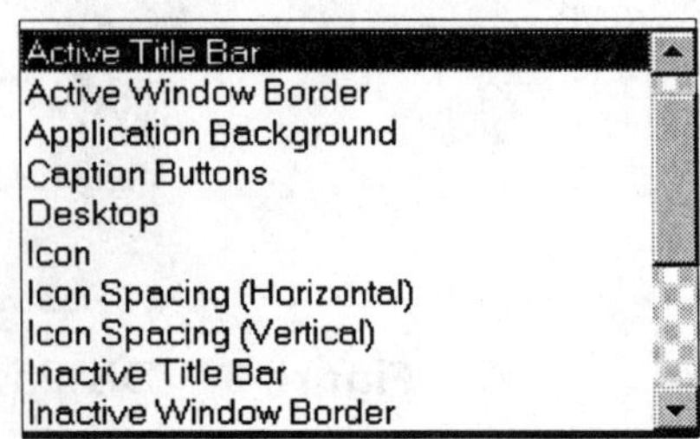

   - Clicking on that element on the Item drop-down list (see the figure at the right).

or

■ Clicking on that element in the preview window area.

For example, if you want to change the look of the active title bar or the text that appears on it, either select Active Title Bar from the Item drop-down list or click on "Active Window" in the preview window.

4. To choose a size for the selected screen element (if this option is available), click on the Size box next to the Item text box, as shown in Figure 6. The number in the Size box gives the height (or sometimes, width) of the object in *points*. There are 72 points per inch, so the height of the Active Title Bar of Figure 6 is 27/72 of an inch, or 3/8".

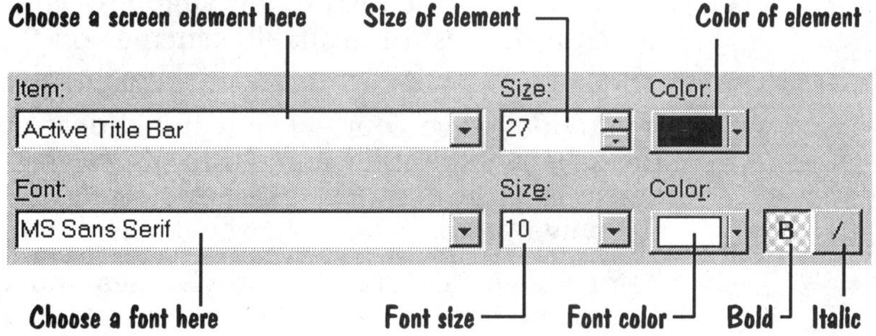

Figure 6   Selecting a Screen Element and its Size, Color, and Font

5. To choose a color for the selected screen element, click on the Color box to the right of the Item text box (Figure 6). A palette of 20 colors will be displayed, as shown at the right. Now, just click on the desired color or, if you want to view additional colors, click on the Other command button, which opens a dialog box with more color choices. (This dialog box also allows you to create your own colors.)

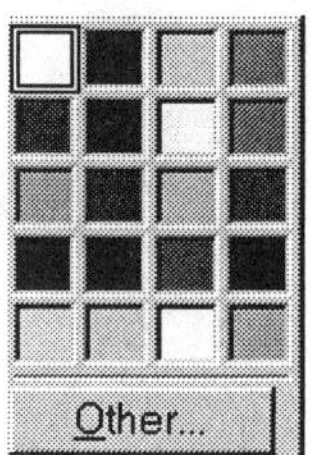

6. If the selected screen element contains text, you can choose the *typeface*, *font size*, *font color*, and elect to use *bold* or *italic* attributes for this text. As you make your selections, the text for the given screen element will change accordingly in the preview window.

■ To select a typeface (the font style), open the Font drop-down list (Figure 6) and select from the available choices.

- To select a font size, enter a new number in the Size box to the right of the Font text box. The number displayed here represents the height of the font in *points*. (Remember: There are 72 points to the inch.)

- To select a font color, click on the Color box to the right of the Font text box and select a color from the resulting palette. (See step 5 for more information on selecting a color.)

- If you want, you can select boldface (thicker) or italic (slanted) type for the text by clicking on the appropriate button (see Figure 6).

7. Save your new window scheme, if so desired, by choosing the Save As command button (see Figure 5) and typing a name for the scheme in the resulting dialog box. This scheme will then be added to the list of available schemes on the Scheme drop-down list.

   If you don't save your scheme, but choose OK or Apply in step 8, the scheme will still be put into effect and used in all Windows sessions until another scheme is selected. After that, however, the only way to retrieve the scheme is to recreate it step-by-step.

8. After you have made all the changes you want, choose the OK command button to put them into effect and close the dialog box, or choose the Apply button to put the changes into effect without closing the dialog box. (To leave the previous settings in effect, choose the Cancel command button.)

Modifying certain screen elements also affects other aspects of the Windows interface. For example:

- The settings for the Menu screen element are used for all Windows menus, including the Start menu.

- The font specified for the Icon screen element is also used in the Explorer folder tree and contents panes (see Section 3.2).

- The font specified for the Active Title Bar screen element is also used for the Taskbar.

The *Settings* and *Plus!* pages of the Display Properties dialog box provide additional ways to customize the screen display. You can explore these options by clicking on the relevant tab to display the corresponding page and then making use of content-sensitive help.

TUTORIAL

Try the following exercise on your own.

1. Turn on your computer, if necessary, to start up Windows NT and close any open windows.

2. Open the Display Properties dialog box: Right-click on an empty part of the Desktop and choose Properties from the pop-up menu.

3. Click on the Appearance tab to open this page of the dialog box.

4. Successively select several window schemes from the Scheme drop-down list and notice their effect on the preview window.

5. Select the Windows Standard scheme.

6. Change the Desktop color to white: Select the Desktop entry in the Item drop-down list, then click on the Color box, and finally, click on the white box in the pop-up palette.

7. Alter the size, color, and text of the active window's title bar:

   - Click on the Active Window title bar *in the preview window.* "Active Title Bar" will appear in the Item text box.

   - Change the height of the title bar to 25 points by clicking on the up-arrow in the Size text box (next to the Item box) until the entry reads "25".

   - Change the color of the active window's title bar to red by clicking on the Color box (to the right of the Item box) and then clicking on the red-colored square in the pop-up palette.

   - Change the active window's title bar font by opening the Font drop-down list and selecting Arial from it.

   - Change the size of the active window's title bar font to 10 points by clicking on the Size text box (next to the Font box), deleting the current number, and typing 10.

   - Add italics to the active window's title bar text by 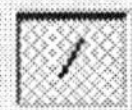 clicking on the Italic button.

8. Choose the Apply command button to put the new scheme into effect without closing the Display Properties dialog box. (Notice that the font used for the Taskbar buttons has changed.)

9. Select the original window scheme from the Scheme drop-down list (or select Windows Standard, if you're not sure what that scheme was).

10. Choose the OK command button to close the Display Properties dialog box and put the scheme just selected into effect.

4.4　Adjusting the Action of Keyboard and Mouse

In terms of your physical comfort while using a computer, some of the most important factors are the look of the screen display, and the operation of the keyboard and mouse. (Another important factor, the chair you sit on, is beyond our control.) In this section, we will discuss how to alter the operation of the keyboard and mouse so that they are easier and more pleasant to use.

Changing the Speed of the Keyboard

Most keys on the keyboard have a *repeat feature*; when you press such a key and hold it down, the character or action corresponding to it is repeated until the key is released. For example, if you press the B key and hold it down for a few seconds, a sequence of Bs will appear on the screen.

The number of times a key repeats in a given period of time depends on two factors:

- The *repeat delay* — how long it takes for a key to start repeating once it is pressed.

- The *repeat rate* —how fast the key repeats after the delay time has elapsed.

To change these parameters:

Keyboard

1. Start Control Panel (if it's not already open) and choose the **Keyboard** icon, as described in Section 4.1. The Keyboard Properties dialog box, shown in Figure 7, will be displayed.

2. To decrease the repeat delay, drag the *Repeat delay* slider toward the word *Short* or click to the right of the slider; to increase the delay, drag the slider toward the word *Long* or click to the left of the slider.

3. To decrease or increase the repeat rate, drag the *repeat rate* slider toward *Slow* or *Fast*, respectively, or click to the left or right of the slider.

4. To see the effect of your changes without closing the Keyboard Properties dialog box, click in the text box; then, observe what happens when you hold down a character key such as B.

5. Choose the OK command button to put your changes into effect, or choose the Cancel button to leave things as they were.

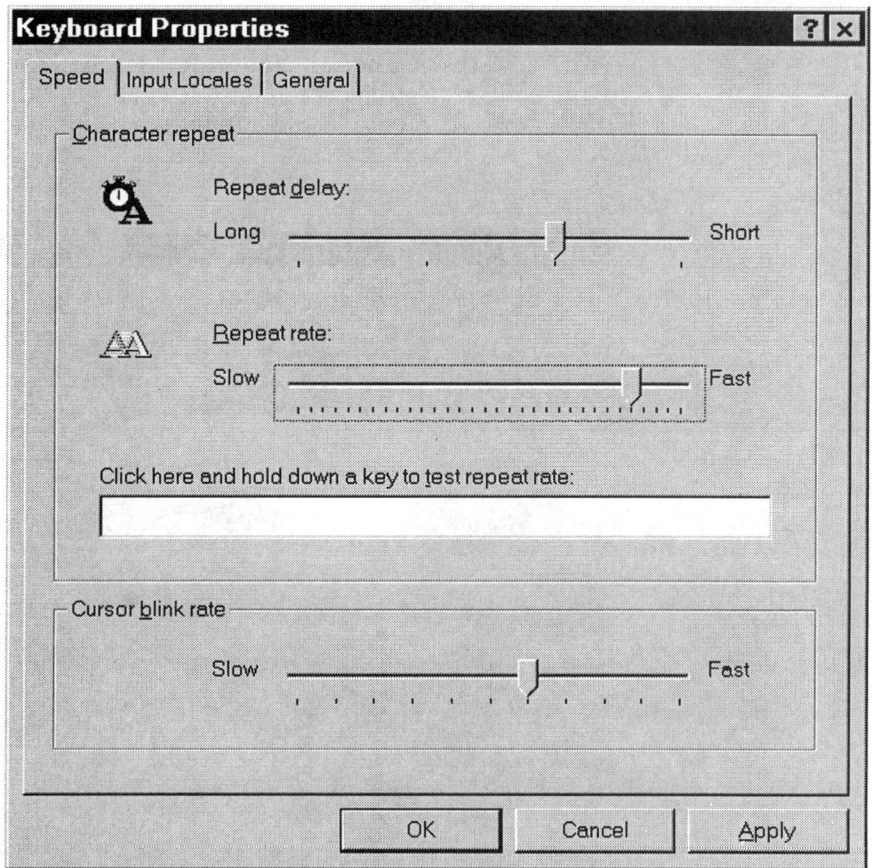

Figure 7   The Keyboard Properties Dialog Box

NOTE

As you can see in Figure 7, the Keyboard Properties dialog box can also be used to adjust the cursor blink rate. To do so, just drag the slider toward the left (*Slow*) or right (*Fast*), or click to the left or right of the slider.

Changing the Action of the Mouse

Different people have different preferences for the way the mouse "feels" when you move or click it. The feel of the mouse affects the ease with which you can choose menu items, double-click icons, move windows, and perform many other tasks.

To change the mouse settings:

Mouse

1. Start Control Panel (if it's not already open) and choose the **Mouse** icon, as described in Section 4.1. The Mouse Properties dialog box, shown in Figure 8, will be displayed.

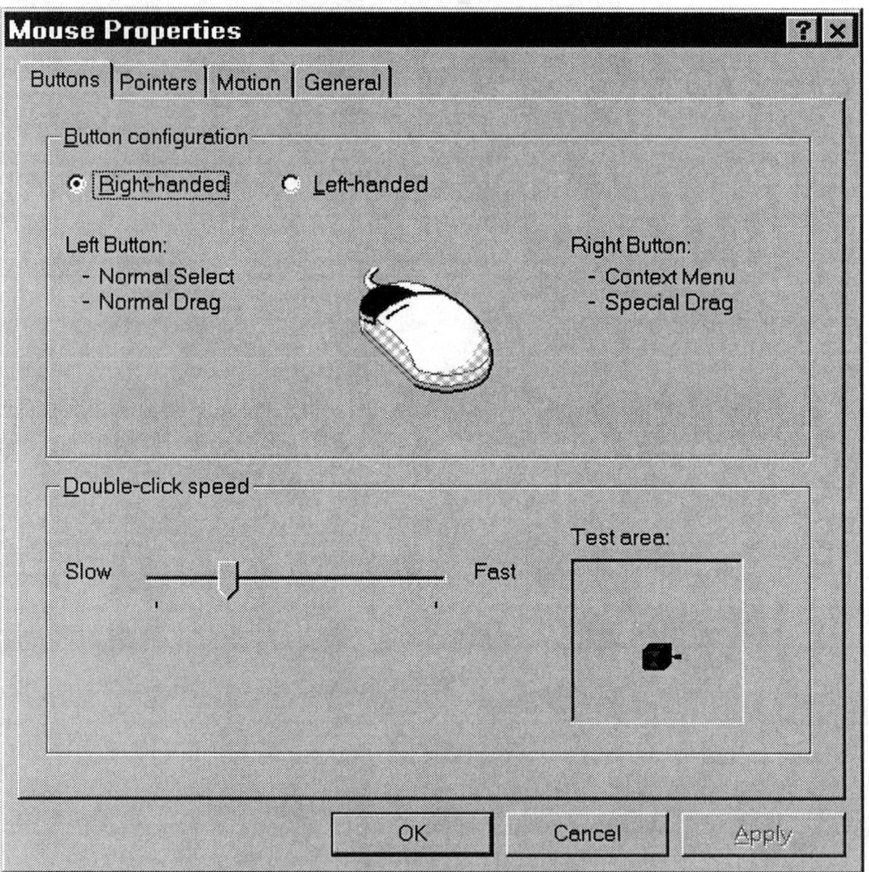

Figure 8   The Mouse Properties Dialog Box

2. On the Buttons page of this dialog box (which is shown in Figure 8), you can:

   ■ Swap the functions of the left and right mouse buttons. By default, the left mouse button is the *primary button* — it is used to choose menu items, select icons, and so on; the right button performs the functions we have referred to as right-clicking and right-dragging. If you want to make the right mouse button the primary one, select the *Left-handed* option button (so-named because it usually makes the mouse easier to use for left-handed people). To return to the default con-figuration, select the *Right-handed* option button.

- Change the double-click speed — the amount of time that elapses before Windows NT interprets a double-click as two sepa-rate clicks. Drag the *slider* to the left (toward *Slow*) or click to the left of the slider to allow yourself more time between clicks. You can test the results by double-clicking on the box in the *Test area*; if Windows interprets your two clicks as a double-click, a "jack-in-the-box" pops out.

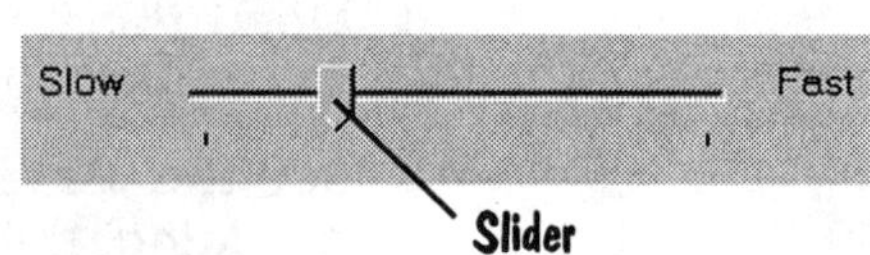

3. Click on the Pointers tab to provide options that allow you to change the shapes of the various Windows pointers.

4. Click on the Motion tab to provide options that:

   - Change the *pointer speed* — the speed with which the poin-ter moves across the screen when you move the mouse on the desk top. To increase or decrease the speed, drag the slider in the appropriate direction:

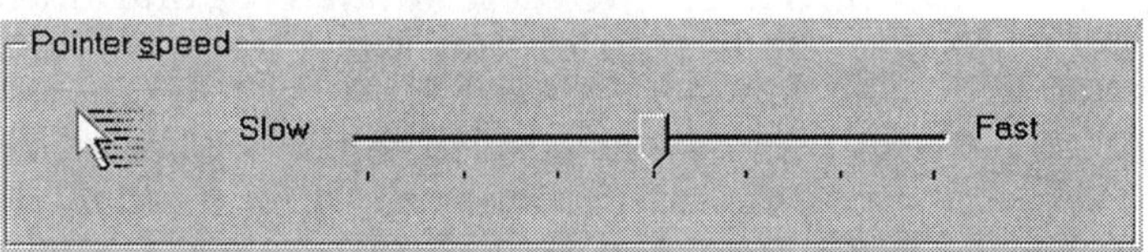

   - Automatically moves the mouse pointer over the default command button when a dialog box is opened. To select this option, click on the *Snap mouse to the default button in dia-logs* check box.

5. Click on the General tab to specify the type of mouse you are using.

6. Choose the OK command button to put your changes into effect and close the Mouse Properties dialog box, or choose the Apply button to put the changes into effect without closing the dialog box.

TUTORIAL

Try the following exercise on your own.

1. Turn on your computer, if necessary, to start up Windows NT and close any open windows.

2. Start Control Panel from the Settings option on the Start menu.

3. Open the Keyboard Properties dialog box by double-clicking on the Keyboard icon in the Control Panel window.

4. Set the *Repeat delay* to Long and the *Repeat rate* to Fast by dragging the sliders to the far left and far right, respectively. With these settings, a key must be held down "a long time" before it starts to repeat, but then repeats rapidly. Click on the test box and hold down a character key (such as A) to see the effect.

5. Set the *Repeat delay* to Short and the *Repeat rate* to Slow by dragging the sliders to the appropriate positions. Click on the test box and hold down a character key (such as A) to see the effect.

6. Set the *Cursor blink rate* slider to Slow; then set it to Fast. Notice the effect of each on the "insertion point" to the left of the slider.

7. Choose the Cancel command button to close the Keyboard Properties dialog box without putting your changes into effect.

8. Open the Mouse Properties dialog box by double-clicking on the Mouse icon in the Control Panel window.

9. Select the *Left-handed* option button and activate the Apply command button. Now, click the left mouse button on the *Right-handed* option button and notice the result. Then, right-click on the *Right-handed* option button and choose Apply again to return the mouse to "right-handed" use.

10. Set the *Double-click speed* slider to Fast and then to Slow. In each case, double-click at a few different speeds on the "jack-in-the-box" to see the effect. Jack will pop up or go down if Windows interprets your two clicks as a double-click.

11. Click on the Motion tab to open the corresponding page.

12. Drag the *pointer speed* slider to the *Fast* setting on the scale (all the way to the right) and choose the Apply button. Note the action of the pointer as you move it about the screen. Now move the slider to the *Slow* setting, choose Apply, and note the action of the pointer as you move it about the screen.

13. Choose the Cancel command button in the Mouse Properties dialog box and then close the Control Panel window.

4.5   Other Basic Control Panel Options

In this section, we will discuss a few other useful Control Panel functions.

Setting the Computer's Clock

Your computer contains an internal clock powered by a battery that keeps track of the date and time for the computer system. These settings are used by the Taskbar Clock, Explorer, and numerous other applications for various purposes.

The internal clock normally keeps fairly accurate time, but it may need to be adjusted every once in a while. To change the system date and time:

Date/Time

1. Start Control Panel (if it's not already open) and choose the **Date/Time** icon, as described in Section 4.1. The Date/Time Properties dialog box, shown in Figure 9, will be displayed.

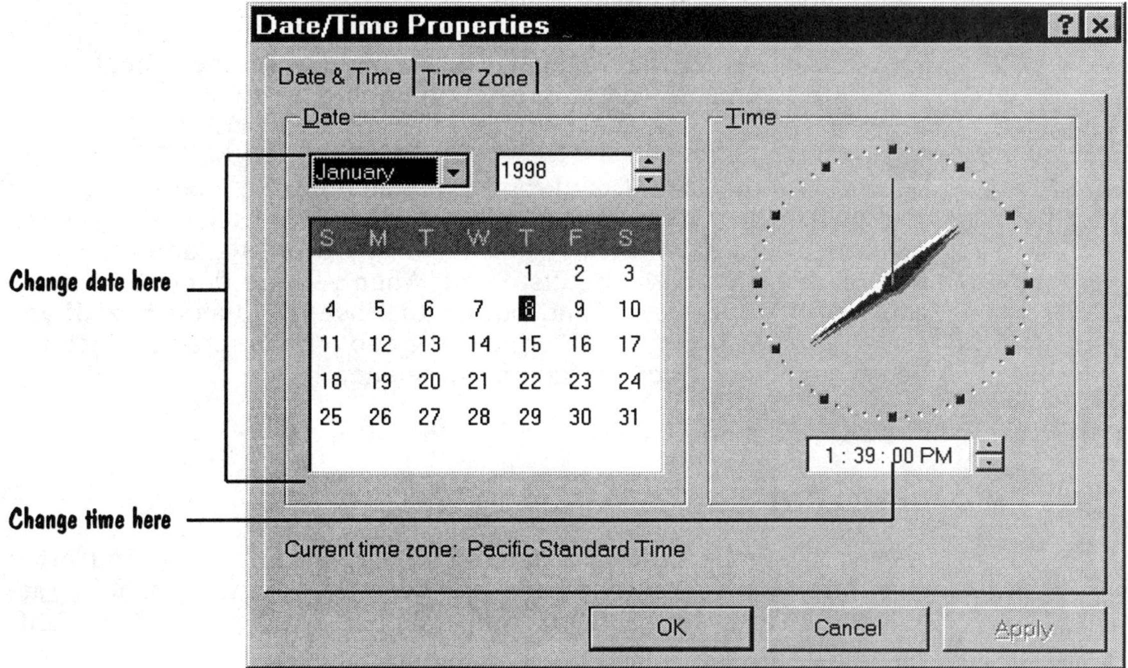

Figure 9   Date/Time Properties Dialog Box

2. Change the time with the aid of the digital clock in the lower right part of this dialog box. 
   The hours, minutes, seconds and AM/PM areas are set separately. To change any of these areas, click on it, use the Backspace or Delete key to delete the current setting, and type in the new one (or click on the up or down arrow button until the correct setting appears).

3. To change the date, use the left side of the dialog box. Select the correct month from the drop-down list and type in the correct year in the text box (or click on the up or down arrow button until the correct year appears). The correct day is set by clicking on the appropriate number on the calendar.

4. Choose the OK command button to put your changes into effect and close the Date/Time Properties dialog box, or choose the Apply button to put the changes into effect without closing the dialog box. (The Cancel button cancels all changes and closes the dialog box.)

Here are a couple of easier ways to open the Date/Time Properties dialog box shown in Figure 9:

- Double-click on the Clock on the Taskbar.

or

- Right-click on the Taskbar Clock and choose the Adjust Date/Time command from the resulting pop-up menu.

You can use the Date/Time Properties dialog box to look up dates as you would with a conventional calendar. To do so, select the desired month and year from their respective drop-down lists, and the calendar for that month will be displayed. When you are done, be sure to choose the Cancel command button to close the dialog box. If you click on OK (or press the Enter key), the computer's internal clock will be set to the date highlighted on the calendar!

Viewing Your Fonts

A **font** is a collection of characters — letters, numerals, and other symbols — of a given design, size, and style. Examples of fonts are "12-point Times New Roman" and "10-point Arial bold"; these fonts look like this:

12-point Times New Roman   **10-point Arial bold**

The design or *typeface* of a font determines the overall look of the characters; the fonts shown above are examples of the Times New Roman and Arial typefaces. The *size* of a font is its height, measured in points; a *point* is 1/72 of an inch. Thus, 12-point type is roughly 1/6-inch high. Fonts are also distinguished by their *attributes*; for example: regular, **bold**, or *italic*.

Some fonts are available in discrete sizes, such as 8-point, 10-point, etc. Others, known as **scalable fonts**, can be used in any size. Times New Roman and Arial are examples of a kind of scalable font called **TrueType**, which is included with the Windows software. TrueType fonts are available from many other sources, as well. (So are scalable fonts of other kinds, notably the widely used *Postscript* typefaces, developed by Adobe Systems, Inc.)

We will show how to make use of fonts in applications in Section 5.2. Here, we describe how to employ Control Panel to view or print samples of the fonts stored on your hard disk. To view or print font samples:

Fonts

1. Start Control Panel and choose the **Fonts** icon, as described in Section 4.1. The Fonts subfolder of the WinNT folder, shown in Figure 10, will open. (The "TT" symbols appearing on the icons indicate that these are TrueType fonts.)

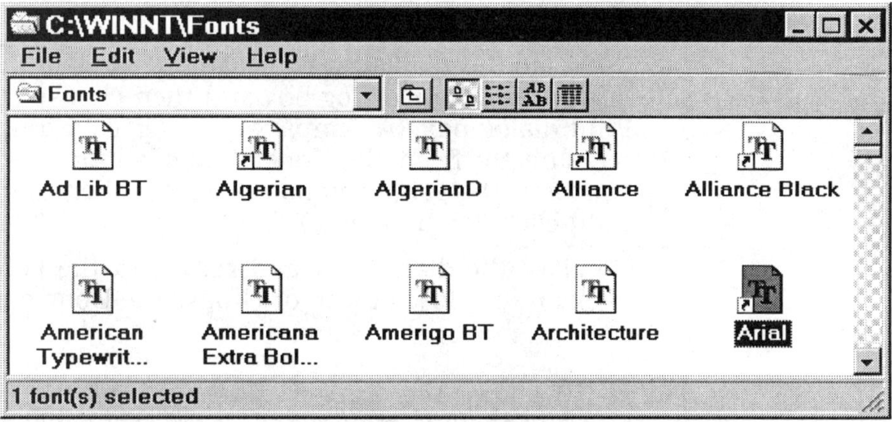

Figure 10   The Fonts Folder (Large Icons View)

2. Select the font in which you are interested by clicking on its name.

3. To view a sample of the selected font:

- Choose the Open command from the File menu or the menu that pops up when you right-click on the selected font.

or

- Double-click on the desired font.

In either case, a dialog box similar to the following one will be displayed:

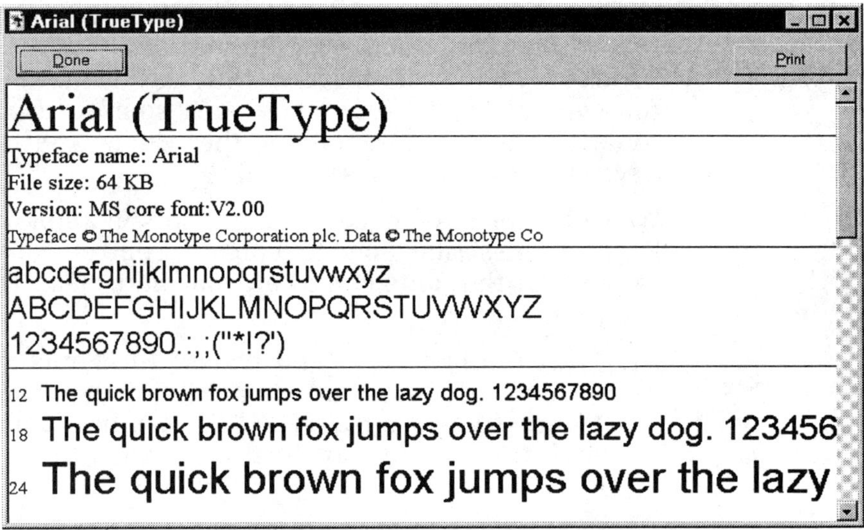

4. To print the displayed font sample, choose the Print command button from this dialog box and then choose OK in the resulting Print dialog box. (A sample of the selected font can also be printed directly from the Fonts folder window — Figure 10 — by choosing the Print command from either the File menu or the right-click pop-up menu.)

5. To close the dialog box and return to the Fonts folder window, click on the close button or choose the Done command button.

Figure 10 shows the "Large Icons" view of the Fonts folder. Even when this window is maximized, it will probably only show a small portion of your available fonts without scrolling. To display more font names and icons:

- Choose the *Hide Variations (Bold, Italic, etc.)* command from the View menu if it's not already checked. Then, instead of seeing (for example) "Arial", "Arial Bold", "Arial Italic", and "Arial Bold Italic", only "Arial" will be displayed.

- Choose either List, Similarity, or Details from the View menu, or by clicking a toolbar button as indicated below. (If the toolbar is not currently visible in the Fonts folder window, choose the Toolbar command from the View menu.)

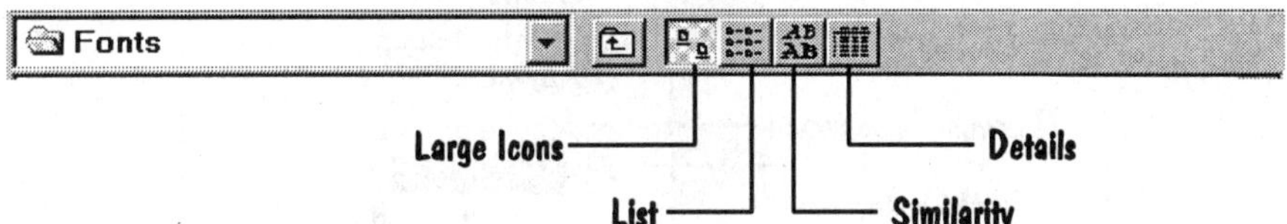

The List option displays the most font names at once; Similarity lists the fonts and describes their degree of similarity to the selected font; Details provides, for each font, the name, size, and creation date of the file that contains it. You will probably find the List view option to be the most useful.

NOTE

You can also use the Fonts folder window to install (add) or remove fonts from Windows.

- To install a new font (usually from a disk supplied by a software company), choose the Install New Font command from the File menu. The Add Fonts dialog box will open, allowing you to specify the disk and folder in which the new fonts are located and to select the desired fonts from a list. Choose the OK command button to complete the process.

- To remove an existing font, select it in the Fonts window and press the Delete key or choose Delete from the File menu. Then, choose the Yes command button in the resulting dialog box.

The Sounds Utility

If your computer is equipped with a sound card and speakers, you can specify that certain sounds be played to accompany certain system "events", such as minimizing an application or exiting Windows. The assignment of a sound to a given event is made from within Control Panel's **Sounds utility**.

To start the Sounds utility:

Sounds

1. Open the Control Panel window and choose the Sounds icon as described in Section 4.1. The Sounds Properties dialog box, shown in Figure 11, will open.

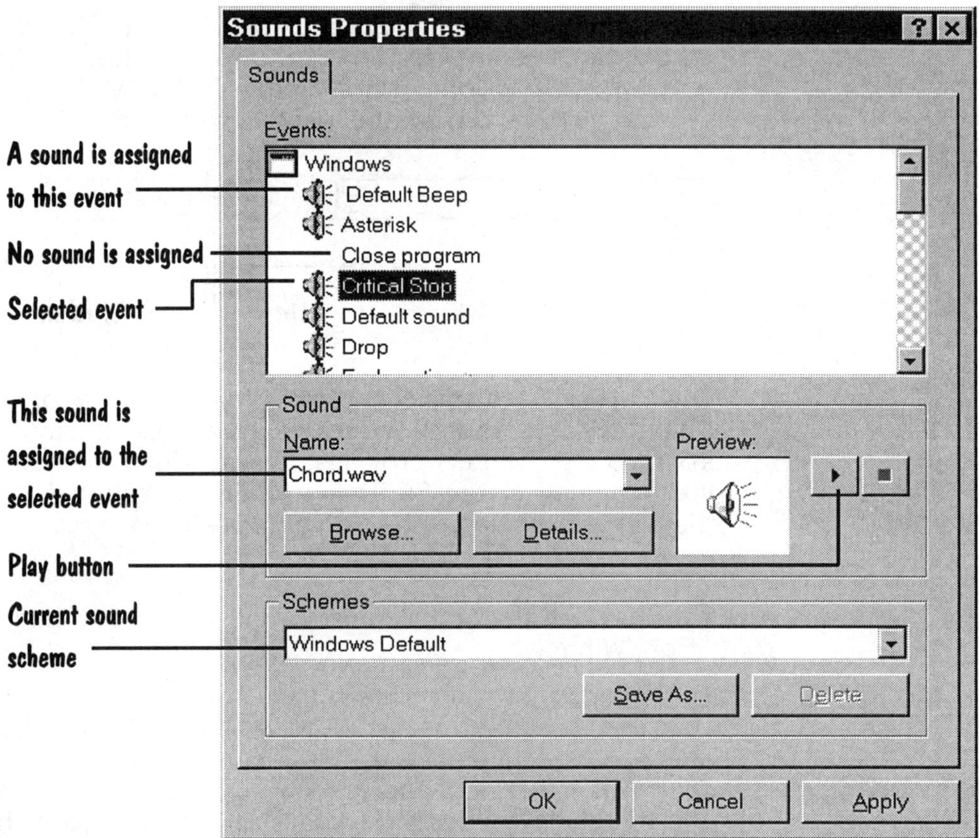

Figure 11   The Sounds Properties Dialog Box

Using the Sounds Properties dialog box, you can:

- Choose a built-in *sound scheme*, consisting of a collection of sounds pre-assigned to system events, or choose not to use sounds at all.

- Create a custom sound scheme by assigning particular sounds to specific events.

Selecting a Built-in Sound Scheme

Windows comes equipped with several sound schemes. To select one of them:

1. Open the Sounds Properties dialog box, as described above.

2. Select a sound scheme from the Schemes drop-down list. Select

"No Sounds" from the list if you do not want to hear sounds at system events.

Previewing sounds

3. To listen to (*preview*) an assigned sound, select the associated event from the Events list box and click on the Play button. To terminate a sound file before it has finished playing, click on the Stop button.

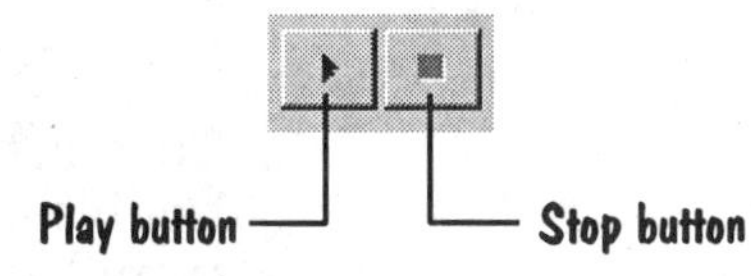

4. Choose the Apply command button, which puts the selected sound scheme into effect without closing the dialog box, or choose the OK button to put the scheme into effect and close the dialog box.

Creating a Custom Sound Scheme　　If you have the time and inclination, you can assign a sound of your choosing to each individual system event, creating a custom sound scheme. To do so:

1. Select a built-in sound scheme from the Schemes drop-down list that is similar to what you want.

2. Select a system event from the Events list box. (This box displays all events to which you can assign sounds; some events, such as Asterisk and Exclamation refer to dialog boxes of certain types.) The selected event will become highlighted.

   If the selected event is already associated with a sound, it will be preceded by the "speaker" symbol shown at the right, and the name of the corresponding sound file will be displayed in the Name text box. To preview the sound, click on the Play button. 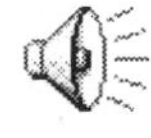

3. To assign a new sound to the selected event, select another sound file from the Name drop-down list. (This list contains all files with extension *wav* in the default folder; to select a sound file from another folder, choose the Browse command button.)

4. Repeat steps 2 and 3 until your sound scheme is complete.

5. If you would like to save your new sound scheme (so that it will be added to the Schemes drop-down list), choose the Save As command button, enter a name for the scheme in the resulting dialog box, and choose the OK button.

6. Choose the Apply command button, which puts the new sound scheme into effect without closing the dialog box, or choose the OK button to put the scheme into effect and close the dialog box. (The Cancel button closes the dialog box and restores the previous scheme.)

Review Exercises

Section 4.1

1. To start Control Panel, point at the ____________ option on the Start menu and then click on the Control Panel item.

2. To start a particular Control Panel utility, select it and either double-click on its icon or choose the ____________ command from the File menu or the right-click pop-up menu.

3. True or false: The type and number of Control Panel functions available for your computer system depend on its configuration.

4. True or false: If you change a Control Panel setting, the original setting will be restored the next time you start Windows.

5. Which of the following Control Panel utilities can be used to change the properties of audio devices connected to your system?

   a. Modems
   b. Multimedia
   c. Sound
   d. Regional Settings

6. Which of the following Control Panel utilities can be used to change settings such as the format of numbers and currencies?

   a. Modems
   b. Multimedia
   c. Regional Settings
   d. System

Section 4.2

7. To place a patterned background on your Desktop, begin by opening Control Panel and double-clicking on the ____________ icon.

8. You can use Control Panel to place ____________, a graphic image, either tiled or centered on the Desktop.

9. A ____________ can be used to cause an animated image to appear on the screen after a specified period of inactivity.

10. True or false: To apply a new Desktop pattern or wallpaper to the Desktop, you must first close the Display Properties dialog box.

11. True or false: When wallpaper is centered (instead of tiled), it always completely covers the Desktop.

12. True or false: The delay time for a screen saver is how long the mouse and keyboard must be inactive before the screen saver appears.

13. To open the Display Properties dialog box without first opening Control Panel:

    a. Right-click on the Taskbar and then click on Properties.
    b. Right-click on the Desktop and then click on Properties.
    c. Double-click on the Taskbar and then click on Properties.
    d. Double-click on the Desktop and then click on Properties.

14. If your computer has been inactive for a while and a screen saver has been activated, to return to your work you must:

    a. Click the mouse.
    b. Move the mouse.
    c. Press a key.
    d. You can perform any of the above actions.

Section 4.3 15. To change the colors of various objects in a window, use the ____________ page of the Display Properties dialog box.

16. To select a predefined window scheme, open the ____________ drop-down list in the Display Properties dialog box.

17. True or false: You can modify certain elements of a predefined window scheme by clicking on an element in the Item drop-down list and then making changes to it.

18. True or false: One-half inch is equivalent to 36 points.

19. From the Appearance page of the Display Properties dialog box, you *cannot* change the size of

    a. Scroll bars
    b. Title bars
    c. Menu entries
    d. The Desktop

20. From the Appearance page of the Display Properties dialog box, you *cannot* change the color of

    a. Scroll bars
    b. Title bars
    c. Menu entries
    d. The Desktop

Section 4.4 21. To change the keyboard repeat rate and delay, begin by double-clicking on the ____________ icon in Control Panel.

22. If it seems as if the functions of the left and right mouse buttons have been interchanged, you can switch them back by using the ____________ utility in Control Panel.

23. True or false: To change the cursor blink rate, use the Cursor utility in Control Panel.

24. True or false: If you choose the "Left-handed" button option in the Mouse Properties dialog box, then the right mouse button must be used to select menu items.

25. The Mouse Properties dialog box:

    a. Cannot be used to change the double-click speed.
    b. Cannot be used to reverse the functions of the left and right mouse buttons.
    c. Cannot be used to change the mouse pointer speed.
    d. Can be used to perform all the above tasks.

26. The Keyboard option in Control Panel cannot be used to

    a. Swap the functions of certain keys on the keyboard.
    b. Change the cursor blink rate.
    c. Extend the time delay for repeating keys on the keyboard.
    d. Increase the repeat rate for repeating keys on the keyboard.

Section 4.5 27. If the Taskbar Clock is displaying the wrong time, you can correct it by using Control Panel's ____________ utility.

28. TrueType is a collection of ____________, some of which are included with the Windows software.

29. To change the sound you hear when Windows starts up, use Control Panel's ____________ utility.

30. True or false: The system date and time must be set every time you start Windows.

31. True or false: Using Control Panel's Sounds utility, you can preview the sounds that accompany certain Windows events.

32. True or false: Every character in an 18-point font is roughly 1/4-inch *wide*.

33. The Fonts utility in Control Panel allows you to:

    a. Change the font used for icon titles.
    b. Change the font used in the active application.
    c. Set a default font for your printer.
    d. View the fonts on your hard disk.

34. Using the Date/Time utility in Control Panel,

    a. You can change the date displayed by the computer's internal clock.
    b. You can display a calendar for each month of the current year.
    c. You can determine the day of the week on which your birthday will fall in the year 2002.
    d. You can perform all of the above tasks.

Build Your Own Glossary

35. The following words and phrases are important terms that were introduced in this chapter. (They appear within the text in bold-face type.) Use WordPad (see Section 2.2) to enter a definition for each term, preserving alphabetical order, into the Glossary file on the Student Disk.

Control Panel	Keyboard utility	TrueType font
Date/Time utility	Mouse utility	Wallpaper
Display utility	Scalable font	Window scheme
Font	Screen saver	
Fonts folder	Sounds utility	

Lab Exercises

Work each of the following exercises at your computer. Begin by turning the machine on (if necessary) to start Windows NT, closing any open windows, and starting Control Panel. If you want to produce a written record of your answers, see the material on WordPad and capturing screens in Sections 2.2 and 2.3.

Lab Exercise 1 (Section 4.2)

a. Start the Display utility from the Control Panel window, which opens the Display Properties dialog box. Which (tab) page of this dialog box is active?

b. Select the "50% Gray" repeating pattern from the Pattern list box. Based on its appearance in the preview window, how would you describe this pattern?

c. Choose the Edit Pattern command button. Based on its appearance in the left side of the Pattern Editor dialog box, what is a better name for the "50% Gray" pattern?

d. Close the Pattern Editor dialog box and return the Desktop pattern to its original setting.

e. Select the Center option button and select the wallpaper images one-by-one. Which, if any, of the wallpapers cover the entire preview window?

f. Select the Tile option button, select a wallpaper from the list box, and then choose the Apply command button. Does the wallpaper cover the entire visible Desktop?

g. Return the wallpaper to its original setting and close the Display Properties dialog box.

Lab Exercise 2
(Section 4.2)

a. Start the Display utility from the Control Panel window, which opens the Display Properties dialog box. Now, click on the Screen Saver tab. Which, if any, screen saver is in effect?

b. Select the 3D Flying Objects screen saver from the Screen Saver drop-down list. Is this screen saver displayed in the preview window?

c. Set the delay time for ".5" minutes and choose the Preview command button. What time is displayed in the Wait text box after the preview is complete? What conclusion can you draw about the possible delay times?

d. Choose the Settings command button. Try various Styles and observe the effect on the preview window. (You will have to choose OK in the 3D Flying Objects Setup dialog box to see the effect of each change.) How many Styles are available?

e. In the Display Properties dialog box, choose the Apply button and wait for a minute or two. Did the screen saver become active? If it did, what action did you take to return to the dialog box?

f. Restore the previous screen saver, if any, and close the Display Properties dialog box.

Lab Exercise 3
(Section 4.3)

a. Start the Display utility from the Control Panel window, which opens the Display Properties dialog box. Now, click on the Appearance tab. Which, if any, window scheme is named in the Scheme text box?

b. Select the Active Title Bar from the Item list. What font and font size are used for it?

c. Open the Scheme drop-down list. How many schemes are listed?

d. Select, in succession, the "Windows Standard", "Windows Standard (large)", and "Windows Standard (extra large)" schemes. What are the respective font sizes for the Active Title Bar? Is the same font (type style) used for all three schemes?

e. By selecting, one-by-one, all the available schemes, answer the following questions:

- Which schemes use no colors other than black and white (for the items displayed in the preview window)?
- Which schemes use the Times New Roman font for the Active Title Bar?

f. Select the Windows Standard scheme and 3D Objects (from the

Item list). Change the font color to bright red. Which objects in the preview window are affected by the 3D Objects color?

g. Choose the Cancel button to close the Display Properties dialog box.

Lab Exercise 4 (Section 4.3)

a. Start the Display utility from the Control Panel window, which opens the Display Properties dialog box. Now, click on the Appearance tab.

b. Select the High Contrast White scheme and change 3D Objects to light gray. Which objects in the preview window changed color?

c. Change:

- The Active Title Bar color to dark blue.
- The Desktop color to teal (blue-green).
- The Inactive Title Bar color to dark gray and its font color to light gray.
- Menu items to light gray.

How does the look of the resulting preview window differ from that of the Windows Standard scheme?

d. *Optional*: Capture the Display Properties window, paste it into WordPad, and print the resulting document. (Try this only if you've already read Sections 2.2 and 2.3.)

e. Choose Cancel to close the Display Properties dialog box.

Lab Exercise 5 (Section 4.4)

a. Start the Keyboard utility from the Control Panel window. Where are the Repeat Delay and Repeat Rate sliders positioned (relative to the "tick marks" that appear just below each slider)?

b. Set the repeat delay as short as possible and the repeat rate as fast as possible. In the test area, hold down a character key for about one second. How many characters were displayed?

c. Now set the repeat delay as long as possible and the repeat rate as slow as possible. In the test area, hold down a different character key, also for about one second. How many characters are displayed this time?

d. Set the cursor blink rate as slow as possible; then set it at the middle of the scale. In each case, with the aid of a watch, estimate how many "blinks" take place in ten seconds.

e. Click on the Input Locales tab. What language appears on the Input locales list?

f.   Click on the General tab. What is your keyboard type?

g.   Choose the Cancel command button to close the Keyboard Properties dialog box.

Lab Exercise 6   a.   Start the Mouse utility from the Control Panel window.

(Section 4.4)   b.   Switch the button configuration from right-handed to left-handed (or vice-versa). What changes do you see in the dialog box?

c.   Set the double-click speed to slow; then to fast. By trying each setting in the Test area, which one requires you to double-click more quickly?

d.   Click on the Pointers tab. Make a list of all the available pointer schemes.

e.   Click on the Motion tab. What options are available on the Motion page?

f.   Set the pointer speed to slow; then, to fast. Do you notice any change in pointer speed?

g.   Click on the General tab. What is the "name" of your mouse?

h.   Choose the Cancel command button to close the Mouse Properties dialog box.

Lab Exercise 7   a.   Start the Date/Time utility from the Control Panel window. What is the name of the "current time zone"?

(Section 4.5)

b.   By using the up and down arrows, determine the earliest and latest years available for the calendar.

c.   Choose the Cancel command button to close this dialog box.

d.   Start the Fonts utility from the Control Panel window. How many fonts are available on your system? (Look on the status bar, at the bottom of the Fonts window.)

e.   Use the View menu or toolbar to switch to List view. How many columns are displayed?

f.   Select the Times New Roman font, view (open) it, and choose the Print command button in the dialog box. (Make sure that the printer connected to your computer is ready before issuing the Print command.)

g.   Close the Times New Roman dialog box and the Fonts window.

CHAPTER 5

Using Windows Accessories

Windows supplies a handful of small and medium-sized applications that are located on the Accessories submenu of the Start button, and are thus often referred to as **accessories**. In this chapter, we will discuss some features of the WordPad and Paint applications and then briefly describe other accessories. More specifically:

- Section 5.1 briefly reviews the material on the WordPad word processor presented in Section 2.2 and then introduces some additional features of WordPad.

- Section 5.2 describes how to format text in WordPad.

- Section 5.3 presents an introduction to the Windows Paint graphics program.

- Section 5.4 provides an overview of other accessories supplied with the Windows NT software package.

5.1   *WordPad Revisited*

Using a word processor to create a document involves several steps. You have to:

1. Enter the text that makes up the document or open a previously created document.

2. Edit the document to correct errors, modify its content, or improve its style.

3. Format the document; for example, set margins and choose fonts.

4. Save the document to disk.

5. Print a copy of the document on paper.

In Section 2.2, we presented an introduction to the **WordPad** word processor that quickly covered a few of these points. In this section, we will review and expand upon some of this material. Then, in Section 5.2, we will discuss additional features of WordPad.

The WordPad Window

To start WordPad:

1. Click on the Start button (or press Ctrl+Esc).

2. Point at the Programs option and then at Accessories.

3. Click on the WordPad item on the Accessories submenu.

A window, similar to the one in Figure 1, will open. The Toolbar, Format bar, Ruler, and Status bar can all be toggled on or off by selecting or deselecting the corresponding item on the View menu. If you don't use one of these features, you can increase the size of the document window slightly by removing that feature from the screen.

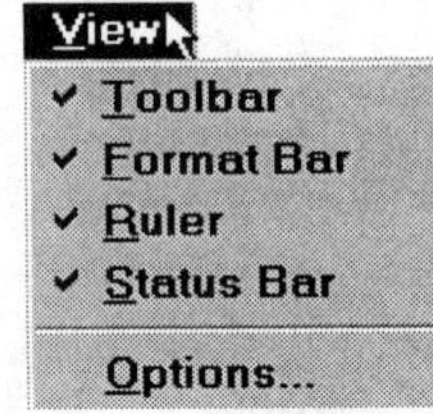

Recall that to create a document, you just begin typing. The text you type appears in the *document window* and is also stored in the computer's internal memory, RAM. The *insertion point* moves to indicate where the next character you type will appear on the screen. When you reach the end of a line, keep typing; WordPad automatically *wraps* the text to the beginning of the next line. Press the Enter key to start a new line only if you want to begin a new paragraph or skip a line. When you reach the bottom of the document window, continue typing; the window will scroll to accommodate the new text.

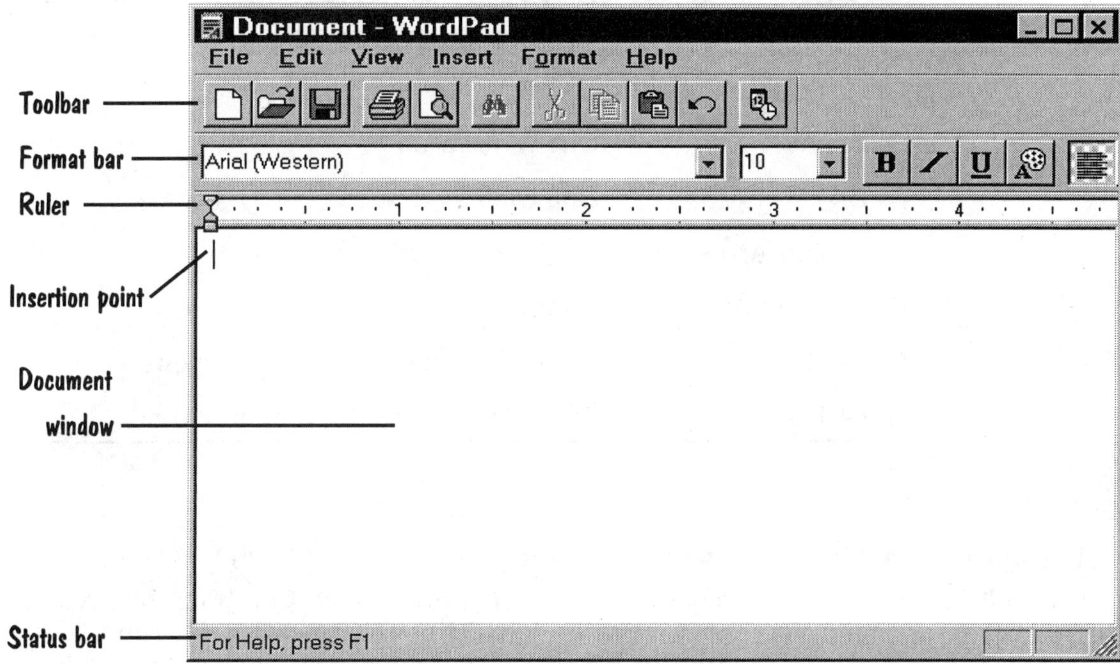

Figure 1   The WordPad Window

Editing a Document

It is inevitable that from time to time you will want to modify the content of the text you have typed. Making changes to existing text, for whatever reason, is called *editing* the document. To modify a piece (or *block*) of text, you have to:

1. Move the insertion point to the text you are changing.

2. Delete the undesirable text and/or insert the new text.

In Section 2.2, we briefly discussed how to use the mouse or arrow keys to move the insertion point within the document window or scroll the window. In some situations, using one of the keys or keystroke combinations described in the following table will move the insertion point more quickly to a desired location in the document.

	Key	Moves the insertion point . . .
Insertion point movement keys	Home	To the beginning of the current line
	End	To the end of the current line
	Pg Up	One window up
	Pg Dn	One window down
	Ctrl + Left Arrow	To the previous word
	Ctrl + Right Arrow	To the next word
	Ctrl + Home	To the beginning of the document
	Ctrl + End	To the end of the document

Deleting and inserting text

After moving the insertion point to the desired spot, you can:

- Delete the character to the *left* of the insertion point by pressing the Backspace key, or delete the character to the *right* of the insertion point by pressing the Delete key. If you want to delete a number of consecutive characters quickly, hold down the Backspace or Delete keys (as appropriate) until the block of text is erased from the screen.

- Insert text at the insertion point by typing it at the keyboard. If the new text just replaces (types over) existing characters, then WordPad is in *overwrite mode*. To return WordPad to the default *insert mode*, press the Insert key.

You can also delete or insert text with the aid of the Windows Clipboard. In Section 2.3, we discussed how to select, cut, copy, and paste text. Recall that:

- To *select* a block of text, position the insertion point at the beginning of the block and then either hold down the Shift key while moving the insertion point to the end of the block or mouse-drag the insertion point to the end of the block. In either case, the selected block of text will become highlighted.

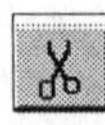

- To *cut* a block of text to the Clipboard, deleting it from its current location in the process, choose Cut from the Edit menu or click on the Toolbar's Cut button.

- To *copy* a selected block of text (which does not delete it from its current location), choose Copy from the Edit menu or click on the Toolbar's Copy button.

 ■ To *paste* a block of text at the insertion point, choose Paste from the Edit menu or click on the Toolbar's Paste button.

These techniques work with every Windows-based application. In addition, WordPad provides some shortcuts for these procedures:

Other ways to select text

■ To select a word, double-click on any letter in it.

■ To select a paragraph, triple-click anywhere within it.

You can also select certain blocks of text by moving the mouse cursor (the I-beam) into the left margin. The cursor will become a right-facing arrow, called the *selection cursor* (see Figure 2). Then:

■ To select the line of text at the cursor, click the mouse (see Figure 2). To select several consecutive lines of text, drag the mouse pointer down the left margin until all the desired lines have become highlighted.

■ To select the paragraph at the cursor, double-click the mouse.

■ To select the entire document, triple-click the mouse. (You can also select the entire document by choosing the Select All command from the Edit menu.)

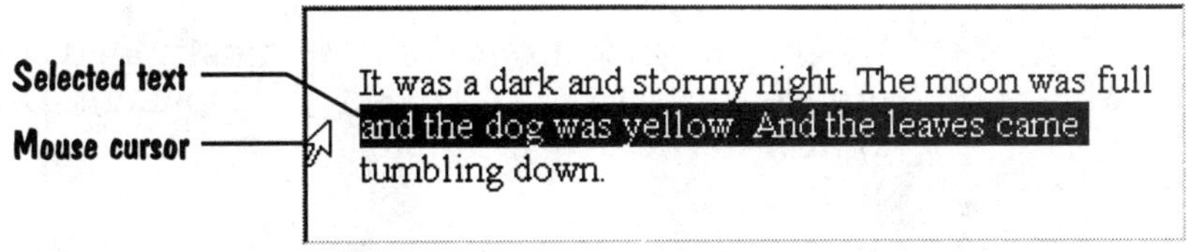

Figure 2   Selecting a Single Line of Text

Deselecting text

To *deselect* a block of text, click the mouse anywhere on the screen or press a cursor movement key, such as an Arrow key. (Do not press any other kind of key while a block of text is selected; the corresponding character will *replace* the selected text!)

Drag-and-drop move or copy

You can also move or copy text from one place in a WordPad document to another using the *drag-and-drop* technique. (In Section 3.3, we used this technique to move and copy files or folders.) Here's the way it works:

1. Select the block of text to be moved or copied.

2. Position the mouse pointer anywhere in the highlighted text (the

cursor will become a left-facing arrow).

3. If you want:

   - To *move* the selected text, press (but do not release) the left mouse button and reposition the mouse pointer at the selected text's new location.

   - To *copy* the selected text, hold down the Ctrl key and press the left mouse button as you move the pointer to the selected text's new location. (In this case, the mouse pointer displays a small box containing a plus symbol.)

   The insertion point moves with the mouse cursor and indicates the exact place the text will be positioned (see Figure 3).

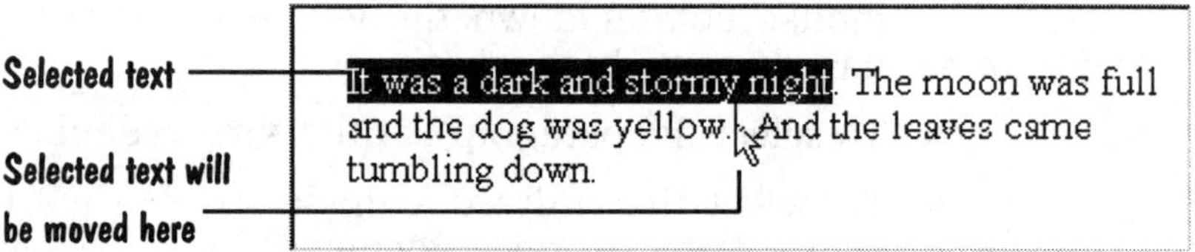

Figure 3   Moving Selected Text by Drag-and-Drop

4. When the insertion point is positioned properly, release the mouse button (and Ctrl key, if copying). The selected text will appear in the new location.

Once you have selected a block of text, in addition to moving or copying it, you can:

NOTE

- Delete the text by pressing the Delete or Backspace key.
- Change the text's font, as described in Section 5.2.

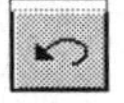

To *undo* your last edit (such as moving or deleting some text), either choose the Undo command from the Edit menu or click on the Toolbar's Undo button.

When using a word processor, you may find it more convenient to perform editing operations using the keyboard rather than by clicking on menu commands or Toolbar buttons. Here are some shortcut keys for the operations discussed in this section:

T I P

Ctrl+A selects the entire document.
Ctrl+X cuts a selected block of text to the Clipboard.

Ctrl+C copies a selected block of text to the Clipboard.
Ctrl+V pastes the text on the Clipboard at the insertion point.
Ctrl+Z undoes the last editing operation.

TUTORIAL

Try the following exercise on your own.

1. Turn on the computer (if necessary) to start Windows NT and open WordPad by clicking on the WordPad item on the Accessories submenu of the Start menu's Programs option.

2. Begin a document by typing the sentences "It was a dark and stormy night. The dogs were barking.", and then pressing the Enter key.

3. Select the first line of this document by moving the mouse cursor into the left margin, where it becomes a right-facing arrow, and clicking. (Because the first line happens to be a paragraph, you can also select it by either double-clicking while the mouse cursor is in the left margin or triple-clicking while the cursor is in the paragraph itself.) The first line of text will become highlighted.

4. *Copy* the selected text to the end of the document by dragging it there: Hold down the Ctrl key (if you forget to do this, the text will be *moved*, not copied), position the mouse cursor within the selected text, press the left mouse button, reposition the cursor (and insertion point) at the end of the document, and release the mouse button and Ctrl key.

5. Select the entire document by either:

   - Repositioning the mouse cursor in the left margin and triple-clicking.

   or
   - Choosing Select All from the edit menu (or pressing Ctrl+A).

6. Copy the selected text to the end of the document: Copy it to the Clipboard (press Ctrl+C), reposition the insertion point at the end of the document (press Ctrl+End), and paste the text there (press Ctrl+V). There should now be four lines of stormy nights and barking dogs.

7. Undo the last action (step 6): Either choose the Undo command from the Edit menu, click on the Toolbar's Undo button, or press Ctrl+Z.

8. Close WordPad, answering No to the "Save changes?" message.

5.2   Formatting Text in WordPad

In Section 5.1, we discussed some of the basic capabilities of the WordPad word processor. In this section, we will describe how you can control the way text appears on the screen and the printed page.

Fonts

Nothing makes a bigger difference in the impact your words will have on the reader than the fonts you use to print them. We briefly discussed the nature of fonts in Section 4.5; we will expand upon that material here and then show how fonts are implemented within a WordPad document.

Recall that a **font** is a collection of characters of a given design, size, and style.

- The *design* or **typeface** of a font refers to the general appearance of the characters, independent of their size, thickness, or other attributes. For example, Arial, Courier New, and Times New Roman are three of the typefaces supplied by Windows.

- The *size* of a font refers to its height, measured in **points**. There are 72 points per inch, so 18-point type, for example, is roughly 1/4-inch high on the printed page. Here are some examples of different sizes of the Arial typeface:

    8-point   12-point   18-point

- The *style* of a font refers to attributes such as **bold** or *italic*.

Some fonts are only supplied in discrete sizes, such as 10-point, 12-point, and so on. Others, called *scalable fonts*, can be scaled to any size. Microsoft includes several scalable typefaces, known as *True-Type fonts*, with the Windows NT software. These fonts are available for use in any Windows-based application.

WYSIWYG   When you type text in WordPad, the corresponding characters appear on the screen in the current font (which is displayed on the Format bar). If you print the document, the fonts that appear on the screen will also be used by the printer. We say that WordPad is a WYSIWYG (What You See Is What You Get, pronounced "whizzywig") word processor. WYSIWYG means that the appearance of the document on the screen, including fonts, graphics, spacing, and so on, previews the way it will appear on the printed page.

Changing the font

There are several ways to change the current font in WordPad. With any of these techniques, the font change will apply to either:

- The currently selected block of text, if text is selected when the change is made.

or

- The text you type after the change is made, if no text is currently selected.

Using the Font Dialog Box   The most flexible way to change the current font is to make use of the Font dialog box, which allows you to change not only the typeface, style, and size of the font, but also other attributes such as underline (<u>underline</u>), strikeout (~~strikeout~~), and color. Here's how to use this dialog box:

1. If you want the new font to apply to existing text, select that block of text. (Otherwise, the new font will apply to the text you type after the change is made.)

2. Choose the Font command from the Format menu. The Font dialog box, shown in Figure 4, will be displayed. The current font's typeface, style, and size are shown in the Font, Font style,

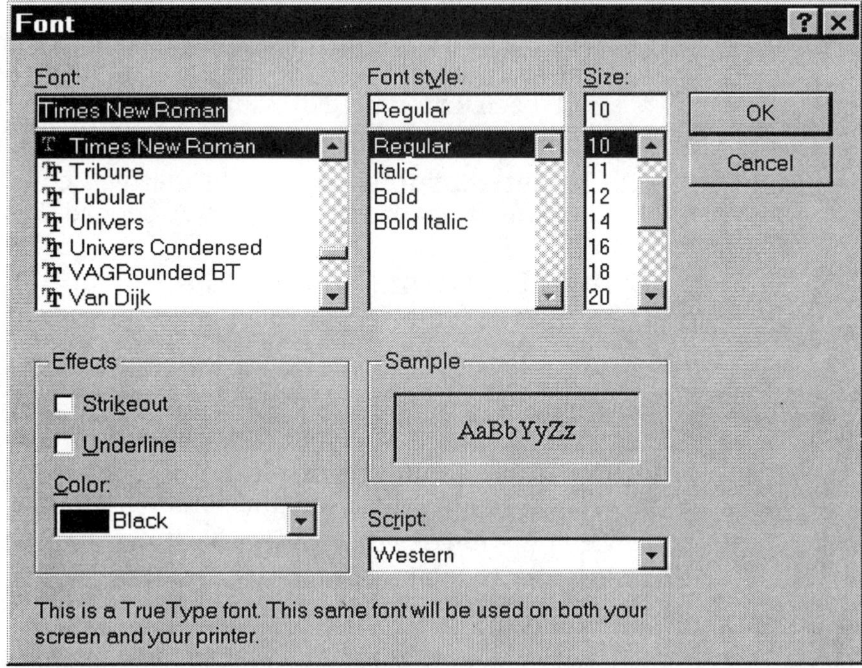

Figure 4   The Font Dialog Box

and Size text boxes, respectively; a sample of this font is displayed in the Sample box. As you make selections to change this font, the sample text changes accordingly.

3. Select a typeface for the new font from the Font list box. Instead of scrolling to the desired name, you might save time by typing its first few letters in the Font text box at the top of the list. For example, to change to Arial, type "ar" in the text box and the Font list box will scroll to display Arial and other "nearby" typefaces.

4. Select bold, italic, or bold italic, if you wish, from the Font style list. Selecting Regular turns off (cancels) a current style.

5. Select a font size (in points) from the Size list. You can select any (whole number) size that your printer can print, even if it doesn't appear in this list. Just click on the text box at the top of the Size list and type in the desired size.

6. If you want to add an underline and/or strikeout line to the text, select the appropriate check boxes.

7. You can select a text color from the Color drop-down list. Of course, to print the resulting text in this color, you need a color printer. (Some black-and-white printers print the various colors in shades of gray.)

8. The Script drop-down list is used to select an alternate character set for use with a language other than English. If Windows has not been configured for another language, you can ignore this feature.

9. To put your font changes into effect, choose the OK command button. To ignore these changes, choose Cancel.

Using the Format Bar   The Format bar provides a quicker, though less flexible, way of changing fonts and their attributes. (Remember: If the Format bar is not displayed in your WordPad window, choose the Format Bar item from the View menu to display it.) The functions of the Format bar buttons that alter the current font are identified in Figure 5. Notice that the typeface and font size of the current font are displayed on the Format bar; if the current font has bold, italic, or underline attributes, the corresponding buttons will appear to be "pressed in".

To use the Format bar to change the font of selected text or the text that you are about to type:

1. Select a new typeface or font size from the appropriate drop-down list.

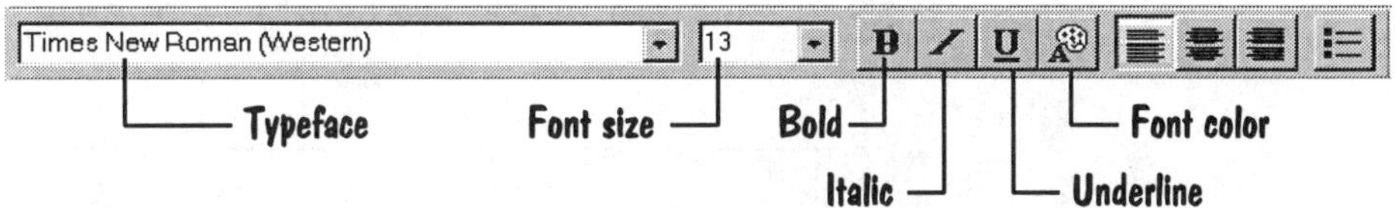

Figure 5   Font Attributes on the Format Bar

2. Select or deselect bold, italics, or underline by clicking on the corresponding button.

3. Change the font color by clicking on the Font Color button and selecting the desired color from the drop-down list.

The easiest way to turn the bold, italics, or underline attribute on or off is to use the keystroke combinations Ctrl+B, Ctrl+I, or Ctrl+U, respectively. For example, to bold a word you are about to type, press Ctrl+B, type the word, and press Ctrl+B again. Or, to remove italics from a word you have already typed, select the word and press Ctrl+I.

Other Text Formatting Features of WordPad

Here is a brief summary of the other ways you can format text within a WordPad document.

Margins   You can set top, bottom, left, and right margins for the document, by choosing the Page Setup command from the File menu and entering the desired margins in the resulting dialog box. Any margin change applies to the *entire* document. (The default margins are 1" top and bottom, and 1.25" left and right.)

Alignment   You can center the text in the current paragraph (or selected paragraphs) or align it with the left or right margins by either

- Clicking on the appropriate Format bar button.

or

- Choosing the Paragraph command from the Format menu and then selecting Left, Center, or Right from the Alignment drop-down list in the resulting dialog box.

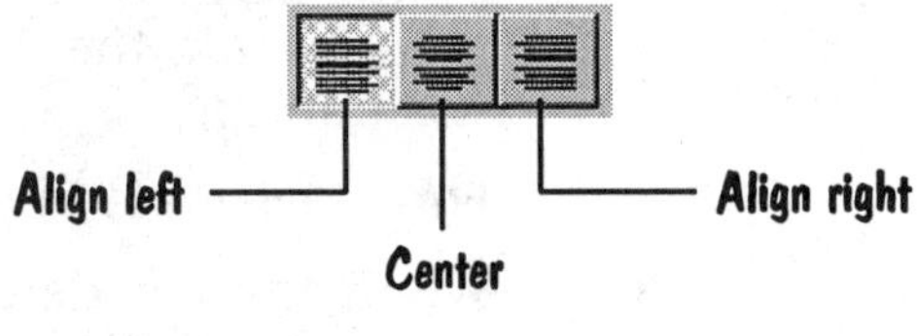

Figure 6 gives examples of centered and left- and right-aligned text.

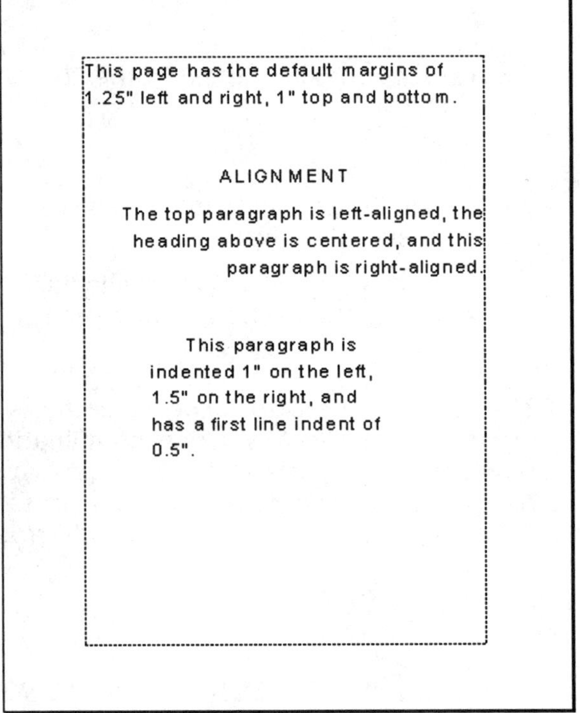

Figure 6   Examples of Formatting Features

Indentation   The margins you set apply to the entire document. If you want to further indent the current paragraph (or selected paragraphs), and/or further indent the first line of the paragraph, choose the Paragraph command from the Format menu and enter the appropriate figures in the resulting dialog box. You can also set left, right, and first line indents by dragging markers on the Ruler to the desired positions.

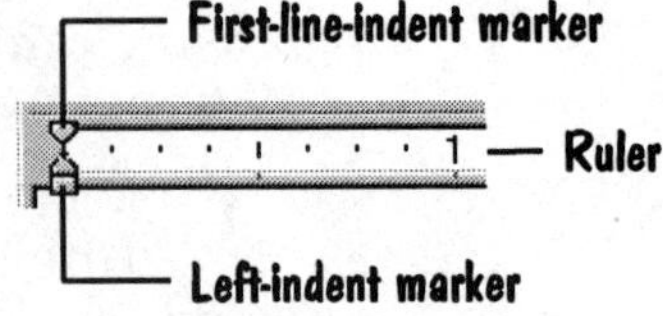

For an example of indentation, see the last paragraph in Figure 6.

Tabs   WordPad sets default tab stops every one-half inch. Thus, if you press the Tab key when the insertion point is 2.75" from the left margin, it will move to a position on the same line 3" from the margin. To set other tabs, either

- Choose the Tabs command from the Format menu and enter the positions of the new tab stops in the resulting dialog box. (You can also *clear* — remove — existing tabs using this dialog box.)

or

- Click on the Ruler where you would like a tab to be positioned. (You can clear an existing tab by dragging it off the Ruler.)

In either case, an L symbol will appear in the appropriate spot on the Ruler to indicate that a new tab has been set.

NOTE

Changes in alignment, indentation, and tab settings automatically apply to the paragraph that contains the insertion point and to the following paragraphs, as well. Each of these settings remains in effect until it is changed again.

Continuing on ...

You can learn more about WordPad by using it! Try out features you see on menus and in dialog boxes, and don't forget that you can always get help from the Windows Help system (see Section 2.5).

TUTORIAL

Try the following exercise on your own.

1. Turn on the computer (if necessary) to start Windows NT.

2. Open WordPad from the Start button's Accessories submenu and maximize its window.

3. Insert the Student Disk in its drive and open the document named Preamble. (For information on opening documents, see Section 2.2.)

4. If the Format bar is turned off, display it by choosing the Format Bar command from the View menu. Notice that 14-point Arial type is used for the title of the document.

5. Change the title's font to 12-point bold italic Times New Roman:

    - Select the title (by, for example, clicking in the left margin).
    - Choose the Font command from the Format menu to open the Font dialog box.
    - In the dialog box, select Times New Roman from the Font list, Bold Italic from the Font Style list, and 12 from the Size list.
    - Choose the OK command button.

6. Notice that the title (which should still be highlighted) is left-aligned and that the Align Left button is "depressed" on the Format bar. Click on the Align Right button, then on the Center button to see the effect of alignment on the text. (Alignment options can also be accessed by choosing the Paragraph command on the Format menu.)

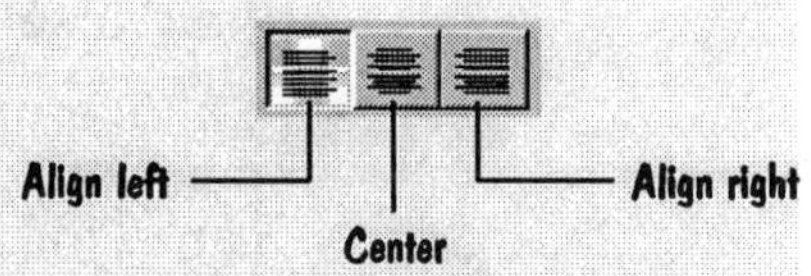

7. Change the text for the preamble from 12-point Times New Roman to 11-point Arial:

   - Select the text of the preamble (by, for example, double-clicking in the left margin next to this paragraph).
   - Select "Arial (Western)" and "11" from the drop-down lists on the Format bar.

8. While the paragraph is still selected, indent it 0.25" on the left and 0.5" on the right, with a first-line-indent of 0.5". To do so, choose the Paragraph command from the Format menu and enter these figures in the appropriate text boxes in the resulting dialog box.

9. Add the words THE END at the end of the document in bold type:

   - Reposition the cursor at the end of the document and press the Enter key twice.
   - Turn on boldface by clicking on the Toolbar's Bold button (or pressing Ctrl+B).
   - Type the words THE END and turn off boldface by clicking on the Bold button (or pressing Ctrl+B) again.

   Notice that the paragraph indentation from the previous paragraph (step 8) is continued in the succeeding paragraph.

10. Set the left and right margins for the entire document to 1.5": To do so, choose the Page Setup command from the File menu and enter 1.5 in both the Left and Right Margins text boxes.

11. Close WordPad (responding No to the "Save changes?" message) and remove the Student Disk from its drive.

5.3 An Introduction to Paint

Creating a **graphic** (a picture) using the **Paint** application is not unlike creating one using conventional artist's tools. (In fact, some Paint tools have familiar names, such as brush and eraser.) Instead of using an artist's brush to apply paint to a canvas or other surface, Paint allows you to manipulate the tiny dots of light (*pixels*) that make up the screen image, coloring them as you wish to create various shapes.

In this section, we will provide an introduction to the graphics-creation process. Using the material provided here, together with the Windows Help system (described in Section 2.5) and a lot of trial and error, you should be able to learn more about Paint on your own.

The Paint Window

To start Paint:

1. Click on the Start button to open the Start menu.

2. Point at the Programs option on this menu and at Accessories on the resulting submenu.

3. On the Accessories submenu, click on the Paint item. The Paint window, shown in Figure 7, will open.

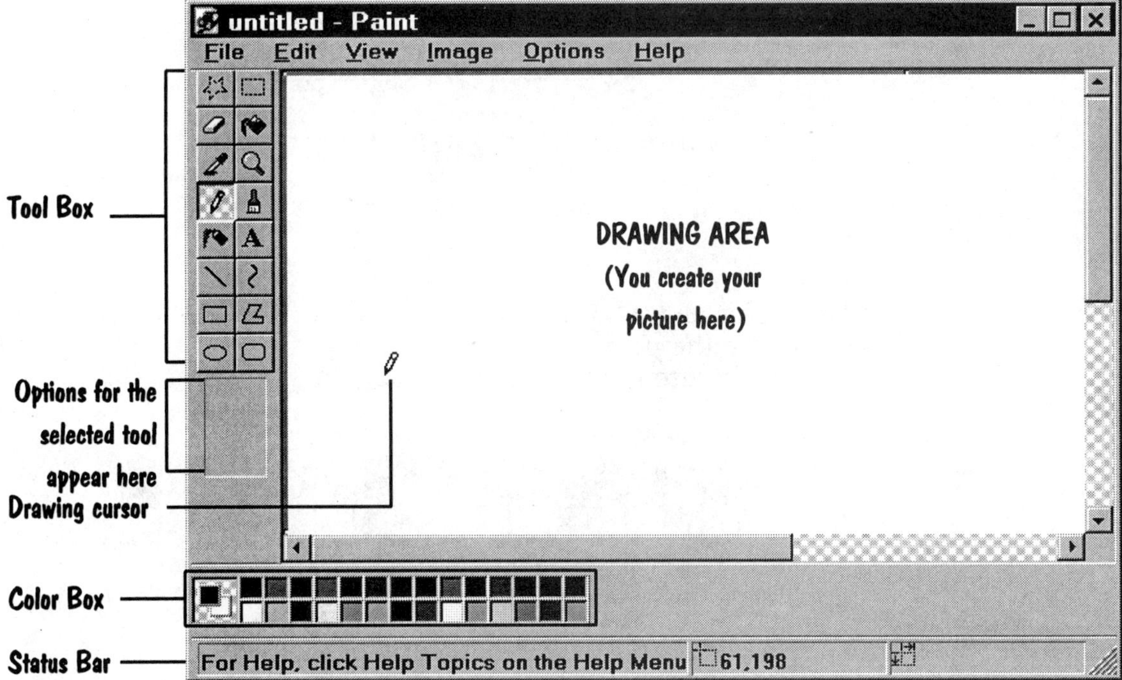

Figure 7   The Paint Window

In addition to the usual components, such as title and menu bars, the Paint window is broken into three main parts:

1. The *Tool Box* contains icons that represent the tools you use to create the graphic. The names of these tools are given in Figure 8; we will describe their use later in this section. Below the icons is a box (see Figure 7) that displays the options, if any, available for the selected tool. For example, for the Line tool, the Options Box (shown at the right) displays the available line widths with the current width highlighted. To select another drawing width, click on it.

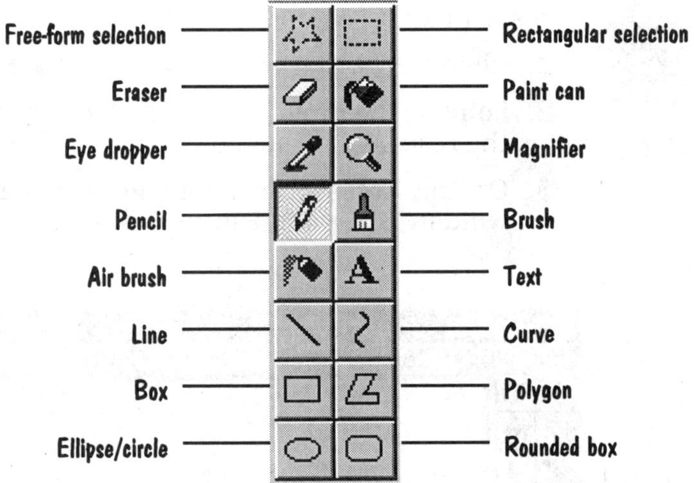

Figure 8   The Paint Tool Box

2. The *Color Box* allows you to select (by clicking on them) the colors for the object you are about to draw. It also displays the current foreground and background colors (see Figure 9).

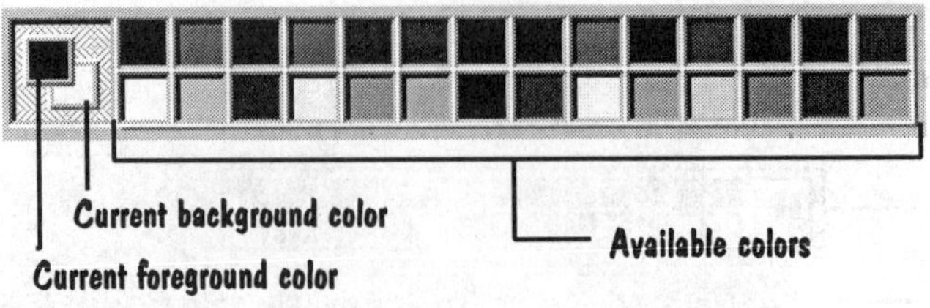

Figure 9   The Color Box

3. The *drawing area* (or *work area*) is the window in which you compose the graphic. Often, the graphic is larger than the drawing area, so only part of it is displayed. In these cases, you can view other parts of the graphic by scrolling the window. To minimize the amount of scrolling you must do, maximize the Paint window.

The Paint window's Status bar (see Figure 7) provides information about the current operation. Perhaps its most useful indicator is the *cursor coordinates* box, which gives the precise location of the drawing cursor relative to the upper-left corner of the drawing area. For example, the coordinates shown at the right indicate that the cursor is 270 pixels from the left border of the drawing area and 40 pixels down from the top border.

Drawing a Graphic

Using Paint to draw a graphic involves these general steps:

1. Select a *background color*, the color of the drawing area, by *right-*clicking on the desired color in the Color Box. Then, choose the New command from the File menu, which clears the drawing area and colors it as you specified.

2. For the object you are about to draw:

    - Select a drawing tool by clicking on its icon in the Tool Box. (The icon will appear to be "depressed".)

    - Select an option for this tool (if available) from the Options Box.

    - Select a *foreground color*, the color with which the object will be drawn, by (left-) clicking on the desired color in the Color Box. (Some tools require that you select a background color as well; this choice does not affect the color of the drawing area.)

3. Draw the object

    - Position the cursor at the location in the drawing area where you want to begin drawing.

    - Drag the cursor to draw the object; release the mouse button when you're done.

4. Repeat steps 2 and 3 until the drawing is complete.

NOTE

From Windows' point of view, the graphic you are creating is a "document". It is saved, opened, and printed in the same ways as a Word-Pad document (see Section 2.2).

To illustrate the drawing process, let's create the graphic image of a signature:

- Leave the foreground and background colors at their default settings: black and white, respectively.

- Select the Brush tool by clicking on its Tool Box icon. The options for Brush are various sizes and styles of "brush tips". Choose the smallest available tip; the one on the right end of the first row.

- Move the cursor (a cross hairs) into the drawing area and position it where you want to begin drawing your first name.

- Drag the cursor to form your first name. Then, reposition the cursor and drag it to form your last name.

It takes some practice to use the Brush tool. To start over, choose Undo from the Edit menu or just press Ctrl+Z. If your name were John Hancock, the completed graphic might look as shown in Figure 10.

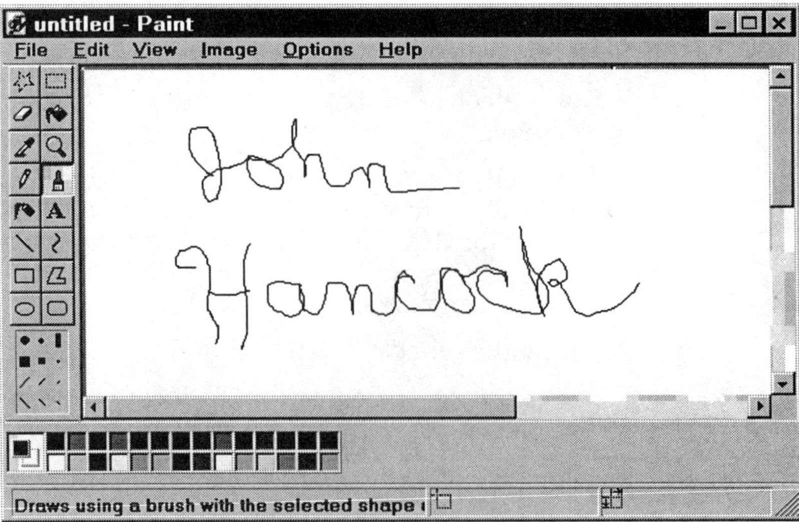

Figure 10   Graphic Image of a Signature

The Paint Tools

Here are brief descriptions of the drawing tools found in the Tool Box (see Figure 8).

The **Free-form Selection** tool selects an irregular region to be moved, copied, resized, and so on. To use this tool, drag the cursor around the object to be selected.

The **Rectangular Selection** tool selects a box-shaped region: Position the cursor in the upper-left corner of the box to be selected, and drag it to the lower-right corner. Rectangular selection is not as versatile as free-form selection, but it's easier to use.

The **Eraser** tool changes everything in the path of its cursor to the current background color. The Options Box allows you to size the cursor.

The **Paint Can** tool fills an enclosed object with the current foreground color. Just click anywhere within the object to color it.

The **Eye Dropper** tool picks up a color from the drawing and establishes it as the foreground color. Just click the cursor on the desired color.

The **Magnifier** tool allows you to "zoom-in", magnifying the drawing area by the amount specified in the Options Box.

The **Pencil** tool draws a free-form figure that is only one pixel in width. As long as you hold down the Shift key while dragging the Pencil cursor, the result will be a straight horizontal, vertical, or diagonal (inclined at 45°) line segment.

The **Brush** tool also draws free-form figures. Unlike the Pencil, you can select Brush "tips" of various widths and styles from the Options Box. On the other hand, holding down the Shift key has no effect when using the Brush.

The **Airbrush** tool draws a free-form figure made up of a spray of dots. The faster you move the Airbrush, the finer the spray.

The **Text** tool allows you to insert text into the graphic. To use it, drag its cursor to form a box in the drawing area within which you want to place the text; select a typeface, font size, and style from the Format bar that pops up at the top of the Paint window; and type the desired text.

The **Line** tool draws straight lines of several different widths, which are selected in the Options Box. Holding down the Shift key while dragging the Line cursor creates perfectly horizontal, vertical, or diagonal (inclined at 45°) lines.

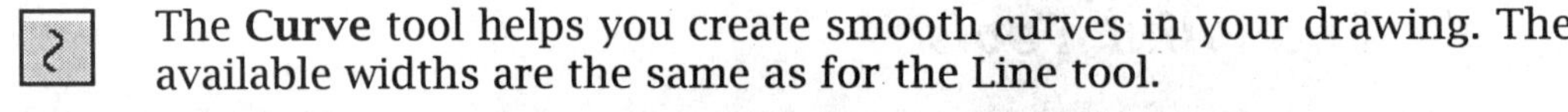

The **Curve** tool helps you create smooth curves in your drawing. The available widths are the same as for the Line tool.

The **Box** tool draws a rectangle. You have the option of a hollow figure drawn in the foreground color, a figure entirely filled with the background color, or a figure bordered in the foreground color and filled in the background color. Hold down the Shift key while dragging the Box cursor to form a square.

The **Polygon** tool helps you draw a polygon (a many-sided enclosed figure). The same options are available as for the Box tool.

The **Ellipse/Circle** tool draws an ellipse (or circle, if you hold down the Shift key). The same options are available as for the Box tool.

The **Rounded Box** tool draws a rectangle (or square, if you hold down the Shift key) with rounded corners. The same options are available as for the Box tool.

TUTORIAL

Try the following exercise on your own, creating a drawing of the truck shown in Figure 11. Remember: The Eraser can be used to correct mistakes and Ctrl+Z undoes the last change to the graphic.

1. Start Windows NT (if necessary) by turning on the computer.

2. Start Paint by selecting it from the Accessories submenu of the Start button, and maximize its window.

3. Draw the road:

   - Select the Line tool from the Tool Box (see Figure 8) by clicking on it and select the second smallest line thickness in the Options Box (see Figure 7) by clicking on it.

   - Position the Line cursor in the drawing area about one inch from the lower-left corner, hold down the Shift key (for a horizontal line), and drag the cursor to the right side of the drawing area.

   - Select the Airbrush tool from the Tool Box, and select a medium thickness from the Options Box.

   - Position the Airbrush cursor just under the left edge of the line you've just drawn and drag the cursor slowly across the screen under this line.

4. Draw the truck tires:

   - Select the Ellipse/Circle tool from the Tool Box and the hollow (top) option from the Options Box.

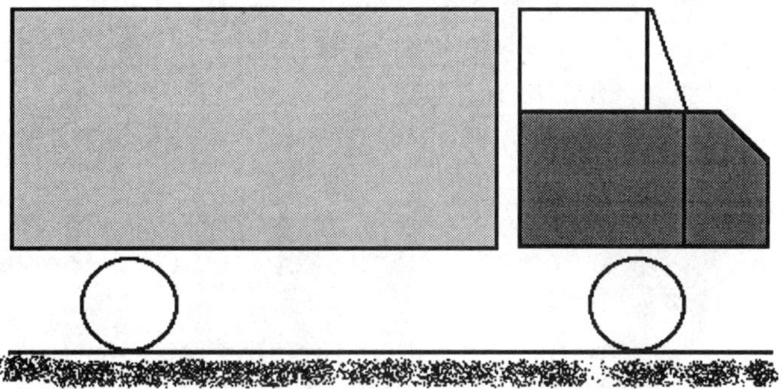

Figure 11   Truck Graphic for Tutorial 5.3

- Draw the rear tire by positioning the cursor about one inch above the road, holding down the Shift key (for a circle), and dragging the cursor down and to the right until the circle touches the road.

- Use the cursor coordinates on the Status bar to help create a front tire of exactly the same size: Position the cursor at the top of the rear tire and note the second cursor coordinate. Then, for the front tire, position the cursor so that its second coordinate has this value, hold down Shift, and drag a circle until it touches the road.

5. Draw the truck's trailer:

- Select the Box tool from the Tool Box and the "filled box with outline" option (the middle one) from the Options Box.

- Select a foreground of black (by clicking on this color in the Color Box) and a background of light gray (by *right*-clicking on this color in the Color Box).

- Start near the rear wheel and drag a box that makes a rectangle about 2" high and 4" long.

6. Draw the lower (shaded) part of the cab of the truck:

- Select a background color of white from the Color Box.

- Select the Polygon tool from the Tool Box and the "hollow" option from the Options Box.

- Hold down the Shift key (for horizontal, vertical, and diagonal lines) and drag the Polygon cursor from corner to corner of the polygon that makes up the lower cab. At each corner, click the mouse to end the previous line segment before dragging the next one. Double-click on the last corner to close the polygon.

- ■ Fill the polygon with color: Select a foreground color of dark gray from the Color Box, select the Paint Can tool, and click inside your polygon.

- ■ Select a foreground color of black, select the Line tool, hold down the Shift key, and draw the vertical line that forms the door.

7. Continuing to use the Line tool, draw the four lines that make up the window area of the cab.

8. Save and/or print the graphic, if you want, and exit Paint.

5.4   Other Windows Accessories

In this section, we will describe some of the other programs that are typically found on the Accessories submenu of the Start menu. To run one of these applications, open the Accessories submenu and click on the appropriate item.

Notepad

Notepad is a very simple type of word processor called a **text editor** because its capabilities are limited to editing text. Unlike more sophisticated word processors, such as WordPad, Notepad cannot format text — there is no choice of fonts and no alignment or indentation options — and it cannot place graphics in your document. (You *can* set margins in Notepad by choosing the Page Setup command on the File menu.)

Advantages of Notepad

Notepad's major virtue is simplicity; it loads more quickly and takes up less memory than WordPad. Notepad is (arguably) more convenient than WordPad for taking quick notes or editing text files. A **text file**, which is also known as an **ASCII** (pronounced "askey") file, is the simplest and most universal format for storing text. A text file is made up solely of characters you can type on the keyboard; it does not contain any special symbols (such as £ or ©) or formatting codes. Some system files (such as autoexec.bat and config.sys) and program files are stored as text files.

Using Notepad

When you start Notepad (its window is shown in Figure 12), *word wrap* is turned off, which means that the text you type continues on

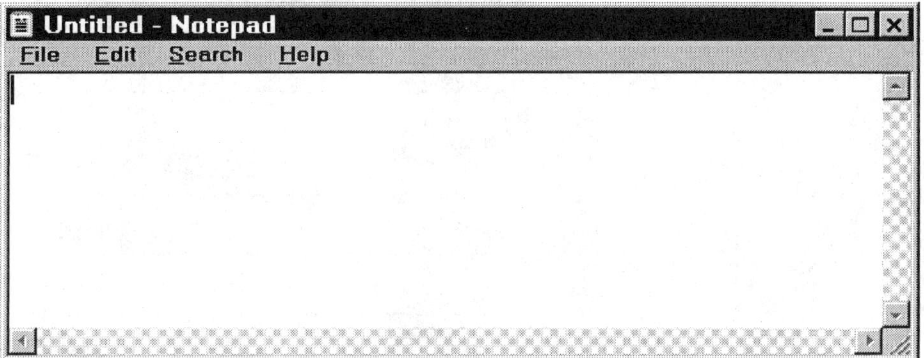

Figure 12   The Notepad Window

the same line until you press the Enter key. If you turn word wrap on (by choosing this item from the Edit menu), text will wrap to the beginning of the next line when it reaches the right edge of the Notepad window. As with any word processor, no matter how simple, Notepad allows you to save, open, and print documents (using the usual File menu commands).

Notepad does possess one major feature that WordPad lacks: It allows you to create headers and footers for a document. A **header** is text that is automatically placed at the top of every page; a **footer** is text placed at the bottom of every page. By default, the header displays the file name of the document and the footer gives the current page number. To change or delete the header or footer, choose the Page Setup command from the File menu and enter the desired information in the resulting dialog box.

Calculator

Windows' **Calculator** accessory provides two types of on-screen calculators — a basic *standard* calculator and a more powerful *scientific* calculator. (The standard calculator is shown in Figure 13 on the next page.) When you start Calculator, it displays the calculator type, standard or scientific, that was being used when you last exited this accessory. To switch from one mode to the other, choose Standard or Scientific, as desired, from the View menu.

Using Calculator   If you know how to use a conventional calculator, then you can use Windows' Calculator; it works in a completely analogous way. Instead of pressing a button with your finger, as you would on a real calcula-

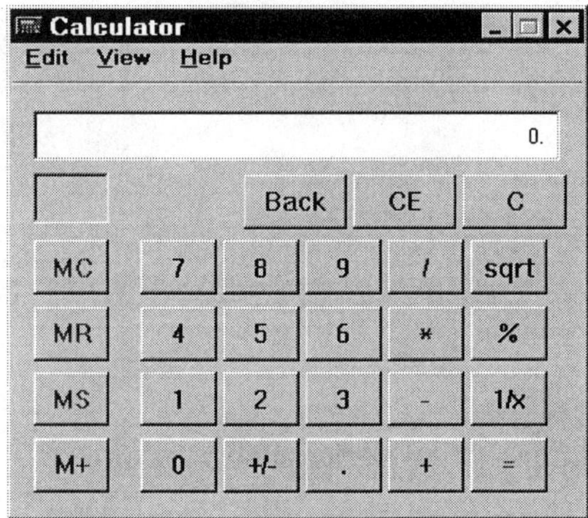

Figure 13   Standard Calculator

tor, just click on that button with the mouse. Or, if you wish, you can use the keyboard to enter numbers and operation symbols.

In standard mode, Calculator contains all the keys usually found on a basic calculator. In scientific mode, Calculator supplies an impressive array of functions. For example, you can calculate trigonometric values, exponentials, logarithms, factorials, and statistical functions.

Copy and paste with Calculator

You can transfer numbers between the Calculator display and another application with the aid of the Clipboard:

- To copy the number displayed to the Clipboard, choose the Copy command from the Edit menu.

- To transfer a number from the Clipboard to the Calculator display, choose Paste from the Edit menu.

Character Map

Character Map lets you insert special symbols into a document open in another Windows application. The Character Map window is shown in Figure 14.

Using Character Map

To use Character Map to insert characters into a document:

1. Select a typeface from the Font drop-down list. The *character set* for the selected font will be displayed in the window.

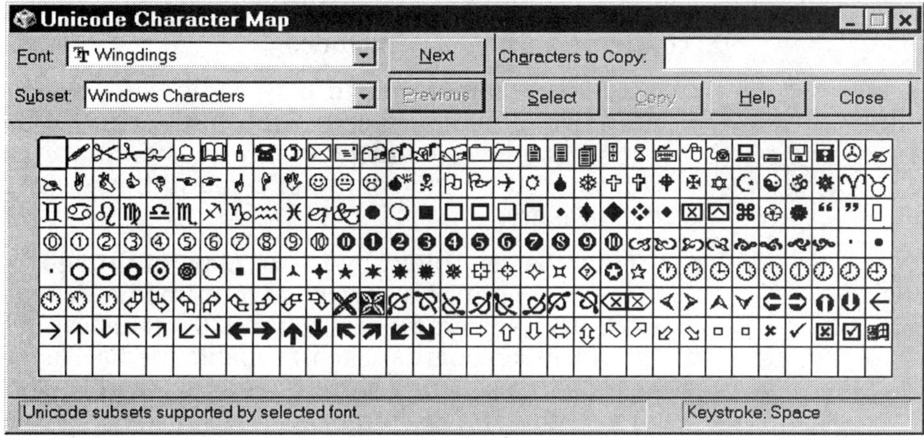

Figure 14   The Character Map Window

2. Select a character from those displayed by double-clicking on it (or by clicking on it and choosing the Select command button). The selected character will appear in the Characters to Copy box.

   With some fonts, additional characters can be displayed by selecting another item from the Subset drop-down list. (You can cycle through this list by repeatedly choosing the Next button.)

3. If you want, repeat step 2 to select additional characters.

4. Choose the Copy command button to copy the selected characters to the Clipboard.

5. Switch to the application and document in which you want to insert the characters.

6. In this document, position the insertion point where you want the characters to be inserted, select the same typeface as the one used in Character Map, and choose the Paste command from the Edit menu.

Multimedia Accessories

Multimedia is a catch-all term that refers to the creation, recording, display, or playback of documents that contain sophisticated sound, graphics, and/or video components. The Multimedia item on the Accessories submenu provides access to programs that manipulate devices such as sound boards or CD-ROM drives. The particular multimedia accessories available to you depend on how your system is configured. They may include:

- **CD Player** allows you to play audio compact discs on your CD-ROM drive. Its interface resembles the control panel of the compact disc player connected to your stereo system. The music is transmitted by the computer's sound board and played through its speakers.

- **Media Player** allows you to play multimedia files of various kinds and control a variety of multimedia devices, including CD-ROM drives, sound boards, and MIDI (Musical Instrument Digital Interface) keyboards. Each available Media Player "device" corresponds to a separate set of files and controls. For example, if you choose the Sound command from the Device menu, a collection of sound files will be displayed. Double-clicking on one of them "plays" the content of the file through the sound board and speakers.

- **Sound Recorder** allows you to record sound (input via a microphone or line-in to the sound board), edit it, and store the result as a file on your hard disk. The Sound Recorder's interface resembles the controls on an audio tape player.

- **Volume Control** lets you adjust the volume and balance for the various sound devices connected to your computer system.

Communications Accessories

If your computer is equipped with a **modem**, a device that translates computer-generated data into signals that can be sent (usually over phone lines) to another computer, you can access information on other computer systems. Using computer-to-computer communication:

- You can access the vast quantities of data supplied by an **online information service**, such as CompuServe, America Online, or the Microsoft Network. With such a service, you will be able to receive *e-mail* (electronic mail), use encyclopedias, obtain stock market quotes, make airline reservations, and even "chat" with other subscribers.

- You can post messages on electronic *bulletin boards* and read messages posted there by others.

- You can make use of the **Internet** — a worldwide system of interconnected computer networks — to send and receive e-mail or browse through the information posted by hundreds of thousands of organizations and individuals on the *World Wide Web*.

- You can connect to your campus computer network and use the software and data on it that has been authorized for public use.

- If your modem contains fax capabilities (as virtually all modems do, nowadays), you can send computer-generated faxes and receive any fax transmitted by others.

To take advantage of these communication possibilities, you not only need a modem and phone line, but also the appropriate software and, in the case of the Internet, a company that acts as a service provider. For this reason, Windows supplies two key accessories:

- **HyperTerminal** is a communications software package that allows you to configure, dial, and pass commands to the modem from your keyboard. It ensures, with your input, that the signals sent by your computer, through its modem and the telephone lines, will be understandable to the hardware setup on the remote system.

- **Dial-Up Networking** is an accessory that allows your computer to connect to remote networks through a modem and phone lines. Once connected, the network's applications work as if they were running on your machine. Internet Service Providers (ISPs) can make use of the Dial-Up Networking program to help establish a connection, through the service provider's network, between your computer and the Internet.

Review Exercises

Section 5.1

1. In WordPad, to move the insertion point to the beginning of the current line, press the ___________ key.

2. To select a word in a WordPad document, ___________ the mouse on any letter within it.

3. To undo the last editing change in WordPad, choose Undo from the Edit menu or just press the ___________ keystroke combination.

4. True or false: To move the cursor to the end of a WordPad document, press the End key.

5. True or false: To select an entire WordPad document, move the insertion point into the left margin and double-click the mouse.

6. True or false: You can copy a selected block of text by dragging it to its new location while holding down the Ctrl key.

7. To paste a block of text into a WordPad document, click on the Toolbar button that looks like:

   a. [✂]   b. [▣]   c. [▣]   d. [↰]

8. Which of the following keystroke combinations can be used to select an entire WordPad document?

   a. Ctrl+A
   b. Ctrl+V
   c. Ctrl+X
   d. Ctrl+Z

Section 5.2 9. To print type that is about one inch high, use a ____________ point font size.

10. To change the current typeface in WordPad, select one from the Format bar's drop-down list or choose the ____________ command from the Format menu.

11. To bold a selected word in a WordPad document, click on the Format bar's Bold button or press the ____________ keystroke combination.

12. True or false: If text is selected when you make a font change in WordPad, the font change applies only to the selected text.

13. True or false: The "strikeout" attribute (selected in the Font dialog box) causes the affected text to become unreadable.

14. True or false: In WordPad, it is not possible to align text with both the left and right margins.

15. Which of the following text formatting features is not accessible from WordPad's Format bar?

   a. Changing the font size.
   b. Changing the font color.
   c. Changing the font style to bold, italic, or underline.
   d. All the above features are accessible from the Format bar.

16. Assuming that no text is currently selected, which of the following format changes applies to *all* existing text in a WordPad document?

   a. Changing the margins.
   b. Changing the tab settings.

      c. Changing the text alignment.
      d. Changing the paragraph indentation.

Section 5.3

17. To select red as the background color in a Paint graphic, click the ___________ mouse button on that color in the Color Box.

18. To draw a horizontal line with Paint's Line tool, hold down the ___________ key while dragging the cursor.

19. An existing polygon can be filled with color by using Paint's ___________ tool.

20. To erase a green circle that is enclosed in a red square using Paint's Eraser tool, set the background color to ___________.

21. True or false: Paint's Brush tool can only produce curves of a single line thickness.

22. True or false: To draw a rectangle filled with the color blue using Paint's Box tool, set the background color to blue.

23. True or false: To draw a perfect circle with Paint's Ellipse/Circle tool, hold down the Ctrl key while dragging the cursor.

24. True or false: The Tool Box icon for Paint's Text tool is the capital letter "T".

25. To select blue as the foreground color in Paint:

      a. Click the left mouse button on blue in the Color Box.
      b. Double-click the left mouse button on blue in the Color Box.
      c. Click the right mouse button on blue in the Color Box.
      d. Double-click the right mouse button on blue in the Color Box.

26. Which of the following Paint tools cannot be used to draw an "L-shaped" pair of lines?

      a. The Polygon tool
      b. The Line tool
      c. The Pencil tool
      d. The Brush tool

27. To fill an irregularly shaped region in a Paint graphic with color

      a. Double-click on that color in the Color Box.
      b. Use the Brush tool.
      c. Use the Paint Can tool.
      d. Use the Airbrush tool.

28. To draw a square using Paint's Box tool, while dragging the cursor, hold down the

      a. Alt key

b. Ctrl key
c. Shift key
d. Spacebar

Section 5.4 29. The ____________ Windows accessory is a text editor that contains no text formatting or graphics features.

30. The Windows Calculator accessory allows you to use two types of calculators: ____________ or ____________.

31. The term ____________ refers to applications that contain sophisticated sound, graphics, and/or video components.

32. True or false: The Notepad accessory allows you to use Arial, Times New Roman, and Courier New typefaces.

33. True or false: To copy a character in the Character Map accessory to the Clipboard, choose the Copy command from the Edit menu.

34. True or false: To use ordinary telephone lines to access an online information service, your computer needs to be equipped with a modem.

35. Which of the following is not a multimedia device?

a. A sound board
b. A CD-ROM drive
c. A modem
d. A MIDI keyboard

36. Which of the following applications deals with computer-to-computer communications?

a. Media Player
b. HyperTerminal
c. Notepad
d. WordPad

Build Your Own Glossary 37. The following words and phrases are important terms that were introduced in this chapter. (They appear within the text in boldface type.) Use WordPad to enter a definition for each term, preserving alphabetical order, into the Glossary file on the Student Disk.

ASCII file	Footer	Multimedia
Accessories	Graphic	Notepad
Calculator utility	Header	Online information
CD Player	HyperTerminal	service
Character Map	Internet	Paint accessory
Dial-Up Networking	Media Player	Point (measure)
Font	Modem	Sound Recorder

Text editor   Typeface   WordPad
Text file   Volume Control

Lab Exercises

Work each of the following exercises at your computer. Begin by turning the machine on (if necessary) to start Windows NT and closing any open windows.

Lab Exercise 1
(Section 5.1)

a. Start WordPad and maximize its window.

b. Type your name and class on separate lines, and skip a line (by pressing the Enter key twice).

c. Type the sentence: This is a test of the copy and paste operations. Then, press the Spacebar to inset a blank space after the period.

d. Select the sentence and the space that follows it. Describe how you accomplished this.

e. Copy the selected text to the Clipboard. What menu command or mouse actions did you use?

f. Paste the text from the Clipboard onto the end of the document. What menu command or mouse actions did you use?

g. Repeat step *f* four times. Try pasting the text without reselecting and recopying it. Did this work?

h. Print the document. (See Section 2.2, if necessary, for information about printing a document.)

i. Save the document if you wish and exit WordPad.

Lab Exercise 2
(Section 5.2)

a. Start WordPad and maximize its window.

b. Insert the Student Disk in its drive and open the document named Preamble on this disk. (See Section 2.2 for information on opening a document.)

c. Display the Format bar (if it's not currently visible) and use it to help determine the two fonts used in the Preamble document. What are they?

d. Break the title into two lines (after "Constitution"), select both lines, and center them. Describe how you centered the lines.

    e.   Change the font for the entire title to 19-point Arial bold. Do you have to use the Font dialog box to do this?

    f.   Within the preamble itself:

- Bold the phrase *We the people.*

- Italicize the word *Constitution.*

- Underline the last four words, *United States of America.*

What keystroke combinations can be used to accomplish each of these text enhancements?

    g.   Skip a line at the bottom of the document and type your name.

    h.   Print the revised document (see Section 2.2, if necessary).

    i.   Save the modified document under another name if you wish, exit WordPad, and remove the diskette from its drive.

Lab Exercise 3   a.   Start WordPad and maximize its window.

(Section 5.2)   b.   Insert the Student Disk in its drive and open the document named Fonts on this disk. (See Section 2.2 for information on opening a document.)

    c.   Follow the instructions on the screen.

    d.   Print the revised document (see Section 2.2, if necessary).

    e.   Save the modified document under another name if you wish, exit WordPad, and remove the diskette from its drive.

Lab Exercise 4   a.   Start Paint and maximize its window.

(Section 5.3)   b.   Create the "Palette" graphic shown below:

- Use the Box tool to create the outer border of the graphic.

- Use the Line tool to subdivide the outer box into 28 compartments. (Use the cursor coordinates on the Status bar as you draw these lines to help create even subdivisions.)

- Use the Paint Can tool to fill each compartment with a different color from the Color Box.

c. Use the Text tool to display your name and class, in 24-point type, below the Palette graphic.

d. Print this graphic (see Section 2.2, if necesary).

e. Save the graphic if you wish and exit Paint.

Lab Exercise 5 a. Start Paint and maximize its window.

(Section 5.3) b. Insert the Student Disk in its drive and open (see Section 2.2) the Factory1 graphic on this disk.

c. Edit the Factory1 graphic, so that the revised version resembles the one pictured in Figure 15, by:

- Using the Eraser tool (with a background color of dark gray) to erase the triangular part of the two existing windows.

- Using the Box tool (with the "filled box with outline" option) to create the new rectangular window.

- Using the Box tool (with the "filled box" option) to create the second smokestack.

- Using the Airbrush tool to create the new (gray-colored) smoke.

Figure 15 Final Graphic for Lab Exercise 5

    d.   Print the revised graphic (see Section 2.2, if necesary).

    e.   Save the modified graphic under another name if you wish, exit Paint, and remove the diskette from its drive.

Lab Exercise 6   a.   Start Notepad and maximize its window.

(Section 5.4)   b.   Open the Edit menu. If Word Wrap is not selected (if a check mark does not appear next to this menu item), choose the Word Wrap command to turn on this feature.

    c.   Carry out steps *b — h* of Lab Exercise 1.

    d.   Save the document if you wish and exit Notepad.

Running DOS Applications

A program that was designed to run under the DOS operating system, but not under Windows, is known as a **DOS application**. Although Windows-based software has many advantages over DOS applications (see the Introduction), the latter often run faster and make more efficient use of computer resources. For this reason, some contemporary graphics-intensive computer games are designed as DOS applications.

DOS applications are normally started in the same ways as Windows programs (see Section 2.1). You can run several DOS and Windows programs at the same time and switch among them using the techniques described in Section 2.3. In addition, Windows NT provides special features for DOS applications that make them easier to use. We will discuss these features in this appendix.

Running DOS Applications under Windows

Unlike Windows applications, which always run inside a window on the Desktop, DOS programs can be run in a window or *full-screen*, in which case the application occupies the entire Desktop, as shown in Figure 1.

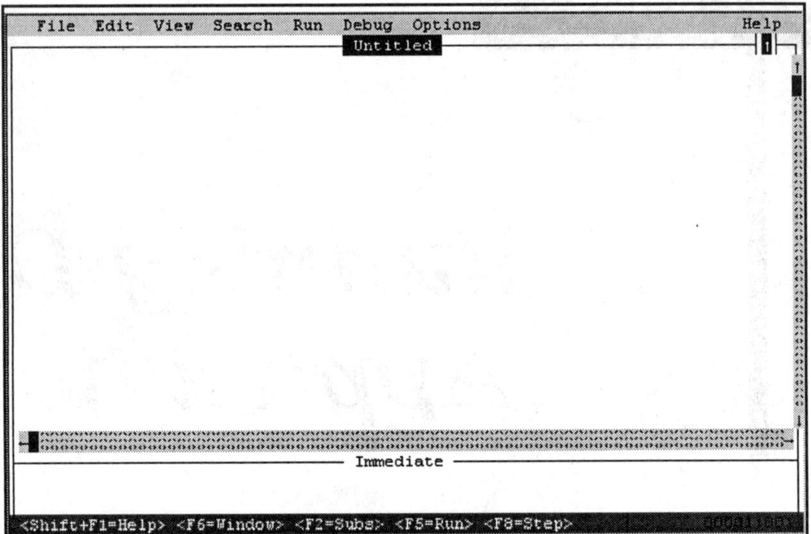

Figure 1   A DOS Application Running Full-screen

To switch from one mode to the other, press the Alt+Enter keystroke combination. If the application of Figure 1 is switched to window mode, the result is shown in Figure 2. Notice that the application window contains a title bar, complete with minimize, maximize, and close buttons and a Control menu icon to the left of the window title (C:\DOS\QBASIC.EXE). We will only consider window mode in the remainder of this section because the special features described below cannot be accessed in full-screen mode.

Mark, Copy, and Paste   Text in a DOS window can be selected and copied to the Windows Clipboard, and information on the Clipboard can be pasted into the current document. (See Section 2.3 for general information about these operations.) These three operations are initiated from the Control menu, which can be opened by clicking on the Control menu icon, right clicking on the menu bar, or pressing the Alt+Spacebar keystroke combination.

Selecting text   To select (or *mark*) text in the document in a DOS window:

1. Open the Control menu (as described above), point at the Edit item, and choose the Mark command on the resulting submenu.

2. Use the mouse or keyboard to position the cursor at the beginning of the block of text to be selected and either mouse-drag the cursor to the end of the block, or hold down the Shift key

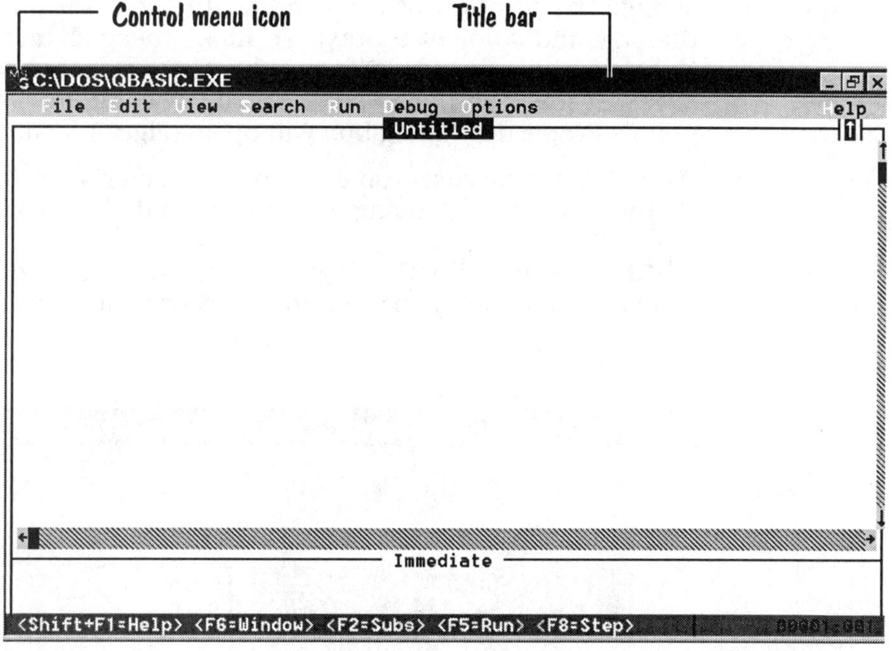

Figure 2   A DOS Application Running in a Window

and move the cursor to the end of the block.

The selected block of text will become highlighted.

Copying text

To copy a selected block of text to the Clipboard, either:

- Press the Enter key.

or

- Open the Control menu, point at the Edit item, and choose the Copy command from the resulting submenu.

Pasting text

To paste text from the Clipboard into a document:

1. Position the cursor where you want to paste the text.

2. Open the Control menu, point at the Edit item, and choose the Paste command from the resulting submenu.

DOS Properties

When a DOS program is running in a window, you can control, to some extent, the way it looks on the screen. For example, you can change the position of the window, the color of its background, and the size and color of its text. To make these changes, pull down the Control menu (by clicking on the Control menu icon or pressing Alt+Spacebar) and choose the Properties item. The running program's Properties dialog box will open. (Figure 3 shows its Font page.)

We will now discuss some of the characteristics of a DOS window that you can change using the Properties dialog box.

Changing the Font   If you want, you can change the font (typeface) used to display the text in a DOS window. To do so:

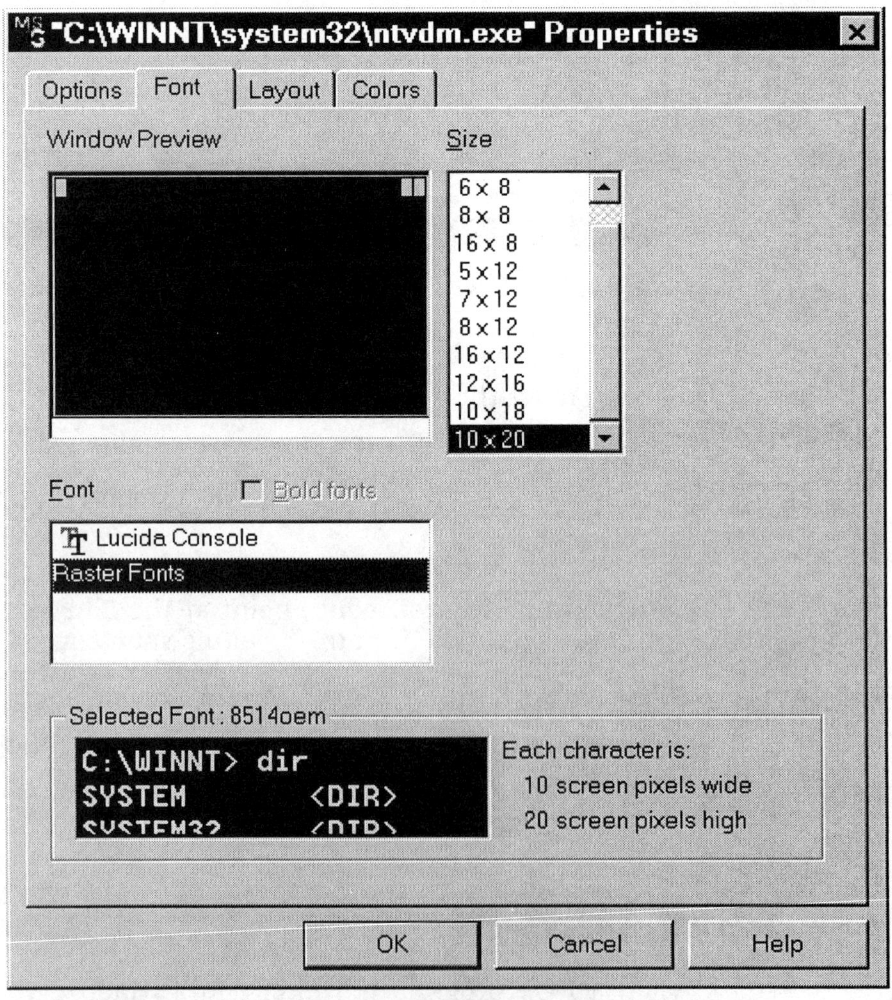

Figure 3   DOS Properties Dialog Box — Font Page

1. Display the Properties dialog box by choosing Properties from the Control menu and clicking on the Font tab. The resulting dialog box is shown in Figure 3.

2. Select a font from the Font list box and a font size from the Size box. If you choose a *raster* font, the sizes listed will be in *pixels*; for example, the current font in Figure 3 is 10 pixels wide and 20 pixels high. If you choose a TrueType font, the sizes listed will be in *points*. (See Section 5.2 for information about fonts.)

   The font and size you choose is previewed in the Selected Font box and the corresponding window size (it changes as the font size changes) is depicted in the Window Preview box. Experiment with the various options until you find one you like.

3. Choose the OK command button. The Apply Properties dialog box will allow you to choose whether to:

   - "Apply properties to current window only", in which case the next time you start up this DOS program the screen will show the font that was in effect before you changed it.

   or
   - "Save properties for future windows with same title", which applies the change to both this *and* future sessions with the program.

4. Choose the OK button in the Apply Properties dialog box to put the font change into effect and return to the DOS program.

Other Properties Dialog Box Options   Here are a few more ways you can use the Properties dialog box to customize a DOS program's window.

- On the Options page, you can select a small, medium, or large cursor size and elect to start the program in a window or full-screen.

- On the Layout page, you can choose the window position and size (given in terms of the number of lines and columns of text displayed) to be used when the program starts up.

- On the Colors page, you can select the colors to be used for the program's text and background.

Running a DOS Session

If you are familiar with the DOS operating system, you may want to issue commands or run programs within DOS from time to time. You can do this — run a *DOS session* — by starting the Command Prompt utility. Command Prompt gives you access to the DOS prompt, so that you can view directories, copy files, start programs, and so on, just as if you were actually running DOS.

Starting Command Prompt

To start Command Prompt:

1. Click on the Start button to display the Start menu and point at the Programs option to open its submenu.

2. Click on the Command Prompt item on this submenu. The window shown in Figure 4, sometimes referred to as a *DOS box,* will open.

Figure 4   The Command Prompt Window

The DOS box provides all the features (described in the first part of this section) afforded to any DOS program running in a window. Using the Control menu, you can mark, copy, and paste text and change certain window properties. Moreover, from the DOS prompt, which is `C:\>` in Figure 4, you can issue any available DOS command.

To exit Command Prompt, close the program that's running (if any), and then either type `exit` at the DOS prompt and press the Enter key, or click on the window's close button.

The Windows NT Find Utility

A typical hard disk contains thousands of files spread across dozens of folders. As a result, locating a particular file or folder (say, to create a shortcut for it) can be a daunting task. Fortunately, Windows NT provides a powerful utility, called Find, that helps you with the search. In this section, we will discuss how to use Find to locate files and folders. (If your computer is connected to a network, Find can also help you search for computers on the network.)

The Find Utility's Window

There are several ways to start the Find utility:

- Click on the Start button, point at the Find option, and choose Files or Folders from the resulting submenu.

- Right-click on the Start button, the My Computer icon, or any folder icon, and choose the Find command from the pop-up menu.

- Click on an empty part of the Desktop and then press the F3 function key.

- In Explorer, either press the F3 function key, or point at the Find command on the Tools menu and choose Files or Folders from the resulting submenu.

In any case, the Find window (Figure 1) will open.

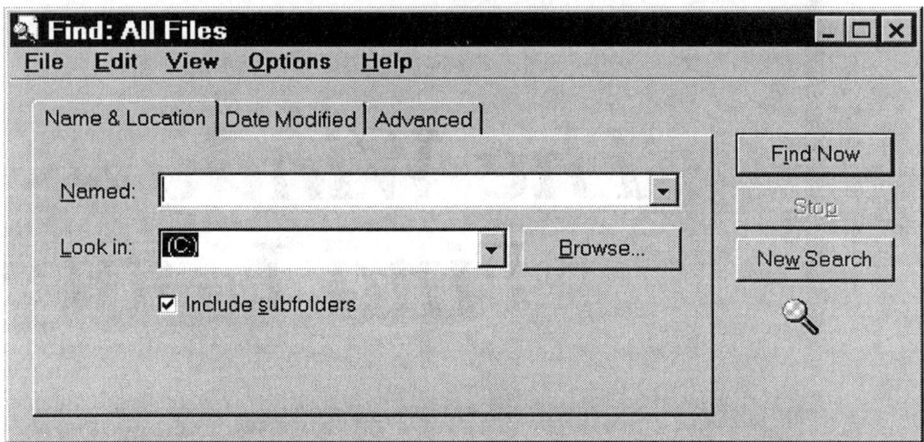

Figure 1   The Find Window

Since Find is an application, its window can be resized, minimized, or maximized. Notice (in Figure 1) that the Find window is somewhat unusual in that it contains both pull-down menus and tabs. The menus provide capabilities that are similar to those of Explorer; the tabs supply options that help you to narrow the search for a particular file or folder.

Performing a Simple Search

In a typical situation, you would use the Find utility to locate a file or folder because:

- You had forgotten its name.

or

- You did not know in which folder it was located.

If you know the name (or at least part of the name) of the file or folder you are seeking, proceed as follows:

1. Start the Find utility, as described above.

2. Type the name (or partial name) of the file or folder in the *Named* text box. (The Named drop-down list contains the entries for recent searches.)

If you know the
name of the file
or folder ...

3. If you know the folder that contains the object you are seeking, enter it in the *Look in* text box or choose the Browse button and then select the desired folder from the folder tree. If you don't know in which folder to look, enter the drive designation of the disk you are searching — for example, (C:) — in the *Look in* box.

4. Select the *Include subfolders* check box if you want to search, not only the *Look in* folder, but all its subfolders, as well.

5. Choose the Find Now command button to start the search. All files and folders (in the specified folders) whose names contain the text entered in the *Named* text box will be displayed in a Search Results window in the lower part of the Find window. The Status bar will indicate the number of files found (Figure 2).

Refining the Search Criteria

If you do not know the name of the file you are seeking or just want to narrow the search (so that fewer files will be found), use the Date

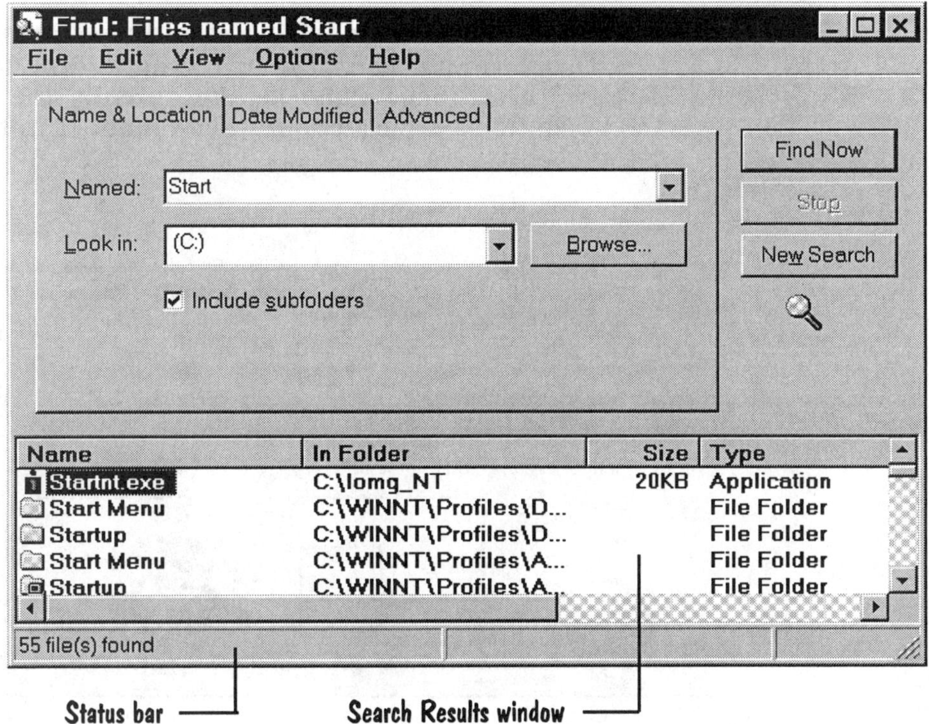

Figure 2   The Find Window After a Search

Modified and/or Advanced pages of the Find window.

The Find windows's Date Modified tab

The Date Modified page is most useful in finding a *document* when:

- You know the approximate date that the file was last saved (perhaps because you have a dated paper copy of the document).

or

- The document was created or modified recently.

To start a search in one of these cases:

1. Start the Find utility, if necessary.

2. Fill in information on the Name & Location page, as described above. If you do not know certain information, leave the corresponding text box blank.

3. Click on the Date Modified tab to display the options shown in Figure 3.

4. Select the *Find all files created or modified* option button.

5. If you know the approximate date that the file was last saved, select the *between* option button and, in the two text boxes, enter dates that bracket the date the document was last saved.

   If the document was modified recently, you could select either the *during the previous days* or the *during the previous months* option button (depending on how recently the document was modified); then enter an appropriate number in the corresponding text box.

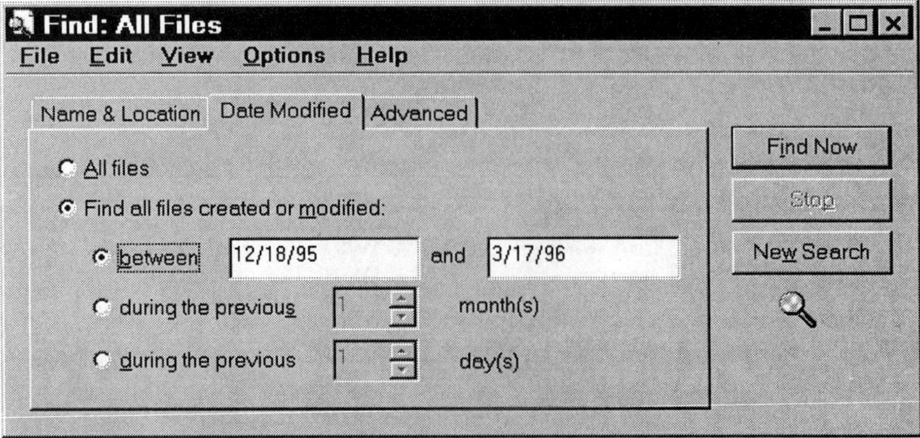

Figure 3   The Date Modified Page of the Find Window

6. Begin the search by choosing the Find Now button. All files that match the search criteria will be displayed in the Search Results window, as shown in Figure 2.

The Find window's Advanced tab

The Advanced page of the Find window allows you to refine a search in a few additional ways. After providing as much information as possible on the Name & Location and Date Modified pages, click on the Advanced tab to display the options shown in Figure 4. Then:

- You can restrict the search to files of a specified type by selecting it from the *Of type* drop-down list.

- You can search for a piece (*string*) of text in a document by entering that string in the *Containing text* box. (This is an extremely useful option for locating a document. Just supply any piece of text that is unique to that document!)

- You can specify the minimum or maximum sizes for the files to be included in the search by using the *Size is* drop-down list and text box.

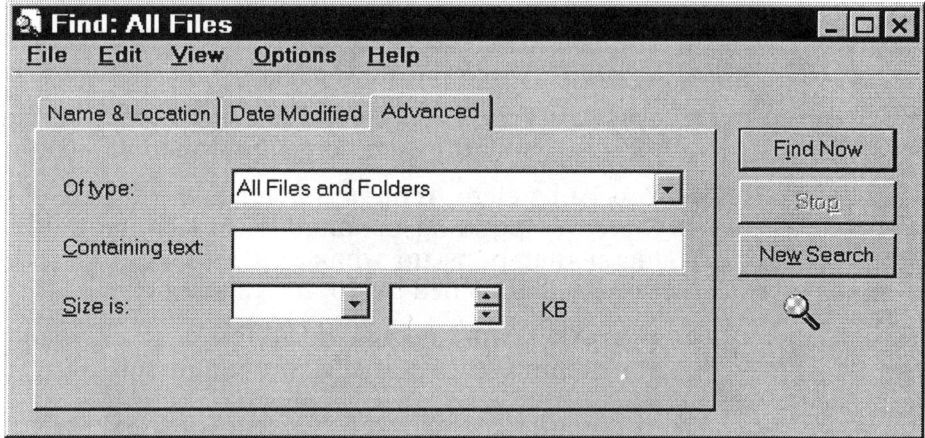

Figure 4   The Advanced Page of the Find Window

In addition to Find Now, there are two other command buttons in the Find window:

NOTE

- While a search is taking place, choosing the Stop button discontinues the search.

- Choosing the New Search button resets all search criteria to their defaults and clears all files and folders (if any) from the Search Results window.

Using the Results of a Search

As you know, when a search is complete, the files and folders found are displayed in the Search Results window at the bottom of the Find window (see Figure 2). For all practical purposes, this window can be used as if it were a My Computer window or the contents pane of an Explorer window. To be more specific:

- You can display the files in the Search Results window in one of four ways by choosing either Large Icons, Small Icons, List, or Details from the View menu. The advantages of each view option are discussed in Section 3.2. (In Figure 2, the Details option is turned on.)

- You can select objects in the Search Results window using the techniques described in Section 3.3.

- Selected objects can be cut or copied to the Clipboard (so they can be pasted into other folders or onto the Desktop) by choosing Cut or Copy from the Edit menu, or by right-clicking on a selected object and choosing Cut or Copy from the resulting pop-up menu.

- You can drag-and-drop objects from the Search Results window to another folder, onto the Desktop, or onto the Recycle Bin.

- You can create a shortcut for an object in the Search Results window using the techniques described in Section 3.4.

- You can delete, rename, or open a selected object by choosing the corresponding command from either the File menu or the menu that pops up when you right-click the object. (An object can also be opened by double-clicking on it.)

- You can print selected documents by choosing Print from the File menu or the right-click pop-up menu.

Answers to Odd-Numbered Review Exercises

Chapter 1

1. icon
3. true
5. left mouse button
7. dialog box
9. false
11. c
13. title bar
15. right border / left border
17. true
19. a
21. A: Control icon   B: Title bar
    C: Minimize button   D: Maximize button
23. OK *or* Close
25. check box
27. true
29. c
31. Start
33. true
35. c

Chapter 2

1. Ctrl+Esc
3. Close *(or* Exit)
5. true
7. c
9. Accessories
11. open
13. true
15. true
17. a
19. Taskbar
21. Clipboard
23. true

25. c	27. install
29. true	31. c
33. Start	35. book
37. true	39. true
41. c	

Chapter 3

1. file	3. true
5. b	7. contents (*or* right)
9. Details	11. true
13. d	15. Ctrl (*or* Control)
17. Send To	19. true
21. a	23. Recycle Bin (*or* Recycled)
25. box (*or* rectangle)	27. false
29. d	31. double-click
33. true	35. d
37. right-clicking	39. true
41. b	

Chapter 4

1. Settings	3. true
5. b	7. Display
9. screen saver	11. false
13. b	15. Appearance
17. true	19. d
21. Keyboard	23. false
25. d	27. Date/Time
29. Sounds	31. true
33. d	

Chapter 5

1. Home	3. Ctrl+Z
5. false	7. c
9. 72	11. Ctrl+B
13. false	15. d
17. right	19. Paint Can
21. false	23. false
25. a	27. c
29. Notepad	31. multimedia
33. false	35. c

Index